Computer-Aided Fraud
Prevention and Detection

Computer-Aided Fraud Prevention and Detection

A Step-by-Step Guide

DAVID CODERRE

WILEY

John Wiley & Sons, Inc.

For general information on our other products and services, or technical support, please
contact our Customer Care Department within the United States at 800-762-2974, outside
the United States at 317-572-3993 or fax 317-572-4002.

Wiley also publishes its books in a variety of electronic formats. Some content that
appears in print may not be available in electronic books.

For more information about Wiley products, visit our Web site at *www.wiley.com*.

Library of Congress Cataloging-in-Publication Data:

Coderre, David G.
  Computer-aided fraud prevention and detection : a step-by-step guide /
David Coderre.
      p. cm.
  Includes index.
  ISBN 978-0-470-39243-0 (cloth)
  1. Fraud.   2. Fraud investigation.   3. Fraud–Prevention.   4. Auditing,
Internal–Data processing.   I. Title.

  HV8079.F7C62 2009
  364.4–dc22

                                                            2008053433

10   9   8   7   6   5   4   3   2   1

This book is dedicated to my mom and dad, who by teaching me right from wrong, contributed much to this book. Also, to my wife, Anne, who tries to keep me focused on the important things in life; and to my children, Jennifer and Lindsay, who are proof that the tone at the top helps guide ethical behavior throughout the organization.

Contents

Case Studies   xiii

Preface   xv

CHAPTER 1   What Is Fraud?   1

Fraud: A Definition   3
Why Fraud Happens   4
Who Is Responsible for Fraud Detection?   7
What Is a Fraud Awareness Program?   11
    Screening Job Applicants   12
What Is a Corporate Fraud Policy?   12
Notes   15

CHAPTER 2   Fraud Prevention and Detection   17

Detecting Fraud   18
Determining the Exposure to Fraud   19
Assessing the Risk that Fraud Is Occurring
    (or Will Occur)   23
External Symptoms   24
Identifying Areas of High Risk for Fraud   25
Looking at the Exposures from the Fraudster's
    Perspective   26
Approach 1: Control Weaknesses   27
    Who Could Benefit from the Identified Control
        Weaknesses?   27
    What Can They Influence, Control, or Affect?   28
    Can They Act Alone or Is Collusion Required?   29
Approach 2: Key Fields   30
    Which Data Fields Can Be Manipulated and
        by Whom?   30

	Additional Fraud Risk Considerations	31
	Understanding the Symptoms of Fraud	31
	Being Alert to the Symptoms of Fraud	34
	Building Programs to Look for Symptoms	36
	Investigating and Reporting Instances of Fraud	37
	Implementing Controls for Fraud Prevention	38
	Notes	39
CHAPTER 3	Why Use Data Analysis to Detect Fraud?	41
	Increased Reliance on Computers	42
	Developing CAATTs Capabilities	44
	Integrated Analysis and Value-Added Audit	48
	Recognizing Opportunities for CAATTs	49
	Developing a Fraud Investigation Plan	49
	Notes	54
CHAPTER 4	Solving the Data Problem	55
	Setting Audit Objectives	55
	Defining the Information Requirements	57
	Accessing Data	58
	Data Paths	59
	Data File Attributes and Structures	61
	Assessing Data Integrity	65
	Overview of the Application System	68
	Overview of the Data	69
	Notes	70
CHAPTER 5	Understanding the Data	71
	Computer Analysis	71
	Analysis Techniques	74
	Filter/Display Criteria	75
	Expressions/Equations	75
	Gaps	75
	Statistical Analysis	76
	Duplicates	76
	Sort/Index	76
	Summarization	77
	Stratification	77
	Cross Tabulation/Pivot Tables	78
	Aging	78

	Join/Relate	79
	Trend Analysis	79
	Regression Analysis	79
	Parallel Simulation	80
	Benford's Law	80
	Digital Analysis	80
	Confirmation Letters	81
	Sampling	81
	Combining Techniques	82
	Assessing the Completeness of the Data	82
	Filter or Display Criteria	83
	Expression/Equation	85
	Gaps	93
	Statistical Analysis	96
	Duplicates	100
	Sorting and Indexing	106
	Notes	110
CHAPTER 6	Overview of the Data	111
	Summarization	111
	Stratification	125
	Cross Tabulation/Pivot Tables	128
CHAPTER 7	Working with the Data	133
	Aging	133
	Join/Relation	147
CHAPTER 8	Analyzing Trends in the Data	159
	Trend Analysis	159
	Regression Analysis	165
	Parallel Simulation	168
	Notes	170
CHAPTER 9	Known Symptoms of Fraud	171
	Known and Unknown Symptoms	172
	Fraud in the Payroll Area	173
	Ghost Employees	174
	Terminated Employees	177
	Overpayment	178

Fraud in the Purchasing Area   185
    Employee Activities   186
    Vendor Action and Employee Inaction   186
    Collusion between Vendor and Employee   187
Symptoms of Purchasing Fraud   187
    Kickbacks   187
    Fixed Bidding   190
    Goods Not Received   191
    Duplicate Invoices   191
    Inflated Prices   191
    Inferior Quality   191
    Excess Quantities   191

CHAPTER 10   Unknown Symptoms of Fraud
                 (Using Digital Analysis)   193

Data Profiling   194
    Statistical Analysis   195
    Stratification   195
    Frequently Used Values   196
    Even Amounts and Rounding   197
    Least/Most Used Categories   198
Ratio/Variance Analysis   199
    Maximum/Minimum   200
    Maximum/Second Highest   201
    Current/Previous   201
    One Business Area/Another   202
Benford's Law   205
Notes   209

CHAPTER 11   Automating the Detection Process   211

Fraud Applications or Templates   213
Fraud Application Development   217

CHAPTER 12   Verifying the Results   219

Confirmation Letters   219
Sampling   223
Judgmental or Directed Sampling   223
Statistical Sampling   224
Quality Assurance   229
Quality Assurance Methodology   230

Preventive Controls 231
Detective Controls 232
Corrective Controls 232
Ensuring Reliability 233
Data Analysis and Prosecuting Fraud 233
Notes 238

APPENDIX A   Fraud Investigation Plans 239

Insurance Policies—Too Good to Be True 239
Paid by the Numbers 244

APPENDIX B   Application of CAATTs by Functional Area 249

Accounts Receivable Tests 250
Accounts Payable Tests 251
General Ledger Tests 253
Materials Management and Inventory Control Tests 253
Salary and Payroll Tests 256
Purchase Order Management Tests 257
Conflict-of-Interest Tests 257
Kickback Tests 258
Bid-Rigging Tests 258
Policy and Administration Tests 259
Vendor Management Tests 260
Retail Loss Prevention Tests 260
Sales Analysis Tests 261
Work in Progress Tests 262
Cash Disbursement Tests 263
Customer Service Management Tests 263
Loan Tests 264
Deposit Tests 264
Real Estate Loans 265
Credit Card Management 265
Life Insurance Tests 266
Travel Claims 266

APPENDIX C   ACL Installation Process 267

Epilogue 273

References 275

Index 277

Case Studies

Soaring Travel Costs	84
Missing Inventory	86
Cash Diverted	87
Invoicing Errors	87
Stamp Out Fraud	89
Telephone Bill Hang-ups	90
Long-Distance Honor System	94
Special Room Rate	95
Missing Inventory	98
Duplicate Serial Numbers	101
Duplicate Payments	102
Duplicate Check Numbers	104
Repurchased Equipment	105
Fictitious Accounts	109
Vendor Address Changes	113
Credit Card Processing Rates	113
Late Payments	115
Set One Aside	116
Unused Accounts	117
Wheeler and Dealer	117
Last Bid Wins	122
Sole-Sourced Contracts	125
Computer Logs	126
Multiple User Authorities	130
False Claims	132
Still on the Payroll	136
Overdue Accounts Receivable	138
Unclaimed Early Payment Discounts	139
Invoices Paid Too Early	141
Insurance Coverage Not Canceled	142
Money-Laundering Scheme	143
Activity on Dormant Accounts	144
Stolen Payments	145

Stolen Bank Deposits   149
Fictitious Vendors   150
Goods Delivered?   151
Short Delivery   153
Wrong Address Deliveries   154
Construction Zone   155
Lots of Parking   160
Inflated Prices   161
Inferior Goods   163
Stolen Credit Cards   166
Heating Things Up   167
No Vacancy   167
Recalculating Move Costs   168
Error of Commission   180
Higher Pay Rates   182
Rounding Up Hours   183
Maxed-Out Meals   198
Doctored Bills   203
Contracting Kickbacks   204
Dormant but Not Forgotten   204
Signing Authority   207
Ex-Employees Still Paid   212
Duplicate Direct Deposit Numbers   214
Purchase Cards   215
Credit Cards   220
Accounts Received?   221
A Confidence Boost for Management   227
Sample Inventory   228
Paper File Review   234
Debt Free?   236
Insurance Policies—Too Good to Be True   241
Paid by the Numbers   245

Preface

How extensive is fraud?

What is it costing your organization?

How can we do more to discourage and detect fraud?

These are some of the questions facing more and more audit departments. The *Report to the Nation on Occupational Fraud and Abuse*, a study conducted by the Association of Certified Fraud Examiners (ACFE), suggests that an average company loses about 6 percent of its gross revenues to various forms of fraud and abuse. This puts the annual cost of fraud in the United States alone at more than $600 billion per year. The report by the ACFE also states that many of the methods used by employees to embezzle money are simple yet largely undetected by auditors. Often they involve some form of larceny, skimming, or fraudulent disbursements. Other sources also indicate that most costly frauds tend to be disbursements through billing schemes.[1]

In recent years, professional auditing bodies have developed new audit standards and statements. These place more pressure on auditors to deter and detect fraud. This deterrence and detection of fraud, waste, and abuse is not new to audit but requires an increasing amount of auditor time and energy. Fraud examiners and investigators are also finding more demand for their services, as companies facing difficult economic times can ill afford to have profits wasted or stolen. To further complicate matters, auditors and fraud investigators are now being asked to deter and detect fraud in an electronic environment where paper trails and manual files may not even exist. Traditional manual techniques are no longer adequate for the task.

One of the principal roles of audit is to provide management with a high level of assurance that internal controls are in place and working as intended. Auditors have long achieved this through the application of "due professional care" throughout an audit. In exercising such care, auditors must be ever alert to the possibility of criminal activity, wrongdoing, conflict of interest, inefficiencies, and other abuses.

Auditing standards require auditors to have a sufficient knowledge of fraud to be able to identify the indicators of fraud. If control weaknesses are detected, additional tests should be performed, including tests to identify fraud indicators.

Despite the involvement of internal and external auditors in the review of a company's operations and financial health, outsiders (police, ex-employees, etc.) are still the main source of information related to fraud. This leads to a disturbing question: Given the huge cost and the often relatively simple schemes used to commit fraud, why are auditors and fraud examiners not more successful in preventing and detecting it? The answer lies in recognizing that (1) the analysis of company data is the single most effective way of preventing and detecting fraud; and (2) computers and data analysis software are generally underutilized in detecting the symptoms of fraud in the analysis of company data.

At professional conferences I often question auditors and fraud examiners about their use of computer-assisted audit tools and techniques (CAATTs). The answer is frequently "Oh yes, we use CAATTs all the time." When asked to explain their use of CAATTs, the answer all too often sounds like this: "We extract the information, dump the data to a spreadsheet, sort the data, produce a report, and then manually review the paper copy." This is "using CAATTs" in the minds of many auditors.

For many audit organizations, these represent important first steps—getting the required data and being able to read it electronically. Historically, the issue of data access has been the most challenging hurdle for auditors wishing to use CAATTs. Today, utilities and options exist for the extraction and downloading of data, making access less of a problem. So, given that many organizations have overcome this hurdle and the data is available in electronic format, why simply sort it and print it out? Once the data is accessed, data-extraction and analysis software provides users with more power to analyze and understand it than ever before. Auditors and fraud investigators who limit themselves to sorting and printing are missing the bonanza of efficiencies available from computerized tools and techniques.

Various surveys have shown that:

- 94 percent of auditors have access to data extraction and analysis software—in effect, they have some form of CAATTs loaded on their system.
- 93 percent of auditors think that the use of computers in business will increase in the coming years.
- 70 percent of auditors use CAATTs to some degree.
- 50 percent of all fraud is found by analysis, as opposed to informant tips or accidental disclosures—and the proportion found in this way is rising.

The electronic environment in which companies operate, along with the controls on that environment, presents an array of complex systems, real-time variances, and worldwide applications. It is a major challenge for auditors to evaluate. But it also provides a broad range of opportunities for the use of powerful interactive audit software and advanced auditing techniques. Thus, while the business environment is rapidly becoming more complex, there is also an increasing array of audit software, tools, and techniques to assist in fraud investigations. Few would dispute that, in the current business environment, data extraction and analysis software is critical to the efficient and effective operations of audit organizations. More than ever before, auditors and fraud investigators have access to data, the tools to translate the data into information, the training and ability to convert information into knowledge, and the skills to transform knowledge into actions and recommendations. In the detection and deterrence of fraud, auditors and investigators can even proactively search for the symptoms of fraud and conduct investigations.

The use of data analysis software not only means that auditors can conduct routine audits more quickly and easily; now they can perform value-for-money audits as well.

Economics plays a role in the current audit environment. Management is pushing all areas of the organization to be more efficient and effective, including internal audit. As a result, auditors must have more than a passing acquaintance with the power and utility of audit tools like ACL (Audit Command Language) and IDEA (Interactive Data Extraction and Analysis).

Auditors need the ability to truly use and understand data by performing analysis such as:

- Creating calculated expressions not available in the data files, such as finding total inventory value by multiplying quantity times unit price for each item
- Selecting records based on user-defined criteria, such as all records with a pay rate greater than $5,000 per month
- Classifying data according to numeric ranges or character field values, such as totals by branch office or aged summaries by invoices 30, 60, 90, and 120 days past a given date
- Creating even more advanced meta-data—for example, regressions and trend analyses that clarify what is happening in the business
- Developing knowledge of what the data and the fields really represent and how they can be used to address specific questions

This book was written as a guide to all persons who are interested in improving their ability to access data and use data-extraction and analysis software to detect and deter fraud and wasteful practices. The focus is on obtaining and cleansing data and on the application of analytical techniques for fraud detection.

The theory and examples presented in text will assist anyone investigating fraud in harnessing the power of the computer and data analysis software to detect fraud, waste, and abuse. The more than 60 case studies presented here demonstrate the application of a wide variety of techniques, each of which is explained in detail.

In many of the cases, several different techniques are combined to detect fraud. It must be stressed that it is the intelligent use of these techniques by auditors, not the blind following of a "cookbook" approach, that is required. Those who commit fraud can be very innovative in hiding their deeds. Auditors and fraud examiners must be equally creative and resourceful in their searches.

The book presumes that CAATTs are being used by the audit organization and that the reader has a basic understanding of the use and importance of CAATTs in auditing. Tips on how to develop CAATT capabilities in organizations, data access issues and techniques, and the testing of data integrity are all discussed in *Internal Audit; Efficiency through Automation.*[2] This book will provide readers with an understanding of CAATTs in auditing and a basis for the use of data-extraction and analysis techniques to detect fraud.

Another useful source of information is *Fraud Analysis Techniques Using ACL.*[3] This book contains details on analysis techniques, including advanced digital analysis techniques, many of which are aimed at identifying fraud, waste, and abuse. It also includes a disk containing an electronic version of the batches to perform the analyses to detect anomalies and possible fraud.

Notes

1. Joseph T. Wells, "An Unholy Trinity: Three Ways Employees Embezzle Cash," *Internal Auditor* (April 1998): 28–33.
2. David Coderre, *Internal Audit: Efficiency through Automation* (Hoboken, NJ: John Wiley & Sons, 2009).
3. David Coderre, *Fraud Analysis Techniques Using ACL* (Hoboken, NJ: John Wiley & Sons, 2009).

CHAPTER 1

What Is Fraud?

Why does someone become an auditor or fraud investigator? What does an auditor or fraud investigator hope to accomplish for him- or herself and the organization?

For some, the notion of fraud, or at least the desire to prevent fraud, factored heavily in their decision to pursue the audit or fraud examiner profession. For others, the concept of fraud only became an issue when they started work and had to deal firsthand with fraud detection and prevention. Since the National Commission on Fraudulent Financial Reporting (known as the Treadway Commission) released its report in October 1987, fraud has been an increasingly important issue, particularly for members of the audit profession. The commission raised the issue of responsibility for the deterrence of fraud, and made it front page news. It also increased awareness in the business community of the prevalence of fraud and laid the groundwork for auditing standards and practices regarding fraud.

Starting in the late 1990s, there has been an even greater increase in the prominence of fraud detection. Further, courts have ruled heavily against internal and external audit companies and auditors who did not adequately address the detection of fraud or the protection of clients and stockholders from the negative effects of fraud. The large-scale problems at WorldCom and Enron have emphasized not only the importance of audit but also the devastating effects fraud can have on a company and its auditors. Accounting firms found themselves liable for millions of dollars and were forced to rethink the issue of fraud detection. In addition, governments have developed new rules and regulations to ensure accurate financial reporting, such as the Sarbanes-Oxley Act.

Fraud is not a rare occurrence or one that happens only in other companies. While the exact magnitude of losses to fraud is difficult to determine, in part because of undetected frauds, one study reported that most organizations lose between 0.5 and 2.0 percent of their revenues to fraudulent acts committed by their employees, vendors, and others. A survey by KPMG Forensic determined that employees were responsible for 60 percent of the losses.[1] A 1997 report by the Association of Certified Fraud Examiners places losses to fraud at 6 percent of gross revenue.[2] A 1997 study by Deloitte and Touche found that international fraud across the European Union costs members 60 billion euros a year.[3] The PricewaterhouseCoopers 2003 *Global Economic Crime Survey* states that 37 percent of companies worldwide have suffered from a fraud in the last two years, with an average loss of $2 million.[4]

All of the studies seem to indicate that the cost of fraud has increased substantially over the past 10 to 15 years. The 2003 PricewaterhouseCoopers survey indicates that most companies expect fraud to increase in the next five years, with the greatest risk being theft of assets, followed closely by computer hacking, virus attacks, and theft of electronic data. Studies also show that fraud occurs in all types of industries and in both small and large firms.

Fraud is costly not only in dollars; it also can have serious nonfinancial effects. To make matters worse, fraud is not something that will go away on its own—it must be discovered and stopped or it will continue to grow. A fraudulent act committed by senior management may affect employee morale and stockholder confidence for many years. About half of the companies responding to the *Global Economic Crime Survey* felt that fraud had its biggest impact on employee motivation and morale. Companies were more concerned that fraud would affect their reputation and business relations than they were about the effect on share price.

What is fraud and why should auditors be concerned about its detection? Surely, this is a management issue; and while most auditors might like to "catch a thief," it is often not their primary role or may not be their organizational role at all. Some organizations even have a separate fraud investigation group. Thus, in the current legal, business, and audit environments, many auditors and audit organizations remain confused about what fraud is, how it happens, who is responsible for its deterrence and detection, and what they should do to deter and detect it.

Auditors, fraud investigators, employees, and management all have roles to play in deterring and detecting fraud. Audit organizations should be well versed in the symptoms of fraud and the steps involved in its detection.

Audit management has an abiding responsibility to ensure that senior management has developed and implemented a corporate fraud policy that details the procedures that will be followed. Senior management is ultimately responsible for the effective and efficient operations of the business, including the protection of company assets and profits from theft and abuse. Management also should foster an atmosphere in which ethical behavior and mutual trust become the first line of defense against fraud. To be successful, antifraud initiatives must begin at the top, permeate all levels of the organization, and be actively documented, communicated, pursued, and enforced. When all players work together and are supported by well-thought-out corporate policies, fraud and its effects can be reduced and even prevented.

Fraud: A Definition

Fraud includes a wide variety of acts characterized by the intent to deceive or to obtain an unearned benefit. The American Institute of Chartered Public Accountants (AICPA) defines two basic categories of fraud: intentional misstatement of financial information, and misappropriation of assets (or theft). Other audit-related agencies provide additional insight into the definition of fraud that can be summarized in this way:

> *Fraud consists of an illegal act (the intentional wrongdoing), the concealment of this act (often only hidden via simple means), and the deriving of a benefit (converting the gains to cash or other valuable commodity).*

The legal definition of fraud refers to cases where a person makes a material false statement—with the knowledge at the time that the statement was false; reliance by the victim on the false statement; and resulting damages to the victim. Legally, fraud can lead to a variety of criminal charges, including fraud, theft, embezzlement, and larceny. Each charge has its own specific legal definition and required criteria, and all of the charges can result in severe penalties and a criminal record.

The *Report to the Nation on Occupational Fraud and Abuse*[5] divides occupational fraud into three major categories: misappropriation (accounting for 88.7 percent of the cases reported), corruption (27.4 percent), and fraudulent statements (10.3 percent).

The median losses reported by type of fraud ranged from $150,000 to over $2 million.

Fraud can be committed not only by an individual employee but also by a department, division, or branch within a company, or by outsiders. It can be directed against the organization as a whole or against parts of the organization. Also, it can be to the benefit of the organization as a whole, part of the organization, or an individual within or outside the organization.

Fraud designed to benefit the organization generally exploits an unfair or dishonest advantage that also may deceive an outside party. Even though it is committed to benefit the organization, perpetrators of such frauds often also benefit indirectly from the fraud. Usually personal benefit accrues when the organization is aided by the fraudulent act. Some examples include:

- Improper transfer pricing of goods exchanged between related entities by purposely structuring pricing to intentionally improve the operating results of an organization involved in the transaction to the detriment of the other organization
- Improper payments, such as bribes, kickbacks, and illegal political contributions or payoffs, to government officials, customers, or suppliers
- Intentional, improper related-party transactions in which one party receives some benefit not obtainable in an arm's-length transaction
- Assignment of fictitious or misrepresented assets or sales
- Deliberate misrepresentation or valuation of transactions, assets, liabilities, or income
- Conducting business activities that violate government statutes, rules, regulations, or contracts
- Presenting an improved financial picture of the organization to outside parties by intentionally failing to record or disclose significant information
- Tax fraud

Fraud perpetrated to the detriment of the organization is generally for the direct or indirect benefit of an employee, outside individual, or another firm. Examples include:

- Misappropriation of money, property, or falsification of financial records to cover up the act, thus making detection difficult
- Intentional misrepresentation or concealment of events or data
- Submission of claims for services or goods not actually provided to the organization
- Acceptance of bribes or kickbacks
- Diversion of a potentially profitable transaction that would normally generate profits for the organization to an employee or outsider.

Why Fraud Happens

Given the risk involved, why do people commit fraud?

Indications from many studies, including interviews with persons who have committed fraud, are that most perpetrators of fraud did not initially set out to commit a crime. Generally, they simply availed themselves of an opportunity. The fraud triangle (see Exhibit 1.1) is used by experts in the psychology of fraud to explain the reasons for persons committing fraud. The fraud triangle consists of: opportunity, pressure, and rationalization.

EXHIBIT 1.1 The Fraud Triangle can be used to examine the causes of fraud.

The *opportunity* exists when there are weak controls and/or when an individual is in a position of trust. While the *pressures* on those who commit fraud are often of a financial nature, unrealistic corporate targets may also influence a person to commit fraud to meet the targets. The *rationalization* for fraud often includes these beliefs:

- The activity is not criminal.
- Their actions are justified.
- They are simply borrowing the money.
- They are ensuring that corporate goals are met.
- "Everyone else is doing it" so it must be acceptable.

The opportunity for fraud often begins when an innocent, genuine error passes unnoticed, exposing a weakness in the internal controls.

Example: System Error

A clerk accidentally processes an invoice twice, and the financial controls do not prevent the second check from being issued.

The internal controls usually exist but are weak; they may have been compromised for the sake of organizational expediency or just eroded over time. A control, such as segregation of duties, may simply be removed as the company downsizes. In other cases controls may be removed or weakened by business reengineering activities. Someone in a position of trust may, because of seniority or position, be able to bypass controls or exploit known weaknesses. Often the internal controls become so weak that there is little or no chance that the person committing the fraud will get caught by the remaining control framework.

Fraud: Action 1

The clerk calls the vendor and requests that a credit be sent to his attention so he can correct the mistake personally.

Psychological and criminal studies have shown that the shift from honest to dishonest behavior results from changes in the fraud triangle. Fraud may start with a perceived opportunity to derive an unearned benefit. It is then rationalized by a belief that the behavior is acceptable or justified. This belief is usually supported and encouraged by a feeling of pressure, often financial.[6] While fraudulent acts may initially be only "questionable," they gradually cross over the line into criminal activity. Yet those caught committing fraud usually do not consider their activities or themselves to be criminal. Rather than being seen as a crime, the fraudulent activity is often seen as a reward for a job well done—such as justified compensation in times when pay increases have been frozen, or other compensation the individual thought was deserved. It may even be viewed as a "temporary loan" to help an employee get through a tough financial crisis.

Fraud: Action 2

When the check arrives at the office, the clerk cashes it and keeps the money.

Pressure

The city raised the property tax bill on his house by 62 percent and he is flat broke.

Rationalization

He has been working a lot of unpaid overtime recently, he deserves the money, and the company can afford it.

Interviews with persons who have been caught committing fraud show that they often are bothered far more by the first illegal act than by subsequent acts. In any case, once the line is crossed from an honest mistake to fraud, the illegal acts tend to become more frequent, even when the original pressure is removed. If the fraud goes undetected, the fraudulent activity will continue and the dollar amounts will increase. The greed of the person committing the crime and the time it takes to detect the activity seem to be the only limiting factors in the extent of the fraud.

Experience has shown that there is no such thing as a small fraud—just frauds that have not reached maturity. The implication for auditors and fraud examiners is obvious: Fraud will occur, and will continue to grow in size, unless stopped. Obviously, there is a heavy onus on management, audit, and fraud investigators to deter and detect fraud.

Who Is Responsible for Fraud Detection?

There has been much debate about the role of management versus audit in deterring and detecting fraud and irregularities. The debate gets hotter when a fraud with a long history is suddenly uncovered. This is particularly so if the fraud was uncovered by accident, even though there were regular audits in the area.

A popular line of argument goes like this: Management is responsible for the business on a continuing basis and has (or should have) intricate knowledge of the day-to-day operations. Management also has responsibility for implementing organizational controls. Management "owns" the systems, people, and records that constitute the controls. Therefore, managers should have a complete picture: knowledge of the business risks and controls, plus the authority to adjust business operations. This provides them with ample means and opportunity to make required changes to company operations. Therefore, management, rather than the auditors, should be responsible for the detection of fraud. Of course, we know that it is not that simple.

The counterargument is this: Auditors, especially internal auditors, have expertise in the design, implementation, and evaluation of internal controls. Auditors are on the front line, and they deal with controls every day. Auditors are also experts in risk identification and assessment and may have knowledge of other similar operations. They should already have access to powerful audit software tools and techniques, so they are in the best position to identify fraud and irregularities and to report them to management. Therefore, fraud prevention and detection should be primarily the responsibility of auditors.

In organizations where a separate group conducts fraud investigations, the question of responsibility for prevention and detection may become even more confusing. Where fraud investigators are called in only when a fraud has been detected, they may not see their role as including fraud prevention. However, management may not have the same view.

So who is responsible?

Part of the answer can be found in a variety of evolving auditing standards, such as the *Standards for Professional Practice of Internal Auditing* published by the Institute of Internal Auditors (IIA). The standards discuss various aspects of internal auditing and provide excellent guidance and direction to auditors. They may also provide useful information and direction to fraud investigators. Unfortunately, these standards are not always read and understood by auditors, let alone by management. However, the most critical part of the answer lies in the corporate culture and a mutual understanding among audit, fraud investigators, and senior management.

In discussing the scope of audit work, the IIA standards clearly charge internal auditors with responsibility for reviewing the controls over the safeguarding of assets and ensuring their accurate reporting. Further, audit is responsible for determining if outputs and results are in keeping with the goals and objectives of the business activities being carried out. In performing these responsibilities, internal audit clearly has a role to play in detecting fraud, irregularities, waste, and abuse.

The IIA standards for professional practice also discuss the concept of "due professional care." Internal auditors are informed of the need to be alert to the "possibilities of intentional wrongdoing, errors and omissions, inefficiencies, waste, ineffectiveness, and conflicts of interest." These ideas are presented in more detail in the Statement on Internal Auditing Standards 3 (SIAS 3), *Deterrence, Detection, Investigation and Reporting of Fraud*.

The American Institute of Certified Public Accountants (AICPA) has also published two key Statements on Auditing Standards (SAS) designed to assist auditors in carrying out their responsibilities. Again, fraud examiners can benefit from the information contained in the standards and statements. SAS 53, *The Auditor's Responsibility to Detect and Report Errors and Irregularities*, provides guidelines for auditors in detecting fraud. SAS 99, *Consideration of Fraud in a Financial Statement*, an update to SAS 82, provides additional operational guidelines which auditors can use when designing audit programs. One of the key features of SAS 99 is a list of fraud risk factors that every auditor should consider during an audit. Applying these risk factors to the development of the audit program enhances fraud detection, obviously, by focusing audit resources on areas with the greatest risk of fraud.

The International Federation of Accountants (IFAC) addressed one of the most important issues facing auditors today—the responsibility for detecting fraud—by releasing an International Standard of Auditing (ISA) entitled *The Auditor's Responsibility to Consider Fraud in an Audit of Financial*

Statements (ISA 240). It states that while the primary responsibility for the prevention and detection of fraud rests with those charged with governance and management of the entity, auditors should be alert to risks of material misstatement due to fraud and are required to assess any such risks encountered during the course of an audit. Auditors are also required to respond to the assessed risk by such actions as testing the appropriateness of journal entries, reviewing the accounting estimates for biases, and obtaining an understanding of the business rationale of significant transactions that are outside of the normal course of business for the entity.

All of the standards stress the duty of auditors to plan and conduct audits in a manner that reasonably ensures that financial statements are free from errors or serious misstatements. They also charge audit with the responsibility of evaluating the organization's controls and the adequacy of management actions to identified weaknesses. The standards require that auditors plan and perform audits in a manner that reduces the risk of fraudulent activities going undetected. However, the standards do not place responsibility for the deterrence, prevention, or detection of these irregularities solely on audit. It remains management's responsibility to oversee the operations of the company and to deter fraud. This situation must be explained in any corporate statement on fraud and clearly communicated to all levels of the organization. The best solution to fraud deterrence and detection is a partnership among management, internal and external audit, and fraud investigators—with everyone working together in a complementary manner to deal with fraud.

Initially, it may be difficult to determine if a fraud has occurred. Something that starts out as an audit may uncover possible criminal activities and become a fraud investigation. Auditors should always be aware of the possibility of fraud and know when or if to call in fraud investigators or police.

Exhibit 1.2 can be used by audit to determine whether an allegation should be referred to fraud investigators or police. It can also be used by audit in developing a fraud policy to map out when audit will be involved and when allegations will be handed over to investigators or police.

How does an organization develop a fraud resistant culture?

The best method to avoid fraud is to stop it before it occurs—through ethics and fraud awareness training. To do so, not only control but also alertness must be created at all levels of the organization. However, fraud prevention must be commensurate to the risk. Care must be taken to avoid creating an atmosphere of distrust and paranoia by overemphasizing fraud deterrence.[7] A corporate ethics program helps to lay a clear foundation for all aspects of employee actions, not just those related to fraud. In recent years, ethics programs have become more common and have demonstrated

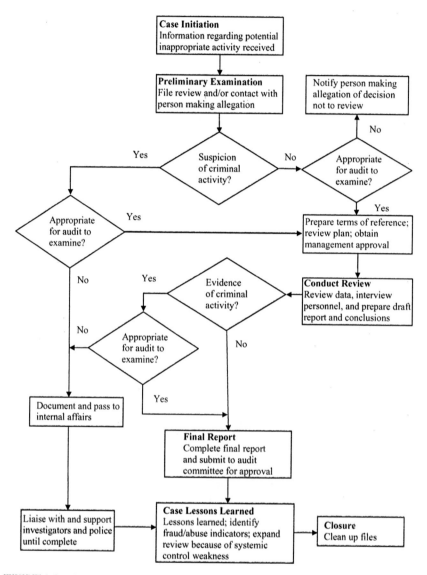

Case Initiation
Information regarding potential
inappropriate activity received

Preliminary Examination
File review and/or contact with
person making allegation

Notify person making
allegation of decision
not to review

Suspicion
of criminal
activity?

Appropriate
for audit to
examine?

No

Yes

No

Yes

Appropriate
for audit to
examine?

Yes

Prepare terms of reference;
review plan; obtain
management approval

No

Yes

Evidence
of criminal
activity?

Conduct Review
Review data, interview
personnel, and prepare draft
report and conclusions

No

Appropriate
for audit to
examine?

No

Yes

Document and pass to
internal affairs

Yes

Final Report
Complete final report
and submit to audit
committee for approval

Liaise with and support
investigators and police
until complete

Case Lessons Learned
Lessons learned; identify
fraud/abuse indicators; expand
review because of systemic
control weakness

Closure
Clean up files

EXHIBIT 1.2 Allegations Flowchart.

considerable value in shaping and guiding employee behavior. An existing ethics program, expanded to include fraud awareness and deterrence
measures, is an excellent method of reducing losses to fraud. Although
experts warn that ethics programs may seem like an obvious way to combat corruption, organizations simply going through the motions of ethics

training and not embracing the real spirit of the effort are just wasting their time.

It is important to understand the underlying cause of the employee behavior, the fraudulent activity, when developing fraud deterrence policies. Often theft is a reflection of how management is perceived by the employees. Any company policy on fraud should be communicated in a manner that stresses the positive. Sanctions must be clearly stated and uniformly enforced. It must be apparent that the rules apply to everyone. The policy must be supported and encouraged by all levels of management, and senior management especially must demonstrate the highest level of integrity—not only following the rules, but appearing to do so. Nothing can foster an attitude that "fraud is acceptable" as quickly as senior management's disregard for financial rules and regulations. The fact that a questionable act is "good" for the company or only affects the competition is not an adequate excuse. Such behavior by senior management may contribute to other types of fraud being considered equally acceptable by employees. Acceptance of any type or level of questionable activity may be seen as a green light to all sorts of activity, including fraud.

By creating a fraud-resistant culture, management can avoid not only the associated monetary losses but also the negative side effects, such as adverse publicity, poor employee morale, and possible loss of goodwill. Fraud can be a public relations nightmare—witness the negative effect that the conviction of a president of the United Way of America had on public and corporate donations, or the negative publicity experienced by Martha Stewart.

A company policy or program emphasizing the general application of ethical standards and practices can help to prevent fraud. A fraud awareness program, mandatory screening of job applicants, and a corporate fraud policy then will complement it.

What Is a Fraud Awareness Program?

A fraud awareness program demonstrates to all employees that the company considers fraud a serious issue. It should cover the company's prevention measures and tell employees what they should do if they are concerned about possible fraudulent activities. It must be clear that fraud will be dealt with swiftly and fairly. A well-constructed fraud awareness program will discuss how, when, and to whom to report possible fraudulent activities. Employees who are aware of the company policy, know the rationale for it, understand the damaging implications of fraud, and know what to do if they suspect fraud are the best line of defense against such activities.

Many companies have added fraud awareness training to existing corporate ethics programs, and some package it with counseling or employee assistance programs. A fraud awareness program is a critical step to deterring fraud and helps to ensure that all employees know what is expected of them. By demonstrating that all employees have a role to play in deterring and detecting fraud, and by addressing various types of fraud (including fraud committed by employees and by outsiders), the program fosters confidence and trust.

Screening Job Applicants

Screening job applicants and temporary employees is a simple and effective way to reduce the risk of employee fraud. Such programs ensure that candidates have been honest concerning educational background and employment histories. All education claims and references should be verified and a search conducted for criminal records. It has been estimated that 10 to 25 percent of resumes include serious misstatements. Where not prohibited by law, some companies also require drug testing of temporary employees, vendors, and contractors. The intent is to keep out those who have committed fraud in the past or may be pressured into committing it in future.

A thorough screening program can reduce fraud, help to ensure that properly qualified candidates are selected for the job, and have the added positive effect of reducing the overall cost of attracting and hiring qualified staff. Screening potential candidates also makes it clear to new employees that the company is serious about the importance of honesty and truthfulness, and lets employees know that they are valued and trusted.

What Is a Corporate Fraud Policy?

One way for an organization to define what constitutes unacceptable behavior and to formalize how fraud investigations will be handled is to have a written fraud policy. A corporate fraud policy formally sets out what an employee is expected to do when he or she suspects that fraud is occurring. It also increases employee awareness of the seriousness of fraud and management's refusal to tolerate such activities. Such a policy is central to any fraud awareness program as it sets the tone for the company and for its employees, demonstrates management's resolve to deter fraud, and formalizes the manner in which the company will handle fraud.

Fraud is committed not only against organizations but also by organizations—or by individuals in an organization—to the betterment of the organization. A strong corporate fraud policy must convey the message that no one has the authority to commit illegal acts on behalf of the company, including fraudulent financial reporting, through which the company may benefit—nor the authority to cover up such illegal acts. The fraud policy establishes a framework for ethical behavior by all employees in all circumstances and details the measures that will be taken to address fraud by individuals inside and outside of the organization. It must also make clear that *any* fraudulent activity will be investigated and the perpetrators prosecuted.

The policy must clearly spell out the procedures to be followed when potentially fraudulent activities are encountered. Such procedures are necessary to ensure the proper handling of possible frauds, to protect employees from wrongful allegations, and to reduce the opportunity for successful litigation by suspects, victims, or witnesses. The procedures reduce the impact of emotions and the opportunity for discrimination, and create an atmosphere of trust by setting the stage for the fair and equitable treatment of all employees.

The fraud policy should be fairly short, simply stated, and contain at least these points:

- A statement of the company's intent to prosecute persons who commit fraud
- A clear statement of who is responsible for the deterrence, detection, and investigation of fraud
- Guidelines and procedures for handling suspected fraud or allegations of fraud
- Instructions on who will be notified at various stages of the investigation of alleged fraud
- Criteria for determining if, and when, legal, law enforcement, and regulatory agencies will be involved
- Guidelines for reporting and publishing the results of fraud investigations.

A well-written corporate fraud policy acts as a deterrent by demonstrating that management has thought about fraud and has taken action to deter such acts. The policy also assists employees who may be placed in compromising situations by giving them concrete direction and guidance. The policy can help to ensure that all instances of fraud are dealt with in a consistent and nondiscriminatory manner, as well as letting employees know that there will be open and equitable treatment of all allegations of fraud. A corporate fraud policy also aids auditors and fraud examiners by setting out procedures to be followed when allegations or suspicions of fraud arise.

Many auditors and fraud investigators find themselves in situations where they are unsure of the next action to be taken, such as whether legal or regulatory agencies should be notified. The corporate fraud policy is the authoritative document on fraud issues, and should be consulted and used as required. Persons investigating fraud will be comforted by the clear statement of the procedures for handling allegations and the investigation of actual fraudulent acts. Also, management can be more confident that the proper steps are being taken and that appropriate authorities notified in a timely manner.

Example of the Main Elements of a Fraud Policy

The senior board of directors wishes to make it clear that (Company Name) has zero tolerance for the commission or concealment of fraudulent or illegal acts. Allegations of such acts will be investigated and pursued to their logical conclusion, including legal action where warranted. All employees are responsible for reporting suspected instances of fraud to their manager.

Management has primary responsibility for the implementation of internal controls to deter and detect fraud. Management is also responsible for referring allegations of fraud to the Chief Audit Executive (or Director of Fraud Investigation, if one exists).

Audit is responsible for monitoring and evaluating internal controls to detect possible weaknesses. The Chief Audit Executive (or the Director of Fraud Investigation) has primary responsibility for the investigation of allegations of improprieties committed by, or against, the company.

During the initial phase of any investigation, the investigators/auditors will protect the reputations of all concerned by restricting access to all information related to the allegations and investigation to those with a legitimate need to know. Where an investigation concludes that a fraudulent activity is "probable," the Chief Audit Executive (or Director of Fraud Investigation) will inform senior management of the nature and possible extent of the activities. The Chief Audit Executive (or Director of Fraud Investigation), with the advice of senior management, will determine whether to inform the legal department, law enforcement, and/or regulatory agencies.

If an investigation determines that fraudulent activities have occurred, the Chief Audit Executive (or Director of Fraud Investigation) is required to inform the head of the legal department, members of the audit committee, and the appropriate law enforcement agencies.

The company will make all evidence collected during the course of the investigation available to legal and law enforcement agencies and will pursue the prosecution of all parties involved in the criminal activities.

Information on detected fraudulent activities will be published in company newsletters and made available to all employees.

Signed President of (Company Name)

Date

Notes

1. KPMG Forensic, *Fraud Survey 2003*, KPMG Forensic, 2003.
2. Association of Certified Fraud Examiners, *Occupational Fraud and Abuse*, (Austin, TX: Obsidian Publishing Co., 1997).
3. Deloitte Touche Tohmatsu International, *International Fraud within the European Union*, Deloitte Touche Tohmatsu International, 1997.
4. PricewaterhouseCoopers, *Global Economic Crime Survey*, 2003.
5. ACFE, *Report to the Nation on Occupational Fraud and Abuse* (Austin, TX: James D. Ratley. 2008).
6. W. S. Albrecht, E. A. McDermott, and T. L. Williams, "Reducing the Cost of Fraud," *Internal Auditor* (February 1994): 28–34.
7. Richard C. Hollinger and John P. Clark, *Theft by Employees* (Lexington, MA: Lexington Books, 1993).

CHAPTER 2

Fraud Prevention and Detection

Programs and activities designed to prevent fraud can reduce its occurrence, but they will not eliminate it. Even companies with excellent fraud deterrence programs are still at risk and will experience fraud from time to time. A study by KPMG reported that 75 percent of companies had experienced at least one fraud in the last two years, 13 percentage points more than in 1998.[1] Given that the median loss from some types of fraud exceeds $200,000, even one act of fraud can be highly expensive. When the potentially negative impact on employee morale and stockholder confidence is factored into the equation, the costs can be devastating. It is, therefore, important for audit organizations to have the ability to detect fraud.

If audit is to contribute to the detection of fraud, it is essential that auditors understand how to build audit programs that address this goal. Such audit programs rely heavily on the evaluation of the control environment and the auditor's knowledge of the organization's exposures to, and risks of, fraud.

Good awareness programs and internal controls can help to prevent crimes of opportunity. Employees not tempted by weak controls, and not encouraged by poor management practices, are less likely to engage in illegal activities. However, there is an ironic side to good controls. The successful prevention of fraud—or at any rate the lack of symptoms—may leave some organizations overly complacent. It is easy to forget the negative effects of fraud when you are not experiencing them. Therefore, the value of deterrence programs is never more widely agreed on than when such programs are allowed to erode, a fraud occurs, and it is eventually detected. The prompt detection of renewed fraud then reaffirms the need for prevention programs and the value of audit. However, the failure to detect fraud will be seen (perhaps unfairly, if controls were allowed to lapse) as a significant shortcoming. But until this happens, the company finds itself in a position of wondering "Is no news good news—or not?" The onus on audit and management is strongest at such times to remain vigilant and maintain the controls. No news *is* good news provided proper controls are maintained.

Audit managers should recognize that keeping a system of strong controls and ensuring that senior management maintains a firm corporate fraud policy are as important as the vigorous search for fraud that has already occurred.

This chapter discusses the preconditions for detecting fraud, the investigation and reporting of fraud, and the role of internal controls. This material is applicable to both audit and fraud investigation. Even though fraud investigators may be called in only to examine cases of known fraud to determine the nature and extent of the activity, a general knowledge of controls is essential to their work.

Detecting Fraud

Auditing is generally concerned with the evaluation of controls for the efficient and effective use of company resources. Sound controls are an essential part of any defense against fraud, but they may not be working as intended or may no longer be adequate. Reorganization, business reengineering, or downsizing can seriously weaken or eliminate controls, while new information systems can present additional opportunities to commit or conceal fraud. Auditors must also be constantly aware that mandated controls that are nominally in effect might be poorly enforced or otherwise irrelevant.

After a thorough examination of the control framework, identified weaknesses and fraud exposures may result in audit performing a fraud examination. The evaluation of the internal controls differs from a pure fraud examination. Whereas the evaluation of controls does not presume a fraud has taken place, a fraud investigation is primarily concerned with the collection and analysis of evidence to support, or refute, allegations of a specific wrongdoing.

Auditors and fraud investigators must be conversant with the key conditions for detecting fraud. There are five such conditions:

1. Determine the organization's risk of fraud by studying its operational and control environments to identify risk categories and exposures.
2. Assess the risks and exposures.
3. Examine the risks and exposures from the fraudster's perspective, to determine what he or she can control or manipulate to make the fraud possible.
4. Thoroughly understand the symptoms of fraud and data sources that may contain those symptoms.
5. Be alert to the occurrence of symptoms and know how to look for those symptoms in the data.

Once these conditions are met, it becomes easier to deter, investigate, and report detected fraud and create new controls to detect any reoccurrence.

Determining the Exposure to Fraud

Auditors must be aware of the areas where their organization could be at risk and the possible impacts. Auditors must understand the various sources of risk and exposure that confront the organization, from the highest to the lowest levels. Risks that are poorly managed or not mitigated are an exposure that can be manipulated to benefit the fraudster. The prevention and detection of fraud will be improved by a thorough understanding of what could possibly happen to the organization in the normal course of operating its business or as the result of some other unusual event. However, simply identifying all the possible exposures, given the likely lack of resources to deal with them, is not sufficient. In order to focus audit attention and the prevention and search for fraud, auditors must not only identify but also assess and prioritize the risks.

The first step the auditor should consider is a review of any fraud risk assessment performed by management. The foundations of an effective risk management program should be rooted in the organization's risk assessment process. As such, management should assess fraud risk on a systematic and ongoing basis.

Audit's assessment of the management of fraud risk should include steps to ensure that management is committed to the prevention and detections of fraud and that fraud awareness training and a process by which management and all employees affirm their knowledge and understanding of fraud and fraud risk are in place. Internal auditors should provide objective assurance that management's assessment is sufficient and that the fraud controls are adequate to address any fraud risks. In addition, during the conduct of all audit engagements, internal auditors should consider the design and operation of controls from a fraud risk management perspective.

The next step is to develop categories that will define the types of fraud risk to which the organization may be exposed. Typical risk categories include external environment, legal, regulatory, governance, strategy, operational, information, human resources, financial, and technology. The development of risk categories can help to identify and assess the risks.

The assessment of risk includes the examination of the controls in place to mitigate against various risks, such as monetary loss, theft of assets, and loss of proprietary data. Each fraud risk should be mapped to the relevant control. Next, auditors must examine the operational environment and its internal controls to identify where weakness and deficiencies can leave the company exposed to fraud. The system of internal controls must be evaluated and tested to ensure it is working as intended. Processes, control points, key players, and risks must be carefully reviewed. Fraud is often largely a crime of opportunity, so the opportunities must be found and if possible eliminated or reduced.

The new requirements of the Sarbanes-Oxley Act (SOX) of 2002 state that it is not enough to simply maintain internal controls; management, and this usually involves audit, must now assert annually as to the effectiveness of those controls, including controls related to fraud detection and prevention. In particular, SOX Section 404 refers explicitly to fraud-related controls. As a result, auditors should evaluate and test the design and operating effectiveness of antifraud controls on an ongoing basis. By doing so, auditors can be proactive: taking significant action to prevent and detect fraud before it becomes an issue that will result in a material misstatement.

While not specifically designed to assess fraud exposures, auditors can obtain guidance from the Securities and Exchange Commission (SEC) and Public Companies Accounting and Oversight Board (PCAOB) Auditing Standard 5 (AS 5). AS 5 encouraged both management and auditors to use judgment and develop a top-down approach to assessing risk, and the same approach can be used to assess and prioritize fraud risk. According to AS 5, auditors should use a top-down approach to assess and select controls to be tested. Beginning at the financial statement level, auditors should develop an understanding of the overall financial risks and controls over financial reporting. They should start by focusing on the entity-level controls and then work down to the significant accounts, disclosures, and assertions. Finally, auditors should select for testing those controls that significantly address the risk of misstatement.

AS 5 is consistent with the AICPA's Auditing Standards Board (ASB) Statements on Auditing Standards (SAS) 104 to 111. They cover topics such as guidance on due professional care, audit risk, and supervision; and focus on the assessment of risk in an audit of financial statements. The statements are:

- SAS 104, *Amendment to Statement on Auditing Standards No. 1, Codification of Auditing Standards and Procedures* ("Due Professional Care in the Performance of Work")
- SAS 105, *Amendment to Statement on Auditing Standards No. 95, Generally Accepted Auditing Standards*
- SAS 106, *Audit Evidence*
- SAS 107, *Audit Risk and Materiality in Conducting an Audit*
- SAS 108, *Planning and Supervision*
- SAS 109, *Understanding the Entity and Its Environment and Assessing the Risks of Material Misstatement*

- SAS 110, _Performing Audit Procedures in Response to Assessed Risks and Evaluating the Audit Evidence Obtained_
- SAS 111, _Amendment to Statement on Auditing Standards No. 39, Audit Sampling_

These statements establish standards and provide guidance to auditors when assessing the risks of material misstatement (whether caused by error or fraud) in a financial statement audit. They also cover the design and conduct of the audit procedures aimed at assessing identified risks. Additionally, the statements discuss the planning and supervision, and the sufficiency of audit evidence in providing an opinion on the financial statements that are being audited.

The statements encourage auditors to develop an in-depth understanding of the audit entity and the business and information system environment, including internal controls. This understanding should be used to identify the key risks of material misstatement in the financial statements and to highlight and assess mitigation activities. A better understanding of the controls, risks, and operations contributes to a more rigorous assessment of the risks of material misstatement and improved linkage between the assessed risks and audit work performed in response to those risks.

Two widely distributed audit standards address fraud exposure concerns directly. SIAS 3, _Deterrence, Detection, Investigation and Reporting of Fraud_, requires auditors to have sufficient knowledge of possible frauds to be able to identify their symptoms. Auditors and fraud investigators must be aware of what can go wrong, how it can go wrong, and who could be involved. Also, AICPA's SAS 99, _Consideration of Fraud in a Financial Statement Audit_, was developed to assist auditors in the detection of fraud. It goes further than its predecessor, SAS 82. New provisions include:

- The need for brainstorming the risks of fraud
- Emphasizing increased professional skepticism
- Ensuring managers are aware of the potential of fraud occurring
- Using a variety of tests
- Detecting cases where management overrides controls

It also defines risk factors for fraudulent financial reporting and theft, and can be used as a basic model for assessing the risk of fraudulent financial reporting. The risks outlined in SAS 99 include factors such as management conditions, the competitive and business environment, and operational and financial stability. The risk factors for theft include employee relationships, internal control, and the susceptibility of assets. The risk factors for fraud are shown in Exhibit 2.1.

EXHIBIT 2.1   Risk Factors for Fraud.

Risk Factor	Typical Issues	Evaluation Strategies
Management environment	Are management's financial targets realistic? Pressures to meet unrealistic performance standards, and management style and attitude, may affect financial reporting. There is a higher risk that performance will be overstated by employees, simply to meet otherwise unattainable targets.	Review production figures for accuracy and key target measures for reasonableness. Evaluate financial targets established by management to see if they are too high.
Competitive and business environment	The rapid pace of technological innovation can make inventory holdings obsolete in a matter of months. Coupled with other pressures, this may encourage the overstatement of inventory values on financial statements.	Recalculate the value of inventory to ensure that it has been correctly calculated and reported.
Employee relationships	An employee's spouse or close relative may receive noncompetitive contracts.	Match employee addresses to vendor addresses.
Attractive assets	High-value, new technology items that are easily transported are at high risk of theft.	Include specific audit objectives to assess risks and controls for physical inventories.
Internal controls	Older manual systems had well-established controls, but new organizational structures and computer systems are typically different.	Verify that the computer system has controls to prevent users from initiating and authorizing the same transactions, and performing other incompatible duties.
Lack of separation of duties	Business reengineering has combined various functions, reduced staff, and eliminated separation of duties.	Ensure that new processes, procedures, and application systems have proper controls to address the lack of separation of duties.

EXHIBIT 2.1   *(Continued)*

Risk Factor	Typical Issues	Evaluation Strategies
Too much trust placed in employees with insufficient monitoring and control over their activities.	The purchasing function is at high risk of fraud, but annual audits of this area are sporadic.	Regularly compare the contract, receipt and invoice quantities, and prices for consistency.

Auditors and investigators must be aware of all types of exposures. When planning audit programs, close attention must be paid to identifying areas of greatest exposure and determining steps to assess the related risks. For example, it is well understood that the purchasing function is an area of serious risk for fraud,[2] yet less than 30 percent of audit organizations conduct yearly audits in the purchasing area. Obviously, auditors cannot afford to ignore such areas as purchasing, where the risks of fraud are well known. Understanding and evaluating such risk factors can focus scarce audit resources on areas with a greater exposure to fraud.

Assessing the Risk that Fraud Is Occurring (or Will Occur)

Once the exposures have been identified, it is important to assess the risk. The identification and assessment of fraud risk is a little different from the usual risk assessment performed. Fraud risk is primarily concerned with a loss, usually financial or likely to have a financial impact. When assessing risk, many auditors restrict themselves to likelihood and severity where "likelihood" refers to the measure of certainty that the exposure will result in a loss and "severity" refers to the extent to which the impact will be felt. But these alone are not sufficient to assess the overall risk, as the assessment of the fraud risk has a number of other dimensions. Many people know that a large earthquake will hit Los Angeles sometime and that it will result in significant loss of life. Likewise, people have known for years that smoking may cause cancer. But people still live in Los Angeles and people still smoke. The reason is not a poor understanding of the likelihood and severity of these risks; it is the impact of other dimensions of the risk equation: imminence, frequency, and breadth, in particular.

The question of imminence—how soon?—is a key factor in management's decision as to whether the risk needs to be addressed. A risk that is several years away may not be addressed today no matter how severe the future impact. Another risk dimension is the frequency—how often?—with which the impact will be felt. In the 1970s, automakers knew of design flaws that could cause a fatality but felt that the frequency of this happening was sufficiently low and did not fix the problem. Another factor is that of breadth—how wide-reaching? Does the risk affect the entire organization or just a small portion of it?

For some, the earthquake fails to score high on imminence, so people continue to live in Los Angeles. For others living outside of Los Angeles, it is not important because the breadth of the damage is restricted to the southwest coastal area of California. For some, cancer fails to be a concern on both the imminence and frequency dimensions. Take the statement: "California will suffer a severe earthquake of at least 8.2 within a month, resulting in the death of at least 3.5 million people in the Los Angeles area." Given that the veracity of the statement could be proven (likelihood), I am sure you would agree that this would have an impact on people's decision to live (or stay) in Los Angeles—this month. If we added the fact that "Aftershocks will continue for at least six months and additional earthquakes of a similar magnitude will occur for many more years" (frequency), real estate prices might be affected for some time. Similarly, "If you smoke one more cigarette, you will get a painful form of cancer that will kill you within two months" may be considered a high enough risk (likelihood, imminence, and severity) to deter a smoker.

Finally, auditors and management must be concerned with the cost of mitigating activities. There will always be a residual risk—risk cannot be totally eliminated: NASA still has accidents; cars (or tires) still have design flaws. While we cannot totally eliminate the risk of fraud, we can address the balance of the mitigation activities by moving resources from overcontrolled areas to those that are undercontrolled. Balancing resources between areas can reduce the overall risk of fraud.

External Symptoms

In addition to the symptoms of fraud in the financial books or application systems, auditors must be alert to other external symptoms. Fraud committed for personal benefit can be related to personal financial difficulties. Some of the possible signs of fraud for personal benefit are:

- Living beyond one's means
- Compulsive gambling or stock speculation
- Excessive use of drugs or alcohol
- High personal debts or losses
- Performing tasks below one's level or position
- Never taking a vacation.

Although it is unlikely that a routine audit would identify such signs, auditors should be aware of them, and, where possible, investigators should search for them. These red flags will almost always be present in cases of fraud for personal benefit. Despite the red flags, fraud remains difficult to predict and may not fit the standard profile. Also, while the red flags cannot be ignored, auditors and investigators must tread carefully. The presence of these signs does not signify that fraud has occurred, only that there is a risk of fraud occurring. The purpose of the audit or investigation is to determine if fraud has occurred.

Identifying Areas of High Risk for Fraud

The next step is to rate the risk exposures of each fraud risk. Combine into a single worksheet information collected and assessed earlier. Using the risk categories, identify applicable risk factors and relevant fraud risk. Then assess the likelihood of the risk occurring and the impact if it does. Since the controls have not been tested, auditors should consider the level of inherent risk.

The risk-ranking process requires input from a variety of sources. Auditors should consider identifying a risk assessment team that includes individuals from areas across the organization. The risk categories can serve as a means for identifying the organizational areas that should be part of the risk assessment team. The team should include persons from: audit, legal, finance, operations, technology (information technology and operations), human resources, and strategic areas of the organization. In addition, senior management and significant business units and processes (accounting, payroll, procurement, etc.) should be invited to participate.

The risk assessment team should engage in an initial brainstorming activity. The work performed by audit to identify risk categories, risk factors, and fraud risks should also be presented and discussed. A table format can be used to organize the fraud risk-ranking process, as shown in Exhibit 2.2. The ultimate objective is to arrive at a risk-ranked (High, Medium, Low) set of fraud risks.

It is important to be flexible in the approach to determining fraud risks. Ideally, the risk categories will be established once, defined and clearly communicated to all risk assessment team members, and used for all subsequent fraud risk assessments. However, the processes of arriving at the risk factors and fraud risks are dynamic and fluid. These two processes are not dependent on each other. Because of this fact, auditors may identify a fraud risk where they will have to work backward to determine the risk factor and risk category; or they may identify a fraud risk that is an orphan

EXHIBIT 2.2   Inherent Fraud Risk Assessment.

Risk Categories	Risk Factor	Fraud Risk	Likelihood	Impact	Inherent Fraud Risk
Financial	Attractive assets	Theft	High	Medium	Medium
	New computer system in A/P	Improper invoicing	High	High	High
		Lack of separation of duties	High	High	High
Governance	Compensation is bonus based	Contracting irregularities	High	High	High
Technology	Rapidly changing technology	Over valuation of inventory	High	Medium	Medium
External Environment	Competitive business environment	Theft of intellectual property	Low	Medium	Low

and has no risk factor. It is important not to ignore these orphan fraud risks; their inherent risk should still be considered and rated.

The items identified as high fraud risk must be considered in more depth by looking at who could be committing the fraud. Doing this requires auditors to employ two approaches: controls and key fields. The same approaches should be used for specific fraud allegations and to investigate known frauds.

Looking at the Exposures from the Fraudster's Perspective

Once the fraud risks areas have been identified and assessed, the next step is to determine if the high-risk frauds are occurring. The saying "It takes one to know one" does not mean that auditors and investigators need to commit fraud. However, if they wish to prevent fraud from happening, they must know who could be involved, what is possible, and how fraud could occur. Often the people who commit fraud are simply opportunists, taking advantage of a weakness or absence of control. If they hope to prevent fraud, auditors must identify the opportunities before fraud takes place and address any weaknesses in the controls. But they also must be able to think like a perpetrator of fraud in order to detect the fraud.

The best defense against fraud is a systematic and ongoing effort to examine possible fraud exposures. Prevention techniques should be established; data analysis and other detection techniques should be employed; and coordinated investigation and corrective action processes should be implemented.

According to a study sponsored by the Institute of Internal Auditors, the Association of Certified Fraud Examiners, and the American Institute of Certified Public Accountants, fraud risk exposures should be assessed periodically.[3] Further, an effective fraud risk management program should be part of the larger enterprise risk management program.

Auditors should identify not only where there is a high risk of fraud but also who the perpetrators might be. For this reason, auditors should examine control activities—considering both the possible fraud schemes and the individuals, within and external to the organization, who could be committing the fraud.

There are two main approaches to assessing fraud schemes from the fraudster's perspective:

1. **The control weaknesses approach** looks at the potential for fraud by examining the key controls, determining who could take advantage of a control weakness, and how they could manipulate a control that may not be working properly.
2. **The key fields approach** looks at potential for fraud by considering the data being entered. Which fields could be manipulated, by whom, and what would the affect be?

Both approaches try to determine who could be committing fraud, what the fraudster could be doing, and what the symptoms of fraud would look like in the data. Exhibit 2.3 illustrates the two approaches for assessing fraud schemes.

Approach 1: Control Weaknesses

Who Could Benefit from the Identified Control Weaknesses?

Identified control weakness must be examined from the point of view of who can benefit. Without a clear understanding of the control weakness and an assessment of who could take advantage of the weakness, auditors are still somewhat in the dark. Assessing the degree to which people could benefit from the weakness provides auditors with a measure of "opportunity." As mentioned, the fraud triangle—opportunity, rationalization, and pressure—is what drives people to commit fraud. Understanding who could

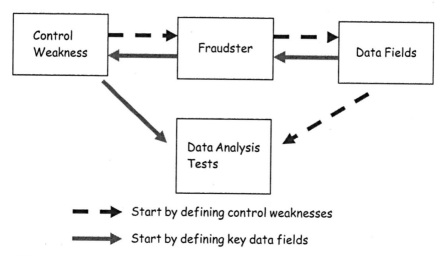

EXHIBIT 2.3 Identifying Fraud Exposures.

exploit the identified control weakness can focus the search for fraud on the persons with the greatest opportunity to commit the fraud.

Example: Received Quantity Greater Than Order Quantity

A review of the controls in the purchasing area determined that there was no control over the quantity received. Previous audit reports had recommended that the *received quantity* be compared to the *ordered quantity* and discrepancies flagged, but system incompatibilities have prevented management from acting on this recommendation.

Once a control weakness has been identified, it is important to consider who might take advantage of this opportunity. In the last example, there are several individuals who could take advantage of the control weakness to commit fraud, including persons internal to the organization, such as the receiving clerk and the contracting officer, and external parties, such as vendors and their salespeople.

What Can They Influence, Control, or Affect?

Fraudsters need to be able to hide the illegal act if they plan to continue committing the fraud. Auditors must look at the control weakness and the persons who could be involved, and determine what they can influence, manipulate, or control. The Barings Bank fraud went undetected largely because Nick Leesson was able to hide transactions in an unused account and then suppress the printing of this account on reports sent to the head office. Had the auditors realized that it was possible to suppress printing of individual accounts, a simple footing of the reports sent to the head office would have identified a discrepancy and led to the early discovery of the fraud.

In the received quantity example, these persons could be involved:

Internal Parties

- ▪ The receiving clerk could knowingly accept more than ordered because she is stealing the excess.
- ▪ The contracting officer could be accepting more than ordered and obtaining kickbacks from the vendor.

External Parties

- ▪ The vendor could simply ship more than was ordered, hoping the order would be accepted, thereby increasing sales.
- ▪ The vendor's salesperson could show that more had been ordered than specified in the contract and be committing the fraud against his company: manipulating his orders to get a bonus.

Can They Act Alone or Is Collusion Required?

The weaknesses in the controls may be such that the person committing the fraud can act alone, without the aid of internal or external accomplices. Auditors must consider whether an individual can exploit the weakness or if collusion is required. They should be aware of the potential for others to be involved, as the fraudsters may work together to hide the illegal act, such as providing a seemingly appropriate separation of duties.

In the example, the receiving clerk and contracting officer could be working in collusion. The receiving clerk could be accepting the delivery of the excess order and the contracting officer signing off on the invoice so that they can steal the excess. Or the receiving clerk may be acting in collusion with vendor, accepting more than ordered for kickbacks or to steal the excess.

The same weakness, with the same symptoms—quantity received greater than quantity ordered—could be an indication of a number of fraud schemes. Once a symptom has been identified, further analysis is required; and the auditors will need to look more closely at the data to see what is really happening.

Approach 2: Key Fields

Which Data Fields Can Be Manipulated and by Whom?

The second approach assesses the fraud risk from the data perspective. For this approach, auditors must identify the key data elements (fields) and determine:

- Who can enter, modify, or delete these
- Why they might do this in terms of both motivation and objective
- What are the key controls to prevent this from happening
- What tests can be performed to see if someone is committing a fraud

Taking accounts payable as an example, the key fields are Vendor Number, Invoice Number, Invoice Date, Quantity, Unit Price, and Amount.

Example: Vendor Number

The *clerk* can enter or modify the Vendor number—and might do this to pay duplicate or to create a fictitious vendor. The key controls would be in the Vendor table—restricting who can create and modify vendor. Tests to determine the adequacy and effectiveness of the controls over the vendor number would include testing for duplicate vendor numbers and verifying the authority of everyone who is creating and modifying vendors.

The clerk can also change the vendor address or bank account number—to misdirect a payment—so a possible test would be to look at the frequency of vendor address and bank account changes.

But a *vendor* can also affect the vendor number. The vendor could use slightly different names or mailing addresses to obtain multiple vendor numbers. The motivation would be to obtain duplicate payments; and the tests would include analyses looking for duplicate invoices (paid to different vendors) and for duplicate vendors (Name or Address or Phone Number or Tax ID, etc.) in the Vendor table.

Invoice Date

The *clerk* could backdate the invoice date to cause the payment to be made earlier than required. The clerk, working in collusion with the vendor, would pay the invoice early—perhaps even causing interest to be paid on overdue invoices when the invoice was not overdue—and split the gain with the vendor. Tests to ensure that invoice dates are not being backdated include comparison of invoice, goods receipt, and contract dates. Auditors should filter for transactions where invoice date is less than goods receipt date (or contract date). Auditors also could check for invoices where the invoice date for a higher-numbered invoice is before that of an earlier issued invoice number.

The *vendor,* working alone, could also backdate invoice dates to obtain earlier payments. Test would be the same: comparison of invoice, goods receipt, and contract dates and looking for invoice dates that are out of sync with the invoice numbers.

A similar fraud risk analysis would be performed on the invoice number, quantity, unit price, and amount fields. Exhibit 2.4 is an example showing the key fields, possible fraudster, why the fraud would be committed (expected gain), the preventive/detective controls, and tests that should be performed to look for the symptoms of fraud in the data.

Additional Fraud Risk Considerations

After considering the fraud risk from both the control weaknesses and key field perspectives, auditors should also review previous fraud investigations and audits and perform Internet searches for companies in the same industry. In the accounts payable example, additional fraud risks might include insufficient separation of duties, accounts payable (A/P) clerks making payments to themselves, and payments to the wrong vendor. The tests for these risks would include checking to see if an accounts payable clerk performs goods receipt and invoice receipt, setting a filter to identify all transactions where the A/P clerk is also the payee, and performing a vendor ratio analysis on payments.

Looking at A/P from control weaknesses and from the key fields, as well as brainstorming, provides a multifaceted approach to the detection and prevention of fraud.

The initial assessment of fraud risk considered the inherent risk. The items with a high fraud risk were then examined by looking at the risk from the fraudster's perspective. Now the effectiveness of the existing controls is assessed by examining the actual data for symptoms of fraud.

Understanding the Symptoms of Fraud

Common characteristics or symptoms of fraud include unauthorized transactions, cash overages or shortages, unexplained variations in prices, missing documentation, and excessive voids or refunds. Auditors should not be satisfied with a generic checklist of possible symptoms of fraud but must

EXHIBIT 2.4   Identification of Fraud Tests for Key Fields.

Info	Who	Why	Controls	Test
Vendor Name	Clerk	Duplicate payments; fictitious vendors	Vendor creation/ modification; duplicate tests on vendor table	Duplicates; blanks in key fields; classify on Created by; vendor usage by clerk
	Vendor	Duplicate payments	Duplicates	Duplicates test on vendor table
Vendor Address or Bank Account	Clerk	Divert payments	Vendor modification; system log file	Modification by clerk
Invoice Number	Clerk	Duplicate payments	Duplicates	Duplicates test on cleaned invoice number
	Vendor	Duplicate payments	Duplicates	Duplicates test on cleaned invoice number
Unit Price	Vendor	Increases unit price to obtain larger payment	Match of invoice and contract unit prices	Filter for transactions where invoice unit cost is more than contract
Quantity	Contracting officer	Works with vendor to receive more than ordered in exchange for kickbacks	Match of invoice and contract quantity	Filter for transactions where invoice quantities are more than ordered
	Vendor	Ships more than ordered to increase sales or charges for more than was shipped	Match of invoice and contract quantity and invoice and receipt quantities	Filter for transactions where invoice quantities are more than ordered or invoice quantity is more than receipt quantity

EXHIBIT 2.4 *(Continued)*

Info	Who	Why	Controls	Test
Amount	Clerk	Overpayment to obtain refund or for kickbacks	Match of invoice and contract amounts	Filter for transactions where invoice and contract amounts are not equal
	Vendor	Overcharges	Match of invoice and contract amounts	Filter for transactions where invoice and contract amounts are not equal
Date	Clerk	Backdate payment due date to pay early	Comparison of invoice, goods receipt, and contract dates	Filter for transactions where invoice date is less than goods receipt date (or contract date)
	Vendor	Backdate invoice date to obtain earlier payment	Comparison of invoice, goods receipt, and contract dates	Filter for transactions where invoice date is less than goods receipt date (or contract date)

identify the characteristics of fraud applicable to their operating environment. An effective approach is to develop a list of symptoms for each type of exposure identified in the planning phase of the audit. This could include items such as adjusting entries in the inventory system, a trend of increasing amount of deposits in transit, unexplained variances or correcting entries in the general ledger files, and so on.

Once symptoms of fraud have been outlined, auditors must determine the most effective way of detecting their presence—generally by computer analysis. A study of audit working papers to evaluate the methods used to identify financial errors found that computer-assisted audit techniques were the single most effective method used by audit teams,[4] even before the advent of powerful audit software and interactive auditing.

With the increase in electronic applications supporting the business environment, auditors must be creative in identifying ways in which the data could be manipulated or unauthorized users could gain access. The complexity of the environment requires a thorough review of the audit plans. Once these risks have been isolated, auditors can identify and assess controls to mitigate them. Many auditors take this approach one step further: All the possible risks are listed, after which specific audit objectives and procedures are identified for each. SAS 94, *The Effect of Information Technology on the Auditor's Consideration of Internal Controls in a Financial Statement Audit*, and SAS 80, *Amendment to SAS 31, Evidential Matter*, describe both the benefits and risks of information technology to internal control. SAS 94 provides guidance to auditors in determining the skills necessary to consider the effect of computer processing on audits. It also goes so far as to state that auditors may not be able to access certain information for inspection, inquiry, or confirmation without using information technology. However, the matching of risks with audit steps will help to ensure that exposures are properly considered, and addressed, by audit.

Auditors, after examining control weakness and key data fields and determining who can manipulate what, must then determine what the symptoms would look like in the data. The control weakness quantity received not matched to quantity ordered—with the symptoms quantity received greater than quantity ordered—can identify frauds committed by different parties, involving different data elements, and different follow-on indicators, as shown in Exhibit 2.5.

Being Alert to the Symptoms of Fraud

While not all fraud can be prevented, early detection and quick, appropriate action can reduce the losses due to fraud. The first two steps in detecting fraud are identifying the exposures and understanding the symptoms. Next, auditors must be vigilant in watching for the symptoms of fraud. Earlier, I suggested developing a list of symptoms for each specific type of exposure identified in planning the audit. That list can be carried into the audit conduct phase and applied with careful scrutiny to spot symptoms of fraud in its early stages. Exhibit 2.6 shows symptoms of fraud in the purchasing function.

Remember, the presence of symptoms does not mean fraud exists, and the absence of symptoms does not mean that everything is all right. It is important to determine the underlying cause of the symptoms and deal with them.

Where symptoms are present, those committing fraud may have a ready, plausible explanation for each question raised by the auditor. Such explanations must be verified, especially those that are in any way questionable. Given that fraud often occurs when there is a long-standing weakness in the controls, the person committing the fraud may not believe that the explanation will be questioned or that it will be independently verified. Many

EXHIBIT 2.5   Analysis of the Symptoms of Fraud.

Fraudster/Scheme	Symptoms	Analysis
Vendor shipping more than ordered to increase sales	Received quantity > ordered quantity	Summarize overshipments by vendor to calculate the number of times and total value of overages by vendor. The secondary symptom is that certain vendors have more overages than others. Audit should investigate these vendors.
Vendor's salesperson places order for more than on contract to receive bonuses	Received quantity > ordered quantity	Summarize overshipments by vendor salesperson to calculate the number of occurrences and total value of overages by vendor salesperson. The secondary symptom is that certain vendor salespersons have more overages than others. Audit should investigate these vendor salespersons.
Receiving clerk accepts more than ordered—acts alone—steals excess	Received quantity > ordered quantity	Summarize overshipments by receiving clerk. The secondary symptom is that more overages occur with certain receiving clerks than others. Audit should investigate these clerks.
Receiving clerk accepts more than ordered—acts in collusion with vendor—steals excess	Received quantity > ordered quantity	Summarize overshipments by receiving clerk and vendor. The secondary symptom is that more overages occur with certain clerk-vendor combinations than others. Audit should investigate these clerks and vendors.
Contracting officer accepts more than ordered—acts in collusion with vendor—for kickbacks	Received quantity > ordered quantity	Summarize overshipments by contracting officer and vendor. The secondary symptom is that more overages occur with certain contract officer-vendor combinations than others. Audit should investigate these contracting officers and vendors.

EXHIBIT 2.6   Symptoms of Fraud.

Symptoms	Potential Fraud
Invoice irregularities	Phony invoices, duplicate payments, or payment for goods not received
Over-billing	Paying too much for the goods received, or paying for higher-quality goods than received, in exchange for kickbacks
Conflict of interest	Employees with personal relationships, shares, or interest in the vendor's business
Purchasing more than required	Purchasing goods in excess of required quantities for kickbacks or in order to steal the excess

examples of fraud have been detected by auditors who would not settle for "We have always done it that way" or who refused to accept the initial plausible explanations provided by the perpetrators.

Building Programs to Look for Symptoms

Sound comprehension of the business processes and their controls is necessary for the auditor to develop and implement audit programs to measure and report on the critical symptoms. In addition, an understanding of the symptoms of possible fraud will help the auditor to determine if more audit work is required. A sudden unexplained increase in cost of goods sold, delinquent accounts, increases in unit prices, and other patterns or anomalies can be assessed to look for early symptoms of fraud.

While auditors and fraud investigators are not expected to have the same level of knowledge as the person with primary responsibility for the area under review, SAS 53, *The Auditor's Responsibility to Detect and Report Errors and Irregularities*, clearly states that auditors must understand the characteristics of fraud. Auditors should be aware of the symptoms of fraud and conduct sufficient tests to determine if those symptoms are present in their organization.

Fraudulent activity can easily wind up ignored because of time constraints: "We only have two weeks to review the operations of the branch office." Fraud investigations can also be derailed by interference by the perpetrators: "If you are going to waste my time with trivial issues involving the petty cash, I'll report to senior management that you were responsible for our performance targets not being met this month." However, due professional care requires auditors to review symptoms of fraud with a healthy degree of skepticism, diligence, and determination. Auditors should perform their review in a manner that ensures the completeness and confidentiality of the investigation and its results.

In addition, most professional audit-related organizations, including the IIA, AICPA, and ACFE, advocate the use of data analysis technologies to assist in fraud detection. The use of trends and transactional analysis is one of the most powerful and effective ways of detecting fraud within an organization. It generally includes a comprehensive series of tests designed to detect indicators of a wide range of frauds. Data analysis allows auditors and fraud investigators to obtain a quick overview of the operations of a company, develop an understanding of relationships among various data elements, and easily drill down into specific control weaknesses or other areas of interest.

Internal auditors who determine that there is a weakness in the control framework cannot ignore the problem simply to comply with time schedules. Once a weakness has been identified, auditors have additional responsibilities. SIAS 3 defines audit's responsibilities for detecting fraud, and includes the requirement to conduct additional tests if control weaknesses are present. Therefore, it is incumbent on the auditor to analyze the company's exposure to various risk factors and to plan and perform audits to assess these risks. Further, as the audit is performed, the audit program should be adjusted based on the results obtained. Auditors should consciously decide when and if additional action is necessary.

The latest standards by the IIA, AICPA, and other audit organizations provide auditors and fraud investigators with guidance to increase their ability to detect fraud and abuse. In particular, when auditors are designing audit programs, they can use the risk factors contained in SAS 99. For more information see: *www.aicpa.org/pubs/jofa/jan2003/ramos.htm*.

Investigating and Reporting Instances of Fraud

After a thorough evaluation of the control framework, the weakness and fraud exposures identified may prompt a fraud examination—but they also may not. However, if symptoms of fraud are found and additional tests have indicated that there is a strong possibility of fraud, the review enters the formal investigation phase. There must now be a clear understanding of:

- Who will conduct the investigation
- Whether legal authorities and regulators will be involved

- Who will determine the scope of the investigation
- How the results will be communicated
- Who will determine the corporate response to the activity if it is proven to be fraudulent

The first source of answers to these questions should be the corporate fraud policy. However, prudence dictates that these answers be reconfirmed at the start of the investigation. If the organization does not have a fraud policy, or if the policy is unclear on these points, audit should seek immediate guidance and clarification. Failure to do so may result in senior management being caught unawares by stakeholders and the press, resulting in auditors being blamed for not finding the fraud. It may also place audit in a position of defending the actions or omissions of the investigating team to senior management. The early clarification of the process to be followed will ensure that all parties are on the same side and are aware of what is happening and what will be done.

Once the investigation is completed, it is important to publicize the results. Companies that are successful in deterring fraud tend to have strong prosecution policies that are not only consistently and equitably applied but also are well publicized. The fear of public exposure and punishment are great deterrents. Results of the investigation can also be used later, possibly anonymously, as an educational tool for auditors, fraud investigators, and other employees.

Implementing Controls for Fraud Prevention

The final step in the fraud detection process is the implementation of internal controls to prevent fraud from reoccurring. Unless steps are taken to address the weaknesses that allowed the fraud to occur, additional fraudulent activity will almost certainly ensue. To mitigate the risk of future losses, audit and management must clearly understand both the effects of the fraud and how it occurred. Audit should focus on key questions, such as:

- Were specific controls compromised? If yes, how?
- Are additional or different controls required to address the exposure?
- Is the problem systemic or localized in the area where the fraud occurred?
- Where else in the organization could this or something similar occur, and what needs to be done about it?
- Are there preventive measures and monitoring systems that could be established?

With these questions as a starting point, audit can research and develop controls that minimize the risk of future occurrences. While the ultimate goal is the safety and security of financial and nonfinancial assets, care and common sense must be exercised to ensure that efficiency is not compromised. The cost of the control must be evaluated against the scale of possible loss or damage to the organization. If an activity cannot be controlled effectively except at a disproportionate cost, perhaps it should not be undertaken in the first place.

The implementation phase must be based on the clear understanding that new controls will have the concurrence not only of audit, the investigations group, and management but also the agreement and commitment of those who will apply them. This is crucial. Once the new controls are in place, audit must perform follow-up tests to be sure that they are being applied, are working as intended, and are sufficient to prevent future criminal activity.

Notes

1. KPMG Forensic, *Fraud Survey 2003*, KPMG Forensic, 2003.
2. M. V. Cerullo, M. J. Cerullo, and T. Hardin, "Auditing the Purchasing Function," *Internal Auditor* (December 1997): 58–64.
3. Institute of Internal Auditors, American Institute of Certified Public Accountants, and Association of Certified Fraud Examiners, *Managing the Business Risk of Fraud: A Practical Guide* (Altamonte Springs, FL: IIA, 2008).
4. R. E. Hylas and R. H. Ashton, "Audit Detection of Financial Statement Errors," *The Accounting Review*, Vol. LVII, No 4, 751–765, 1982.

CHAPTER 3

Why Use Data Analysis
to Detect Fraud?

D o more with less, and do it better, is the battle cry of many chief executives. The audit department is not exempt from these pressures. The current business environment demands productivity increases from all areas of the company. Fortunately for auditors, however, data analysis can be the answer to demands for increased efficiency and effectiveness.

As the use of information technology (IT) grows, more fraud will involve the use of—and be detected by—computers. Computerized techniques and interactive software can help auditors focus their efforts on the areas of greatest risk. The use of analysis software allows auditors to exclude low-risk transactions from their review and to focus on those transactions that contain a higher probability of fraud. The step-by-step analysis of the data and the patterns contained therein can lead to the identification of fraudulent activity.

An important step in detecting fraud is an examination of the available data to identify if the symptoms of fraud are present. Computer-assisted audit tools and techniques (CAATTs) are ideally suited to this purpose. But the use of CAATTs demands an understanding of the audit software as well as the underlying data. It also requires auditors to be innovative in their use of computer-based tools and techniques and to have access to the required data files.

Although computers and information technology have complicated the auditor's job, they also offer a host of new opportunities to employ computer-based analysis tools and techniques to detect fraud. Computers and CAATTs have the ability to improve the range and quality of audit and fraud investigation results.

Establishing CAATTs as organizational assets can present a number of hurdles. Management, the audit staff, and the information system depart-ment must agree on the program and work together to implement it. A critical factor in the successful implementation will be ongoing and effective communication between all concerned parties.

Implementing CAATTs in an organization is only the beginning. Fundamental to the application of CAATTs to fraud investigation is the ability to access the right data and the development of a sound understanding of what the data mean. Auditors must also change their outlook, since most of the established, manual practices of auditing no longer apply. Data extraction and analysis software gives auditors and fraud investigators a new set of tools that they can use to examine the electronic business environment. The goal is now to seek out and recognize opportunities to apply CAATTs as a means of detecting fraud.

Increased Reliance on Computers

It has been said that there is more computing power in a birthday card that sings "Happy Birthday" than there was in the entire world in the 1940s. While some may debate the validity of this statement, it is difficult to argue against the fact that most homes have more computing power in total—in their personal computers, microwaves, VCRs, DVDs, watches, and other electrical devices—than was available in the first mainframe computers. This computing power has become an integral part of our daily lives, and is even more pervasive in the business world. Many businesses would suffer serious damage if they were without computing power for as little as one week; some might even cease to exist. Often the old manual processes that computers replaced no longer exist. Companies are completely dependent on information technology to process accounts receivable, generate invoices, order inventory, and so on, in every facet of the business.

The growth in the pervasiveness of automation in the business environment has also resulted in more complexity in the internal control environment. The technological revolution, with distributed processing, worldwide networking, and remote access to corporate systems, requires us to constantly redesign our audit programs to keep pace with business risks and exposures of a rapidly changing environment, with increased incidents of fraud and more fraud involving computer systems.[1] This has made the audit profession much more dynamic, difficult, and challenging. The "tried-and-true" techniques and practices of audit are often no longer universally applicable. Paper trails do not exist, and the entire control framework with its related risks is completely different. Yet the spread of computers in business has actually increased the ability of auditors to conduct audits and detect fraud.

Before the era of computers, auditors relied on manual reviews that often required them to dig through mountains of paper. A standard practice was to open the file cabinet and select every tenth file. Today, the depth of audits has vastly improved. Hylas and Ashton[2] reviewed hundreds of working papers to identify the audit techniques most commonly used to find financial errors. They determined that analytical techniques identified almost 30 percent of all reported financial errors, more than any other audit technique. It is significant that even as early as 1982, before the widespread availability of interactive audit software and integrated computer systems, CAATTs were already the most powerful audit tools for detecting financial errors. Since then, analytical techniques have become not only more powerful but also more widely used by auditors. Today, the same study would in all likelihood show CAATTs accounting for a much larger share. In the last 10 years, the use of CAATTs became a standard audit practice, with 73 percent of auditors using more than one data extraction and analysis tool.[3] Such tools permit auditors to obtain a quick overview of the business operations and to quickly drill down into the details of specific areas of interest. Equally important, with the use of CAATTs, audit programs can now be expanded to a 100% verification of the transactions, and a recalculation of important figures, such as totals, ratios, and other indicators.

Statement on Auditing Standards 56 (SAS 56), *Analytical Procedures,* explains that analytical procedures can be used to assist in planning the audit steps and in determining the timing and nature of work to be done. SAS 56 also encourages auditors to use analytical procedures to examine relationships between various financial and nonfinancial data elements and to identify trends. But computers and audit software provide more than opportunities for analysis. Analytical procedures can be used in performing substantive testing, improving the identification of risk, quantifying results, and allowing auditors to focus on the main areas of risk and exposure. This is probably why the Institute of Internal Auditors has published Implementation Standard 1210.A3, which states that auditors should have knowledge of information technology risks and controls and available technology-based audit techniques. In addition, Implementation Standard 1220.A2 states that auditors should consider the use of CAATTs and other data analysis techniques.

To find fraud, auditors need to know what it looks like. Auditors must also know how corporate or organizational data can be used to identify the occurrence of fraud. Doing this requires that the auditor understand the company's data, the internal controls and their weaknesses, and what the fraud will look like. Given that most businesses have millions of transactions, the process of manually reviewing all documents is neither time nor cost efficient. Data extraction and analysis software can assist the forensic accountant or general auditor by highlighting individual transactions that have characteristics often associated with fraudulent activity. With audit software, millions of records can be examined, data from previous years can be used to identify anomalies, and comparisons can be made between different locations. The number of records is not a problem for audit software, and for certain advanced techniques, a large number of transactions is preferred when searching for the anomalies.

Computer-based data analysis tools are invaluable when examining operations, performance, and possible frauds. Yet only 50 percent of auditors are using fraud prevention/detection software.[4] Auditors and fraud investigators not taking advantage of these tools, and the access they provide to electronic data, are not providing their best services to their organizations. Further, Sarbanes-Oxley requires disclosure to the public, on a rapid and current basis, of material changes to financial conditions or results of operations—an impossible task without the aid of data analysis.

Developing CAATTs Capabilities

Computers are a powerful tool in combating fraud. However, the development of CAATTs capabilities continues to be a major stumbling block for many audit departments. Halfhearted or poorly planned attempts to introduce CAATTs will almost surely fail. Implementation of CAATTs will be successful only if carefully planned and executed. It requires more than a change in the status quo.

As a first step, it is necessary to secure and cultivate the commitment of both management and audit staff. There must be more than passive acceptance; in effect, there must be a vision of what can and should be done.

As is the case whenever change is being introduced, communication is central. Everyone must have a clear understanding of what will be expected of them and what part they will play in the development and implementation process. They must also be aware of the value of adopting CAATTs and the importance of data analysis techniques in improving operations and detecting fraud. To obtain maximum benefits from CAATTs, auditors and fraud investigators must receive sufficient information systems training. They must be comfortable with the technology if they are to apply it successfully in a variety of situations. Further, a mixture of information systems and audit or fraud detection expertise is highly desirable in implementing an effective CAATTs program.

There is no single approach to the development of CAATTs that will work in every company. Using the computer to detect fraud poses a range of challenges, as well as opportunities, many of which will be unique to the organization. The staff knowledge and the organizational requirements will dictate what will be audited, and when and how it is to be audited. Still, there are some fundamental issues that must be considered in any CAATTs development.

Issues in CAATTs Development

Issue: Current information technology environment

Item	Description/Options
The company	Hardware and software, IT policies and plans
Audit department	Knowledge levels and expertise of the audit staff

Comments: The company's current information technology environment will provide an indication of the likely level of support for CAATTs. Although audit may be on a different place on the technology curve from the rest of the company, it should be in step with the main business. Race too far ahead and senior management may view CAATTs as "bleeding edge" technology. If management does not see the value of technology in operational areas, it is unlikely that it understands the value of technology in the audit area. However, if audit is too far behind the rest of the organization, technological incompatibilities can lessen the potential gains from CAATTs, and the auditor's efforts may be viewed with less credibility.

Issue: Future information technology environment

Item	Description/Options
Computer platform	Mainframe, mini, micro, LAN, WAN
Operating system	Client server, MVS, NT
Application software	ERP (SAP/R3, PeopleSoft, etc.), legacy systems
Interfaces	IMS, DB2, Oracle, TCP/IP
Organizational changes	Structure, size, reporting relationships
Training and budgets	Who, how much, what kind, and when

Comments: The implementation of CAATTs is a phased and protracted process. The investment of time and resources should have a life span well beyond the planned implementation date, before becoming obsolete or incompatible with the business environment. Where the company is going with its information systems environment is a critical

(continued)

consideration in CAATTs implementation. Training audit staff will also be a key factor in the successful implementation of CAATTs. To be effective, the training should be closely tied to the use of the newly acquired skills.

Issue: Hardware and software

Item	Description/Options
Hardware	Laptop/desktop, LAN, or standalone
Software	Spreadsheet, database, word processing, time reporting, flowcharting, presentation, project management, Internet
Specialized audit software	Custom-built or off-the-shelf—what is being used now, and does it need to be upgraded or replaced?
Other capabilities	Other foreseen needs

Comments: The selected hardware and analysis software should contribute to, and be determined by, the working environment of the auditors, whether it is telecommuting, in the office, on the road, or working primarily at client sites using laptops. The software suite must be compatible with that of the company as a whole. Specific audit software (IDEA, ACL) must run on the current platform and be compatible with future platforms. Audit software must be capable of accessing and analyzing legacy data and data in the newly developed, or planned, applications.

Issue: Audit-specific hardware and software

Item	Description/Options
Hardware	Servers, storage devices, fax/modem
Software	Risk analysis, audit universe, recommendation tracking, electronic working papers, control self-assessment, data extraction and analysis

Comments: The size of data files, where data resides, and where it will be stored; where the analysis will be performed; backup and security; and other questions relating to hardware must be decided early in the process. Audit has specialized requirements and must continually examine the next generation of tools, both hardware and software.

In addition, the standard suite of hardware and software provided to typical users may not meet the unique needs of audit.

Issue: Information technology training requirements

Item	Description/Options
Comprehensive training plan	What training is required? Who should receive training? How much training is required? When should training be scheduled?
Type of training	In-house, external, instructor-led, video, computer-based

Comments: Will auditors be trained on the technology or programmers trained in audit? Will CAATTs experts be employed, or will self-sufficient audit teams be developed? Performance gaps must be identified and solutions found to reduce these gaps.

Issue: Support requirements

Item	Description/Options
Transition technical support	Assistance in building interfaces, setting up servers, and so on
Long-term technical support	Maintenance and upgrading of hardware and software to remain current
Source of support	Within audit department? Information systems department? External?

Comments: Will the audit department support its own staff or use a corporate help desk? Is support required for mainframe or for PC-based applications only? Will hardware be purchased or leased? What about ongoing assistance related to data access, data analysis, and so on?

Issue: File management and security

Item	Description/Options
File management	Version tracking, backup, restore, file naming conventions
Data protection	Data cleanup and security, virus protection, remote access policies and procedures

(continued)

Comments: How long will data files be kept? Daily or weekly backups? Can auditors connect remotely? How will the integrity of client information be ensured—protection against hackers, viruses, and loss? Are there legal and privacy issues that must be addressed?

Issue: Quality assurance

Item	Description/Options
Integrity and accuracy	How will the integrity of the data and the accuracy of the analyses be ensured?

Comments: The use of data extraction and analysis tools will change the nature of the audits undertaken and the methods for arriving at the final conclusions. Who will ensure the integrity of the data and that data analyses are planned and reviewed for accuracy, completeness, and relevance?

Integrated Analysis and Value-Added Audit

The use of computer-assisted tools and techniques is not restricted to audit or fraud investigation. An interesting and valuable spin-off of using audit software is the ability to develop tailored best practices for performing value-added audits of a variety of business operations. Value-added audits can reduce opportunities for waste and abuse, which is fertile ground in which fraud can take root. Waste and abuse can exist only when risks are not identified and addressed.

Management's ability to capture and analyze information often is key to successfully reducing fraud. For example, healthcare fraud can be reduced by:

- Organizing the data by member, not just by date or type of care, giving a different view of the data—one that is centered on the healthcare recipient rather than the caregiver
- Developing cost accounting data to understand business costs, and comparing these to industry standards
- Assembling the data in flexible relational databases—allowing the information to support a variety of uses and aid management in making key decisions

By understanding their operations and the information pertaining to their business, managers can better develop business goals. They can also measure performance to assess critical success factors and risk, and reduce fraud.

Even if management has not developed computerized applications to manage healthcare data, audit software can still sort and summarize data by member to provide a complete history of care received, identify detailed cost breakdowns, and answer a wide range of requests.

The power of audit software can be used to effectively identify risks and exposures in any industry. The key is the interactive and flexible nature of the tools. Auditors need only learn one tool, which they can then apply to a wide variety of situations, data formats, and information sources. The ongoing adoption of data analysis tools by management is a sign that the power of these tools reaches beyond audit and provides support for the use of audit software to fight fraud.

Recognizing Opportunities for CAATTs

The use of CAATTs to detect fraud will depend to a large extent on the willingness and ability of auditors and fraud investigators to recognize opportunities. The interactive nature of CAATTs means that auditors have complete flexibility in what they do and how they do it. The most productive approach is to actively consider the use of CAATTs in all cases where there are allegations of fraud. Rather than missing opportunities to apply CAATTs, the assumption should always be that CAATTs are applicable—so the issue is then to determine how they can be applied to the situation at hand. The failure to recognize CAATTs opportunities is often the single biggest impediment to the successful application of these tools and techniques in fraud detection.

The next section outlines the basic steps that can be followed in determining how computer-assisted techniques can be applied to fraud detection. These steps only present a starting point. Although individual circumstances will vary depending on the integration of technology in the business environment, the basic approach to the use of CAATTs in the detection of fraud is applicable to most organizations. However, if auditors wish to make the best possible use of CAATTs, they must strive to move beyond these minimal requirements.

Developing a Fraud Investigation Plan

The Fraud Investigation Plan describes the "who, what, when, where, why, and how" of the investigation and serves as a guide to the investigating team. It provides a framework for the analysis to be performed and will be useful where the case leads to criminal prosecution. It allows the audit team to plan the analysis, the rationale for the testing, and the expected results. It must not constrain the auditor's judgment, but simply get ideas flowing and organized.

The Fraud Investigation Plan should answer at least six questions:

Why? The plan should provide a clear statement of the fraud risk or allegations, including regulations or laws that are applicable to the area, as well as the reason for conducting the fraud investigation and a statement of anticipated results. This is similar to the planning phase of many audits, where the auditor sets the objectives and scope and performs a preliminary assessment. The auditor also should identify by name and paragraph number all applicable policies, procedures, and regulations as well as potential risks and control weaknesses.

For example:

> *Allegations have been made that the contracting manager is favoring certain vendors during the contract bidding process by providing information on the bid values of other firms and accepting bids after the bid-close date. Foreknowledge of the bid submissions of other firms would likely result in a case where the last bid wins. The disclosure of information related to the contracting process or submissions made by other firms is a serious violation of the corporate contracting policy (ADM II A.3.ii).*

Who? The plan should identify not only the number of resources required but also the type of resources. It should address whether external forensic auditors or fraud investigators will be used and what role they will play. It should also address the mix of skills required. For example, it should clarify whether CAATTs specialists, contract experts, or human resources personnel will be needed to address the specifics of the allegation.

> *The audit team will consist of the team leader, two financial auditors, and a contract specialist from the head office procurement section, and will be supported by a CAATTs specialist.*

When? Often fraud investigations are unplanned activities that must pull auditors off other projects. The plan should identify the priority of the investigation and the projected schedule.

> *The investigation is a high-priority request from senior management. All team members will suspend or transfer other responsibilities in order to make themselves 100 percent available for the investigation. The work*

is expected to take five to six weeks, with the team leader working an additional week to finalize the report.

What? The plan should list the specific objective of the investigation and the symptoms of the fraud.

The audit team will review the contract submissions data to determine if there is evidence that a contractor received an unfair advantage and was submitting bids after the bid closing date. The analysis will examine bid dates for irregularities and look for cases where the contract submission date is later than the bid closing date.

Where? The sources of the data to be used for the analysis, including the location (mainframe or personal computer), the application, the structure of the data, and the access and security requirements, must be listed.

The contracting application is an Oracle database that runs on the contracting section's server. It has a Visual Basic front-end reporting program that will be used to extract detailed bid submission information. The owner of the data is the VP of Procurement, and the application programmer is Kathy Arthur. We will have to write a letter to the VP requesting access in order to obtain the required data as we do not currently have access to this system.

How? The plan should include details regarding the types of analysis to be performed by the investigation team and the time frame to be included (months or years worth of data). In addition, it should address the access method (against the production data, a snapshot, or an extraction) and where the analysis will be performed (client computer system or auditor's system).

The analysis will include the six months since the incumbent became manager of the contracting section as well as the previous six months. An extract of the detailed transaction file will be downloaded to the auditor's laptop and the analysis run there. For each contracting officer, and for each firm submitting a bid, the number of days between bid submission and bid close will be calculated. These will be compared to identify anomalies and trends. The contract file will be pulled for all cases where the bid submission was after the bid close date and will be examined in detail.

The plan must identify the steps to be taken to ensure the integrity and security of the original data and the analyses. Any scripts or programs developed and the results of analysis must be protected until the close of the investigation and the conclusion of any legal action or appeals.

> *A backup of the contracting database will be stored on CD-ROM and the auditors will seize the automatic backup tapes from the server where the contracting database resides. The analysis tests and results will be saved as part of the working papers, with a copy stored on the LAN.*

The Fraud Investigation Plan should be reviewed, agreed to, and approved by the audit manager. All potential problems, such as access to data, should be identified and the potential solutions evaluated. As the analysis progresses, the audit team may take unforeseen avenues. Therefore, the analysis plan should be considered as a living plan that is adjusted and updated, when appropriate. New lines of inquiry can be added as the results of the initial analyses are reviewed and interpreted.

> *During the analysis we noted a strong correlation between one of the contracting officers and the vendor ABC Ltd. No other contracting officer raised contracts with ABC, so a sample of contracts for ABC was selected and reviewed. The review examined the statements of work and the justification for sole-sourcing.*

A typical first draft of a fraud investigation plan follows:

Fraud Investigation Plan Example

Allegation

Pat Currie, a new receiving clerk, reported that the received quantity is not being compared to the order quantity before the items are accepted and the invoice paid. While she has been on the job for only three months, she has noticed that the discrepancy tends to occur more often when Tom Fremont is the officer and the vendor is Steel Cases Limited. Corporate contracting policy has a clear statement (Section J, para. 42) that prohibits the payment if the order quantity, receipt quantity, and invoiced quantity do not agree.

Objective

The audit will review contracts to determine if proper procedures are in place and being followed to ensure that the receipt equals the order quantity. All contracts where there are differences will be examined, specifically to determine if there are problems related to quantities ordered and received with contracts raised by Tom Fremont or with Steel Cases Limited.

Audit Team

Terry Persson will be the team leader. Sam Bedford (financial auditor) and Jackie Wilson (contract specialist) will be the other full-time members of the team. Dave Dorland will provide CAATTs support and will interface with the systems people to obtain the necessary data.

Schedule

All team members will cease other projects effective immediately to concentrate on the investigation, with the exception of Jackie Wilson, who will join the team in two weeks. An interim report will be presented to the audit committee on July 8 and a final report should be prepared for signature by audit committee chairman on July 22.

Data Source

The receipt information is stored on a PC in the receiving dock office in a Microsoft Access database. It contains information regarding the contract number and quantity received by product number. A contract may involve several shipment or receipts.

The contracting information is stored in a DB2 system running on the mainframe computer. It contains total quantity ordered by contract, and by product number.

> Contract database—fields required: contract number; date; contracting officer; vendor; product number; order quantity; unit price; total price
> Receipt database—fields required: contract number; vendor; date goods received; product number; received quantity; receiving clerk

Analysis

The contracting database will be backed up to tape and the receipt data to CD-ROM. Information from the contracting database will be extracted

(continued)

for the last 12 months and compared, by contract and product number, to the receipt database.

The audit team will determine the total amount received by contract and by product number, and compare this to the total quantity ordered, by contract and by product number. If the order quantity differs from the receipt quantity, the detailed receipt information will be extracted to a file called Receipt_LT_Ordered (where the receipt quantity is less than the order quantity) and to Receipt_GT_Ordered (where the receipt quantity is more than the order quantity). Further analysis will determine the vendors with the highest variances (by number of items; by number of products; and by value of the variance [unit price × quantity]) and the contracting officer with the highest variances (items, products, and dollars).

Note: Partial shipments may be a possible reason for receipt quantity being less than order quantity.

Legal Authority

The legal department has been apprised of the allegation. If the analysis indicates that there is a systemic issue and points to one or more contracting officers and/or vendors, audit will immediately notify Ms. K. Lindsay of the legal department.

Audit Director _____ Date _____

Audit Team Leader _____ Date _____

Notes

1. Association for Financial Professionals, *2007 AFP Payments Fraud Survey*, Association for Financial Professionals, Bathesda, MD: March 2007.
2. R. E. Hylas and R. H. Ashton, "Audit Detection of Financial Statement Errors," *The Accounting Review*, Vol LVII, No 4, 751–765, 1982.
3. Glen L. Gray, "An Array of Technology Tools," *Internal Auditor*, (August 2006): 56–62.
4. Ibid.

CHAPTER 4

Solving the Data Problem

D ata analysis, as a method of detecting fraud, requires access to the data. Although many auditors struggle with this, there are really only a few steps involved:

1. Identify the objectives of the investigation.
2. Meet with the data owner and programmer.
3. Define the parameters for the required data.

Once you have the data it will be important to:

1. Assess the integrity and completeness of the data provided.
2. Develop an understanding of what the data means.
3. Perform the analysis and verify results.

Exhibit 4.1 gives an overview of the steps that should be covered during the planning phase of the investigation or audit to ensure the availability of the required data files. The computer-assisted audit tools and techniques (CAATTs) checklist also contains the initial steps to be taken to ensure the integrity of the data and that the auditor understands what the data represent and how they can be used to address the specific audit or fraud investigation objectives.

Setting Audit Objectives

The first step in defining the information required to detect fraud is to identify the goals and objectives of the investigation. Although this step is essentially the same in any audit or fraud review, whether computer assisted or not, the main difference is to try to avoid being constrained by old modes of thinking. Auditors must have a clear understanding of what they are trying to accomplish before defining the information requirements.

EXHIBIT 4.1   CAATTs Checklist.

Step	Description
Set objectives and identify data sources	Identify the key objectives of the audit or investigation and the owner of the possible data sources required to address these objectives.
Meet with data owner and programmer and define the data requirements	Meet with the owner of the data and the application programmer. Based on the objectives of the audit or investigation, determine the best data sources and the key fields or data elements that are required by the audit team.
	Obtain the name and phone information of the programmer or system analyst and a copy of the data dictionary and other documentation for the application system.
Request the data	Prepare a formal request for the required data, specifying: <ul><li>Data source and key fields</li><li>When the data will be needed</li><li>Timing of the data (e.g., as of Mar 31, 2008)</li><li>Data transfer format (floppy, tape, CD-ROM, FTP, LAN)</li><li>Data format (DBF, delimited, flat file, ADO, ODBC, ASCII print file, EBCDIC)</li><li>Control totals (number of records, key numeric field totals)</li><li>Record layout (field name, start position, length, type, description)</li><li>Print of the first 100 records</li></ul>
Import/access the data	Ensure that the software that will be used to analyze the data can read the data file correctly.
Verify the transfer process and perform an initial assessment of the integrity of the data	Check that the data transfer was successful and that all the information was correctly received and interpreted by the software to be used to analyze the information. <ul><li>Ensure that all requested fields are present in the data.</li><li>Check totals against control totals (number of records, key numeric fields).</li><li>Verify the time period covered by the data to ensure proper file has been sent.</li><li>Verify with the client that this data can be used to address the stated objectives.</li></ul>

EXHIBIT 4.1 *(Continued)*

Step	Description
	• Ensure the fields contain the proper data—print the first 100 records and compare to printout from application system. • Ensure the analysis software is properly interpreting fields—numeric fields contain numeric data and date fields have valid dates. • Select a few records and compare what is in the application system (online query).
Understand the data	Use various high-level commands, such as summarize and sort, to get a better understanding of the data. Total numeric fields, determine ranges of values for key numeric and date fields, and determine all possible values for key character fields (summary).
Perform required analyses	Perform the required analyses, as outlined in the fraud detection plan, to address the audit or investigation objectives.
Verify results	Review the results obtained and compare with expected results. Where possible, ensure that results are verified against independent sources and obtain original documents.

Auditors must identify what needs to be accomplished, not how this will be done. The how will be determined at a later stage.

In setting the objectives, audit management should determine the knowledge, skills, and disciplines needed to effectively carry out the investigation. Auditors or fraud investigators must have the appropriate type and level of technical expertise. This should include assurances on such matters as professional certifications, licenses, and reputation, and that there is no conflict of interest. At the same time, it is important to assess the probable level and extent of complicity in the fraud within the organization. This can be critical to ensure that auditors are not providing information to, or obtaining misleading information from, persons who may be involved.

Defining the Information Requirements

At this stage auditors must identify what information is required to address the identified objectives and determine the possible sources of that information. Auditors and fraud investigators should strive to find, collect, analyze, interpret, and document automated sources of information to support the results. The information collected should be factual, verified to source, relevant, and useful, and should provide a sound basis for the results.

In searching for sources of information, auditors should start by assuming that the information exists in electronic form, and where possible:

- Determine the possible sources and application systems.
- Identify the owner of the information—their permission may be necessary before the programmer will provide access to the application system or the data files.
- Identify the programmer/system analyst responsible for the application system.
- Obtain all necessary documentation—such as data dictionary, record layout, system overview, and business processes.

Auditors should not be constrained by the first information system they discover. A more vigorous search will often find better or corroborating sources of the information required.

The business process and system owners can be invaluable in this process. Discussions with the owners of the data and application programmers/analysts can assist in determining the best source of information. These discussions also can serve to identify key fields and other sources of useful data. Auditors always must consider both local office and headquarters data sources—where two sources of data exist, comparisons of the data can prove to be extremely fruitful in fraud investigations. Focus on any discrepancies between data sources.

The next step is to design procedures that will identify the perpetrators, the extent of the fraud, the techniques used, and the cause of the fraud. SAS 47, *Audit Risk and Materiality in Conducting Audit*, states that when planning an audit and evaluating results of audit procedures, the auditor should consider the possibility of fraud, illegal acts, and conflicts of interest. These can form the basis of objectives and should be verified by management, legal counsel, and other specialists as appropriate throughout the course of the investigation. Owners of the business processes and information systems in the area under investigation can assist in identifying risks. It is also important to be aware of the rights of the alleged perpetrators and other personnel within in the scope of the investigation, and the reputation of the organization itself.

Accessing Data

Audit departments that have not secured electronic access to their company's data are running out of excuses and, perhaps, out of time. With advances in both hardware and software technologies, data access is no longer a major technical problem and does not require specialized hardware or the involvement of information systems personnel. Audit software can read and analyze most data structures and PCs can handle large volumes of data.

Often, rather than being a technical problem, the lack of access is a result of management's or the client's reluctance to provide audit with access to the application systems. Support from management is often necessary for audit to obtain logical and physical access to the required information. This may require a strongly worded statement from senior management to the effect that "audit will be given access to any and all application systems and information required to perform their duties." Having secured management support and direction for access to systems and information, auditors must ensure that data owners are well informed of their access rights and requirements. For application systems where the data is regularly required by audit, this means ongoing read-only access. For systems less frequently used by audit, access may be granted "as required." For example, audit may always have access to the inventory system but may require only temporary access to the personnel records, while auditing the company's progress toward employment equity in hiring practices.

To use CAATTs effectively, access to the information in electronic format is necessary. For mainframe and client-server systems, security-cleared read-only access is required. There are four main access methods, all of which should be pursued. Auditors should.

1. Obtain logical and physical access to the client system and sign on as a user with read-only access rights. This will allow review of individual transactions within the system.
2. Run copies of standard reports; if possible, save reports in electronic format for further analysis. If this is not possible, auditors may have to electronically capture screen images, or cut and paste information from the screen to a file, and analyze the data with audit software.
3. Run ad hoc queries or generate reports with a report writer.
4. Obtain direct access to the system's data files, bypassing the application's software, and extract and prepare the data for use with the audit software.

Data Paths

Today's audit software allows auditors and fraud investigators to read diverse data types, including mainframe legacy systems, client-server and Internet-enabled systems, or enterprise applications such as SAP and People-Soft. The flexibility of audit software like ACL and IDEA makes it possible to easily read, combine, and analyze data from various systems and platforms to detect fraud.

Before a CAATTs analysis can begin, the data file must be accessible by the auditor. This often requires the transfer of the data from the client system to the auditor's computer. Today, there are many different methods to achieve this transfer. The most common data paths used for data transfer include:

* Zip disk
* CD-ROM and DVD
* Memory stick
* Telecommunications
* Infrared wireless transfer
* Network connections
* FTP (file transfer protocol)
* E-mail
* Mainframe tapes

Zip disks and memory sticks have numerous advantages, including:

* They are inexpensive, easily attainable, and allow for the quick transfer of data between personal computers.
* Small file size limitation can be increased using compression and backup utilities.
* Zip disks can hold hundreds of gigabytes of information.
* Memory sticks are plug-and-play, and are treated like a removable hard drive, holding gigabytes of information.

One important drawback is that all such systems are PC based and therefore unable to transfer data from mainframe computers unless another type of connection is available.

CD-ROM and DVD also have significant advantages; they are

* Included in new PCs and laptops
* Capable of handling hundreds of megabytes of data
* Write-Once/Read-Many or Read/Writeable

Communication or network links are perhaps the most common method for data transfer within medium- to large-size corporations. Using communication links such as a local area network (LAN) or a wide area network (WAN), a PC can be connected to servers or mainframe systems. However, auditors will require file permissions (read access) and some form of downloading software. Also, the communication links have a baud rate associated with them and may be too slow—depending on the bandwidth of the link—when downloading larger files.

The LAN may provide for a direct link to the mainframe; if so, auditors must ensure the system is in a secure area. A network's file transfer speed is much faster than a communications link and is a reliable means of transferring larger files. Many networks now support TCP/IP, and hundreds of megabytes can be downloaded from the mainframe in minutes.

An advantage of audit software over general-purpose software, such as Excel and Access, is that audit software packages often can read mainframe data in its native (EBCDIC) format. If the analysis software can read EBCDIC characters, auditors should select "Binary" or "No Conversion" when transferring mainframe data to the PC, especially when downloading packed numeric fields. If the analysis software cannot read EBCDIC characters, auditors will have to unpack any packed numeric fields, convert the data, and download it in ASCII format.

Physical connections between PCs also can be achieved through built-in infrared capabilities. The data can then be transferred from the client PC to the auditor's PC.

E-mail messaging and FTP are growing means of accessing and transferring data via the Internet. Using the Internet, auditors can log on to an FTP site and download the data to a PC. Alternatively, the client can send a data file as an attachment to an e-mail message. However, e-mail systems usually have a message size limit of less than 10 Mb. Data files can be compressed to increase the maximum size considerably. Auditors should contact their system administrator if they intend to transfer files via e-mail.

The final category of data transfer is mainframe tape. The two primary types of mainframe tapes are 9-track and 3480/3490. The 9-track tape has existed for more than 35 years and was the worldwide standard for storing mainframe data for many years. Many organizations have switched to 3480/3490 due to increased data storage and automated access, positioning, and retrieval capabilities. Mainframe tapes can be an ideal data path for acquiring mainframe data external to an organization if a PC is connected to a tape reader.

Data File Attributes and Structures

There are several file types to be considered when asking for, and transferring, data:

- Fixed-length flat files
- Variable-length files
- Delimited files
- Multiple-record type files

- Relational files
- Standard formats—DBF files and spreadsheets
- Open database connectivity (ODBC)

A *fixed-length flat file* stores all of the information for a given record in one place on a file. The data is independent of other files because all information is stored in the one file. Each record is structured identically, with a fixed record length. A simple inventory system may be flat file—with each record containing the product number, product description, quantity on hand, required quantity, and so on.

As the name implies, in a *variable-length file*, the record length varies according to the information stored in the individual record. Often this type of record is comprised of both fixed and variable portions. The fixed portion contains the same fields for each record, while the variable portion will be different from record to record.

Note that with some variable-length files, a carriage return and line feed (CRLF) are added to the end of each record. The CRLF identifies the end of the record and increases the record length by 2 bytes for each record. However, with IBM variable-length files, the record length will be contained at the beginning of each record, and the analysis software uses this to determine the length of each record.

COBOL often uses variable-length records to store record segments that may occur one or more times ("occurs depending on" or ODO format). This type of record usually has a counter that indicates how many segments are contained in the record. For example, a customer record may have a fixed portion that contains the customer name and address. The variable portion may be a segment that details all of the customer's purchases (item, quantity, and cost). One customer may have a single purchase segment; another may have many purchases, and therefore, many purchase segments of information on the same record.

A *delimited file* is a special type of variable-length file. The end of each field is marked by a field separator, and the end of the record is marked with an end-of-record marker. A delimited file differs from a fixed-length flat file because, while each field in a fixed-length flat file is the same length for each record, with a delimited file, the length of each field depends on the data contained therein. A file containing the employee ID, last name, first name, and position number of all persons working in an organization is shown in Exhibit 4.2.

Delimited files can use any character to indicate the end of field marker, but a common type is comma-separated-values (CSV). Tabs and semicolons are also common separators. The first record of the delimited file may contain the field names, with the data starting on the second record. Many

EXHIBIT 4.2   Sample File.

Flat File

0199283	Williams	Bill	44564
2288431	Currie	Anne	33400
3355500	Whitemore-Smith	Jennifer	221197

Delimited File

0199283, Williams, Bill, 44564
2288431, Currie, Anne, 33400
3355500, Whitemore-Smith, Jennifer, 221197

data analysis packages require a delimited file to be converted to a flat file before analysis on the data can occur.

A *multiple-record type file* has records that are of different lengths and contain different pieces of information (different fields) on the different record types. The same segment on different record types contains different information. Using a customer accounts receivable file as an example, columns 1 to 25 may contain the name of the customer for one record type and the description of what was purchased for another record type.

In Exhibit 4.3, record type "1" contains information about the customer (name and address) and each record type "2" contains details on the purchases.

Often electronic versions of printed reports can be considered as a multiple-record type file—with distinct record types for the title, column heading, detail, subtotal, and total lines.

A *relational file system* stores common information in one file and detailed information in other files. Historically, storage space was expensive on the mainframe systems, so programs and methods were developed to use minimum amounts of disk space. As a result, relational files are very common because they are more efficient than flat files for storing information. For example, in a claims file, customer name, address, and phone number usually remain common or constant. Rather than store

EXHIBIT 4.3   Multiple-Record Type File.

1 Jennifer Lindsay	1223 Grey Rock Street		Houston
2 Red paint	4	$29.99	2008-09-02
2 3" brushes	2	$3.99	2008-09-02
2 Turpentine	1	$6.50	2008-09-03
1 Anne Currie	40 Maple Street		Chicago
2 Sandpaper	10	$0.97	2008-06-07

all information with each record, a relational system stores the common information once and refers to it using the key field, such as customer number.

Many application systems support the export of data into database (.DBF used for dBASE, FoxPro, etc.) and spreadsheet (Excel) formats. These formats are so popular that they have become *standard formats*. Most data analysis packages can read files stored in database or spreadsheet format, so this may be an easy way to request the required data. However, these formats also may have a maximum number of records or total file sizes—meaning that auditors may not get all of the records in the database because of record or file size limitations. Auditors always must verify the data you receive with the control totals.

Note: Applications developed using database formats allow users to delete records. Usually the records are not physically removed from the database but only marked for deletion until the database is packed and marked records are removed from the physical database. Database users may not realize that a record they thought they had deleted was only "marked for deletion" and can still be viewed. This issue can be extremely useful in a fraud investigation. At the same time, if auditors do not exclude these "deleted" records, they will have problems when trying to compare control totals with the original database. The software used to develop the database may automatically exclude "deleted" records, whereas analysis software may require filtering out the deleted records before working with the data.

Open database connectivity (ODBC) allows a variety of applications to read and understand databases developed with ODBC-compliant software packages. A PC must have the ODBC drivers for the given application. The drivers are often sold independently of the software, so one does not have to have a copy of the application. For example, using a Microsoft Access ODBC driver, many different software packages can read Microsoft Access databases. While ODBC-compliant software will allow auditors to read the data from various database applications, they have access only to the physical database, not the logical structure (the way the relational databases are connected using key fields). Auditors will have to use analysis software to recreate the logical structure—combining relational tables using key fields.

Accessing and using data from almost any source requires a good understanding of the record layout. It is important to not only understand the data file structure at the macrolevel—will the data be provided as a flat file, a delimited file, or a number of relational files, and so on—but also at the field level. A record layout contains information about how the records are structured and which fields are stored in a data file. It is used as a reference when defining data for the data analysis package, providing information on

EXHIBIT 4.4   Record Layout Using COBOL Convention Example.

Name	X(25)	(Character, length=25)
Address	X(25)	(Character, length=25)
Phone	X(10)	(Character, length=10)
Claim No	X(5)	(Character, length=5)
Claim Amount	S9(10)v99	(Signed numeric, length=12 with 2 decimals)
Date	X(8)	(character, length=8, format YYYYMMDD)

the field names, data types, field lengths, and decimals. Exhibit 4.4 is an example of a record layout using COBOL conventions.

If using ODBC to read more than one table, or if a relational file was extracted into various tables, auditors also will need to know the logical database structure. Auditors must understand how the tables can be related to give the required information. With this knowledge, auditors will be able to use analysis software to read the various tables, build the necessary relationships, and analyze the data properly. When requesting information from a system that contains relational files, a useful tip is to request that all the information be provided in a single flat file. This will eliminate the need to understand the logical structure of the database.

Fraud examinations place additional pressures upon audit, as they must be conducted in a manner that protects the reputations of the innocent from wrongful allegations. The access to data required for fraud investigations should be carried out in accordance with the corporate fraud policy. Evidence must be gathered, analyzed, and maintained in a manner that supports future actions by the organization, including prosecution of perpetrators. Access to data may need to be discreet, and backups of databases may be required as evidence in court at a later date.

Assessing Data Integrity

CAATTs can improve the efficiency and effectiveness of any audit, whether in the financial, personnel, inventory, or other areas of the company. They can pinpoint transactions that merit investigation. It is possible to select a statistical or directed sample, perform a complete examination of the data, identify trends, conduct detailed analyses, and much more. The data can be extracted from a variety of sources and downloaded to the auditor's computer where all the necessary analyses can be performed. However, the use of CAATTs in analyzing data for fraud detection is dependent not only on access to the data, but also on the integrity of the data, and a sound understanding of the related file layouts and structures.

In the world of programming, there is a well-known term, *GIGO*, meaning "garbage in, garbage out." The "garbage" usually refers to the data itself, but this can be expanded to include an improper understanding, or definition, of the data that leads to incorrect conclusions. Simply stated, if the auditor's queries are not properly related to the underlying data and its structure, the results of the data analysis will almost certainly be flawed. A powerful software tool in the wrong hands is a dangerous weapon and without proper care GIGO can become "garbage in, gospel out," as people too often place a high degree of reliance on incorrect data, simply because it came from the computer. The greater the reliance placed on the results of the analysis, the more critical it is to fully understand the data, the software, the techniques used to perform the analysis, and the actual facts the data represent. Auditors seeking to improve their effectiveness by employing CAATTs must invest the time and training required to understand the tools, techniques, and data.

The concern over data integrity, or the lack thereof, will vary in complexity and nature, depending on whether the computer application itself is being audited or data from the application itself is being used to support an audit or fraud investigation. The audit of a computer application typically contains steps to assess the integrity of the application, including the completeness, timeliness, and accuracy of the data. When using the data from an application to review a client's operations or investigate a fraud, auditors will not likely include all the steps necessary to fully assess the integrity of the application's data. However, the integrity of the data remains crucial to the results of the investigation and demands that an assessment of data integrity be performed.

Any evaluation of the data integrity begins with an assessment of the reliability risk, which is dependent on the auditor's knowledge of the system. The importance of data integrity will be proportional to the reliance placed on the data analysis. In cases where fraud is suspected, the integrity of the data and the accuracy of the analysis may be central to the successful investigation. A wrongful accusation of a person can seriously damage the reputation and the well-being of the accused, not to mention create a potential legal liability for the organization and the accuser. Auditors and fraud investigators must apply due diligence in assessing the integrity of the data before using it as the basis for conclusions about, and accusations of, fraud.

But how and to what degree must the integrity be examined? How much is too much (overauditing), and when is it not enough (underauditing)? The answers to these questions lie in assessing the consequences of relying on faulty results, and determining the amount of testing and verification necessary to reduce those consequences to an acceptable level.[1] If this is not possible, it may be necessary to eliminate that data source from the fraud investigation. The requirement for due diligence and the potential penalties for error mean that auditors and fraud investigators can never assume that the computer-based data is reliable. Active steps must be taken instead to ensure it. The issue of data integrity and reliability risk is addressed in detail in the book.[2] There are numerous ways in which an auditor who relies too much on abstract analysis can fail to arrive at correct conclusions. Auditors must avoid:

- **Improperly extracting the source data.** Care is required when extracting information from systems. Fields can be lost, decimal places shifted, or data corrupted.
- **Misinterpreting the data.** Even if the data is correct, it can be misread. For example, a file containing both debits and credits may be read as debits only. Auditors also can falsely assume that a field marked "location" in the personnel file will consistently designate an employee's physical location or that there are no additional employees at the same location who are not so coded.
- **Forgetting to consider real-life issues.** Even with uncorrupted data that is correctly understood, practical factors can make a huge difference to one's conclusions. Consider a data entry section whose increased error rate at the new facility was caused by the afternoon sun's glare and a case of color blindness among the operators.

The reliability of the data analysis and accuracy of the interpretation of the results can be increased by:

- Challenging all aspects of what is received, the analysis done, and the results obtained
- Asking others for input—use team members, CAATTs experts, and the application system's programmers
- Keeping all team members informed—ensure they are aware of and support the analysis, results, and interpretation
- Involving the CAATTs experts at every step of the audit or investigation—from the initial access and extraction of the data to the interpretation of the results
- Requesting a quality assurance review—have the analysis checked by an independent source
- Verifying the results against another source—(original documents, other systems, or different reports)

A proper fraud investigation plan, good communication, and professional skepticism are the main quality control methods. Everyone—audit management, audit team leaders, and audit team members—has a role to play in ensuring the reliability of all analysis results. The data reliability risk is significantly reduced when auditors and investigators have an adequate understanding of the business operations and the supporting data. A further reduction of risk is achieved when the controls over the application are sound and when the data analysis is supported by other sources. Still, any electronic analysis identifying fraud should be supplemented with hard evidence wherever and whenever possible. The existence of manual records, interviews with staff in the area, and supporting reports or analyses help auditors and investigators ensure that their analysis is correct and the results are accurately interpreted.

Overview of the Application System

When using the data from the application as part of an investigation, auditors must develop an adequate understanding of the application and the business it supports. This may be time consuming, but if the application is to be used to detect and deter fraud or to support other audits, the benefits are well worth the effort.

An effective way to address the issue of familiarity, understanding, and appreciation of the data is to establish an ongoing CAATTs working group. Such a group would be responsible for:

- Identifying the applications to which the audit department requires access
- Determining which of these are most critical
- Negotiating access rights
- Developing a good working knowledge of these applications and their controls
- Ascertaining the integrity of the data and the degree of reliance that can be placed on the data
- Determining which information—key fields and databases—is relevant to audit
- Deciding if, when, and how the information can be used by audit
- Developing extraction and downloading capabilities
- Creating standard audit scripts or reports

CAATTs working groups usually are established to assist regular audits, but fraud investigations can make use of the results of the working groups. A working group should not be the only source of information concerning application systems useful to fraud detection. All auditors must be aware of the importance of identifying electronic sources of information inside and outside of the company. For example, auditors doing fieldwork in branch offices may discover locally developed applications that could be of use for subsequent fraud investigations.

If an organization uses CAATTs working groups, a good understanding of the application may already exist. Auditors who are not supported by CAATTs working groups can obtain a basic understanding from the existing documentation by:

- Reviewing the general system description documentation—user and programmer manuals, system flowcharts, copies of input documents, sample output reports, and descriptions of the controls
- Interviewing system users and programmers
- Reviewing standard reports and exception reports

A more in-depth knowledge of the system can be acquired by:

- Analyzing detailed system flowcharts and/or a narrative of the data flows
- Examining copies of all input and output documents
- Studying record layouts for all data files—including field descriptions and explanations of possible values for each field
- Examining transaction counts, exception reports, and summary reports, and comparing these to other reports or systems

Overview of the Data

The area of fraud investigation is especially prone to errors in interpretation of the data or the results. This is frequently due to a lack of understanding or familiarity with the application systems or a failure to appreciate the importance of CAATTs. Auditors and fraud investigators must have a sound understanding of the application system and the underlying data supporting it. Understanding the data under examination before making any allegations of impropriety is critical to a successful fraud investigation. Failure to understand what the data represents will invariably lead to false conclusions that fail to identify fraud or subject the innocent to accusations of fraud. The time and effort spent developing an understanding of the data (and ensuring its accuracy and completeness) will help to render an accurate analysis. An understanding of the data can be achieved by:

- Reviewing the key data fields and data elements
- Reviewing meta-data created by functions applied to the data
- Ascertaining the timeliness of the data—is the information current, how often is it updated and when was the last update?

- Determining if the information is complete and accurate
- Verifying the integrity of the data (sometimes broken down into syntactic, semantic, and pragmatic data integrity) by performing various tests, such as reasonability, edit checks, and comparison with other sources, such as previous investigations or audit reports

Given that all auditors are a potential source of information concerning local and corporate applications, communication is a critical issue to the understanding of the information sources. A CAATTs working group is a formal means of collecting information about specific systems, and the results of the working group should be made available to all. The knowledge gained from informal and other channels also must be shared. Audit departments should develop mechanisms, such as Intranet or groupware, to ensure that all auditors have access to information systems and the associated documentation.

Auditors and fraud investigators must understand the importance of data analysis for the prevention and detection of fraud. Powerful computer-assisted analysis techniques and sophisticated audit software commands and functions allow one to conduct fraud examinations electronically. It becomes easy to search for duplicates, whether there are hundreds or millions of transactions. However, reliable data and correct analysis must support the use of data analysis for fraud detection. Auditors and fraud investigators must ensure the integrity of not only their analysis but also the data and their interpretation of the results. Involving all auditors in the process of identifying possible sources of information can help to change the audit outlook from traditional thinking to viewing CAATTs as an integral audit tool.

Notes

1. U.S. General Accounting Office, Assessing the Reliability of Computer-Processed data, GAO/OP-8.1.3, United States General Accounting Office, 1991.
2. David Coderre, *Internal Audit: Efficiency through Automation* (Hoboken, NJ: John Wiley & Sons, 2009).

CHAPTER 5

Understanding the Data

The previous chapters discussed fraud and fraud detection, the use of analysis to detect fraud, and the importance of defining data requirements and assessing the integrity of the data. This chapter discusses how various analysis techniques can be used to understand the data. However, the same techniques and approaches can be used to find fraud. Also presented are cases illustrating some of the potential uses of computer-assisted audit tools and techniques (CAATTs) for detecting fraud. The goal is to stimulate auditors into thinking about possible applications of audit software in their operational environment. The cases illustrate principles that can be applied to actual fraud situations, but they are not exhaustive, as the inventiveness of those committing fraud, and the applicability of the tools and techniques discussed, is limitless. The cases also omit nonessential details to focus on CAATTs analysis. For example, diversion of payments is central to some of the schemes discussed here, but how it is accomplished is a side issue for our purposes. The point is that check fraud, however cleverly executed, remains detectable when the records are analyzed closely. Auditors should use the cases and techniques described as a starting point and expand on them to address the risks they confront.

Computer Analysis

The ongoing evolution of software provides auditors with an ever-improving arsenal of tools and techniques that allow auditors and investigators to gain a better understanding of the data and the application systems. Although these tools were designed specifically for audit, they are equally applicable to fraud detection and investigation, supporting a virtually unlimited range of techniques for data interrogation. The only limit to their use is the imagination and ability of the auditor or fraud investigator.

Audit software has many commands that support the auditor's requirement to review transactions for fraud, such as the existence of duplicate transactions, missing transactions, and anomalies.

These include the ability to:

- Assess the completeness and integrity of the data.
- Compare employee addresses with vendor addresses to identify employees who are also being paid as vendors.
- Search for duplicate check numbers to find photocopies of company checks.
- Search the list of vendors to identify those with post office boxes for addresses or frequent changes of address.
- Analyze the sequence of all transactions to identify missing checks or invoices.
- Identify all vendors with more than one vendor code, or more than one mailing address, or vendors with the same mailing address.
- Sort payments by amount to identify transactions that fall just under financial controls on contract limits.

The power of audit software helps auditors and forensic accountants interrogate a company's data files and develop a detailed understanding of what the data is telling them. By understanding the data, auditors learn to recognize and identify data patterns that may be indicative of fraud: negative entries in inventory received fields, voided transactions followed by "No Sale," or a high percentage of returned items. Transactions meeting auditor-specified criteria or forming an unusual pattern constitute a potential fraud profile and can trigger a detailed review. A fraud profile can uncover possible fraud early by isolating these transactions, reducing the amount of the loss. The profile highlights the high-risk transactions, enabling resources to be focused on them. Systems can also be built to continually monitor transactions, as frequently as dictated by the level of risk, as a proactive approach to the early detection of fraud.

CAATTs are powerful and readily available assets to help auditors and fraud investigators focus on high-risk areas, perform systematic in-depth analysis of data, and isolate transactions that have the symptoms of, and a high potential for, fraud. However, while computers are unquestionably faster at many tasks—indexing, summing, matching records, and recalculating values—they are only a tool to assist auditors in more efficiently and effectively applying their skills and knowledge. CAATTs are not a replacement for auditor experience and know-how. Software can search for relationships among data items and make comparisons across years or between locations, as well as sort, search, and join files. Still, the evaluation, verification, and interpretation of CAATTs-generated results will always demand an auditor's judgment. The key to the effective application of CAATTs lies in the auditor's ability to query data interactively and carry out additional analysis based on the interpretation of previous queries.

The principal benefit of audit software is that it enhances the ability of auditors to interact with the data, turning raw facts and figures into information that supports recommendations and subsequent actions. The interactive nature of modern audit software allows auditors to discover the meaning behind the numbers and develop a better understanding of both the data and the reality it supports. The software makes "what if" analysis easy to formulate and perform. Hypotheses can be formulated, tested, and revised as necessary, based on the results of initial interactive analyses.

Audit tools provide auditors with the ability to quickly and efficiently extract information from several databases with disparate database management systems, and identify underlying patterns or relationships in the data. For example, reviewing data from the accounts payable database may identify a trend in the payments to a particular vendor. Combining this information with the contracting database may uncover the fact that one contracting officer raised all contracts with that vendor. Finally, a search of the personnel system may reveal that the vendor and contracting officer have the same address. This in turn may raise concerns about possible kickbacks and conflicts of interest.

Statistical, directed, and discovery sampling, stratification, regression analysis, and digital analysis are but a few of the techniques available to identify indicators of fraudulent activity. By employing such techniques, auditors can identify the symptoms of fraud before large losses occur. The use of scripts, a method of storing computer software commands in a file for use at a later date, can make analyses developed for one situation easily reusable by the auditor in similar situations. The sharing of techniques and specifically developed tests is quick and easy, further assisting in the detection of fraud. Continual routines that monitor key symptoms and track trends can also be a major deterrent, preventing or identifying fraud almost as soon as it occurs. Data analysis allows auditors and fraud investigators to understand the symptoms of fraud and easily dull down into specific areas of interest. Such a proactive approach can be instrumental in reducing the incidences of, and losses from, fraud.[1]

Auditors now have the largest array of tools and techniques in the history of the profession to detect and assess the symptoms of fraud in the early stages, before losses escalate or goodwill is destroyed. In particular, early detection of fraud may reduce the likelihood of losses being so high that criminal prosecution is the only recourse. A fraud detected at its beginning may only warrant a slap on the wrist to be fully deterred, and effective detection of fraud may deter people from committing a fraud.

The Statement on Internal Auditing Standards 8 (SIAS 8), *Analytical Auditing Procedures*, discusses various types of, and uses for, analytical auditing procedures. The standard states that analytical techniques and procedures can assist auditors in identifying abnormal conditions that may warrant further attention. It also discusses possible analyses and their uses. SIAS 8 includes a discussion on:

- Analysis types, including:
  - Reasonableness and completeness tests
  - Gaps and duplication tests
  - Period-over-period comparisons
  - Business entity-to-entity comparisons
  - Regression analysis
  - Statistical analysis
  - Transaction matching
  - Threshold comparison
- Uses for analysis, including:
  - Detecting unexplained differences
  - Finding sequenced or ordered transactions where none is expected (the absence of differences)
  - Identifying anomalies or nonrecurring transactions
  - Charting trends across periods or years to identify blips or dips
  - Examining relationships between related and unrelated items
  - Comparing data from similar business units to identify anomalies
- Factors to be considered when performing analysis, including:
  - Strength of the control framework
  - Auditor's understanding of the application and its data
  - Availability and integrity of data
  - Materiality of areas being examined

Analysis Techniques

How can fraud be detected and prevented? What are the leading techniques?

Data extraction and analysis software allows auditors to analyze data, form and test hypotheses, and check their results, interactively and quickly. However, the usefulness of a particular technique will vary depending on the type of fraud being investigated. A combination of techniques often will be required to detect fraudulent activity. Auditors and fraud investigators must therefore be aware of all the available techniques and know which is most applicable and under what circumstances.

Even the simplest of frauds is difficult to discover manually when faced with millions of transactions. As a result, data extraction, analysis, and reporting software has become mission-critical for detecting and preventing fraud. Such software offers a wide range of commands and functions specifically designed to assist in analyzing and understanding data. Although the techniques are extremely useful for routine audit work, they are also readily applicable to identifying and quantifying fraud and waste. Brief descriptions of the most useful analysis techniques follow.

Filter/Display Criteria

A filter identifies only those records meeting user-defined criteria. After obtaining an overview of the data, the investigator can drill down into the details by specifying criteria that select only certain records for review. The use of display criteria can focus attention on transactions outside of the ordinary and reduce the review time. The criteria can be used singly or in combination.

Example. The listing of detailed invoice transactions for period "04" may contain invoices from previous periods. A filter to isolate transactions outside of the invoice period can focus attention on these questionable transactions.

Expressions/Equations

This capability allows you to build new equations to verify key values or test logical relationships in order to confirm the application system's internal calculations. Auditors can confirm amounts by creating expressions, recalculating the key figures for the entire data file, and highlighting all records where the recalculated value differs from the stored value.

Example. To test for invoicing fraud, auditors can use the quantity and unit price fields to calculate the total price and compare this with the amount charged for the products on each invoice. This is a vast improvement over sampling transactions and manually recalculating the amount.

Gaps

An important test is the search for missing items in a series or sequence. If the transactions should follow a specific sequence or order, this technique can quickly find gaps in the data. The entire file can be examined to see if all items are accounted for and properly recorded.

Example. In reviewing health claims, claim numbers that are missing can help focus the search for erroneous claim. Missing check numbers, inventory tags, and other prenumbered items may also point to a control weakness or ongoing fraud.

Statistical Analysis

The calculation of statistical information provides a quick overview of the data before detailed analysis begins. It can quickly detect anomalies in numeric fields, help to establish a direction for additional audit tests, and give an indication of the materiality involved. The command provides details including average value, standard deviation, absolute value, and highest and lowest values for any given numeric field.

Example. To test the controls over purchase cards, auditors can use statistics to determine the highest and lowest transaction amount. Statistics will also quickly highlight transactions that are over the limit, large credit entries, and the average value of purchase card transactions.

Duplicates

This technique can quickly review the file to highlight duplicate values of key fields. In many systems, the key fields should contain only unique values (no duplicate records). Although not necessarily proof of fraud, the presence of duplicate check numbers, invoices, vendor names, and other data often merits investigation.

Example. In reviewing invoices from vendors, the presence of duplicate invoice numbers can indicate that invoices have been paid twice, either by accident or by design. Although the frequency of duplicates can be an indicator of fraud versus accident, it should not be the only indicator of materiality. A single duplicate can be in the tens or hundreds of thousands of dollars.

Sort/Index

Sorting or indexing arranges the file in ascending or descending order based on one or more auditor-specified key fields. The commands can arrange information on any number of key fields quickly and easily. The person committing the fraud may rely on the sheer number of transactions to hide an inappropriate series of items. But unusual transactions can be found simply by sorting on a field such as the date.

Example. If health claims are required to be submitted on a standard form that is preprinted with the claim number, sorting/indexing the data will help the auditor to determine if all the claim numbers correspond to the expected numbering series. Looking for claim numbers at the beginning and end of the sorted list can help focus the search for erroneous claims.

Summarization

Summarizing the data will count the number of records falling into each unique category of a character field and accumulate the total of specified numeric fields for each of the categories. The summarization allows auditors to identify and quantify all the values for given character fields. With a single command, the auditor can determine the total revenue and expenditures by account, for every branch in the company. Not only does this provide a basis for comparative analysis, but it also serves as a quick method of identifying incorrect data, such as invalid accounts, where fraudulent transactions may be placed. Summarized data can be used to determine if system edit checks are working as intended, by identifying all possible values of a given field. The auditor can calculate the total number of records or total monetary value associated with each possible field value and compare these to the acceptable values, such as totals by general ledger (G/L) account.

Example. Applying this technique to a medical claims fraud review, the auditor could identify questionable medical procedures by looking at the type and number of procedures by sex:

Procedure	Sex	Number
Hysterectomy	F	127
Hysterectomy	M	3
Hysterectomy		12

The analysis highlights three transactions where a male had a hysterectomy. These are obviously incorrect and must be reviewed to determine the nature of the error. But the analysis also identifies 12 cases where the value in the Sex field was blank. These point to a weakness in the application system's controls and should also be investigated.

Stratification

A stratification of the data examines the possible ranges, or strata, of specified numeric fields. It counts the number of records falling into specified strata, or intervals. It also allows the auditor to total the value of the numeric fields for each of the strata. By reviewing the number and value of items in each strata, the auditor can identify anomalies.

Example. Stratifying the contract amount will determine the different levels of contracts raised (e.g., ranges 0–4,999, 5,000–9,999, 10,000–24,999, etc.). This technique focuses attention on transactions of high materiality, but it can also identify possible symptoms of fraud, such as transactions exceeding, or just below, an individual's financial limit.

Contract Amount	Count	Total Contract Amount
0.00–4,999.99	0	$0.00
5,000.00–9,999.99	3	$28,394.00
10,000.00–24,999.99	176	$3,350,984.00
25,000.00–49,999.99	444	$16,674,390.00
50,000.00–99,000.00	342	$21,985,213.00
100,000.00–500,000.00	1	$404,182.00
Total:	966	$42,443,163.00

Cross Tabulation/Pivot Tables

Cross tabulation (or pivot tables) is a method that makes it easier to view the data for anomalies. It takes a record, such as pay transactions for each employee, and creates a two dimensional table—pay by employee by type of payment (regular salary, overtime, shift premium)—that will quickly highlight invalid or unusual combinations.

Example. Creating a cross tabulation of overtime payments by employee classification can quickly highlight cases where classifications not eligible for overtime are receiving overtime payments. A cross tabulation of G/L accounts used by branch can highlight G/L accounts that are only used by one branch or that, in comparison, have an unusually high level of activity and should be investigated.

Aging

In financial, inventory, and other types of data, it is often useful to calculate the number of days that a financial transaction has been unpaid or that an item has been sitting in inventory. The number of days between two dates can be calculated and used to find the lapsing of funds, inefficiencies in accounts payable or accounts receivable, and a variety of other irregular transactions.

Example. An audit can review overdue accounts receivable transactions by calculating the total number and value of transactions falling between 1–29, 30–59, 60–89, and greater than 90 days overdue. In detecting fraud, aging transactions can be used to determine if claims are being submitted after the end of the warranty period, if insurance claims are being made before or after the policy effective or end dates, and if contract bids are being accepted after the bid close date.

Join/Relate

Joining and relating combine information from different data files and can highlight unusual transactions. Though the information may be stored in different files or databases, join/relate allows the user to physically, or logically, combine the information from many files, creating a view of the information that contains fields from the separate files. There are different ways to combine files. For example, the results may contain only matched or unmatched primary records. It also could be a many-to-one or many-to-many match. Therefore, before combining files, auditors and fraud investigators must thoroughly understand the different methods of combining files that are supported by their software and the meaning of each result.

Example. In an investigation of travel claims, this technique would easily identify a person who submitted a claim for the use of a private vehicle and who also rented a car, or used a company car, for the same trip. It can also be used to highlight records where there is no match. For example, all employees should have payroll deductions. Joining the personnel file and the payroll file can identify all employees with no payroll deductions. Alternatively, combining data would highlight all payroll transactions to employees not in the personnel file.

Trend Analysis

Trend analysis compares information from several years or locations to identify anomalies. Audits conducted in the same operational area each year are ideal candidates for the use of trend information. The current year's data can be compared to previous years and trends used to examine and highlight areas that deserve further attention. Also, comparisons of business operations in different locations can quickly identify discrepancies worthy of audit follow-up.

Example. Comparison of the rate of return due to defects, by vendor, may indicate a potential fraud in which someone is buying inferior goods and receiving a kickback from the vendor.

Regression Analysis

Regression analysis is a means of predicting values, or comparing actual values with predicted values, to identify anomalies in the data. It can identify relationships in the data or cases where transactions do not follow expected relationships.

Example. A building manager collects cash for an apartment rental and fails to register the lease with the property manager/owner. Regression analysis can predict the number of apartments leased based on the usage of electricity or water.

Parallel Simulation

Parallel simulation can be used to verify an application system's internal programming logic by simulating the processing it performs. Usually this is done using a programming language, but audit software can also be used for parallel simulation. The approach takes the idea of recalculation one step further by using audit software to duplicate the functioning of a portion of the application.

Example. A programmer has altered the benefits calculation to overpay friends. It is possible to verify entitlements by obtaining the input data and performing the necessary calculations to determine the correct benefit amounts. Follow-up is required where the auditor's results differ from those of the payroll application.

Benford's Law

Benford's Law compares the frequency of the occurrence of digits in the data to the theoretical frequency distribution. Auditors can compare the number of occurrences of the first, first two, or first three digits of any numeric field to the Benford predicted frequencies, to highlight anomalies in the data.

Example. A comparison of the contract amount can highlight a higher-than-expected occurrence of contracts with amounts starting just below the sole-sourcing limit (e.g., starting with "49" when the limit for sole-sourced contracts is $50,000). Further investigation of these contracts could identify a situation where an individual is raising contracts below the competitive limit to direct them to friends or relatives. A review of accounts payable (A/P) invoices can highlight cases where invoice amounts (with only the cents altered to avoid detection as a duplicate) occur more often than predicted.

Digital Analysis

Digital analysis refers to a variety of techniques that examine the data for trends and anomalies. The analysis of the data may include an analysis of patterns in the digits of a numeric field, an assessment of the frequency of occurrence, or the calculation of ratios. The aim is to identify transactions that look different from normal transactions and may be indicators of fraud.

Examples. The analysis of travel claims highlighted employees with a high frequency of meal claims that were for even dollar amounts. In another audit, the analysis of the dates indicated that the bank reconciliations on Wednesday were incorrect more often than all other days combined. This led the auditors to a part-time worker who was stealing money from the deposit bag after the bank slip had been completed.

Confirmation Letters

Confirmation letters are a simple and commonly used method of verifying corporate data by seeking confirmation of specific details from the client. Audit software can automate the process of extracting details from the application system for each client and producing confirmation letters and address labels, making the process more efficient.

Example. A letter is sent to the client (vendor, claim holder, etc.) asking them to verify their purchase or account status. The response is compared to the corporate data and variances are followed up. Even "Return to Sender" responses provide significant information about the likelihood of recent activity being legitimate.

Sampling

Sampling selects a set of transactions for review. Audit software supports a variety of statistical sampling methods, including record, monetary or dollar unit, and stratified sampling. In addition, by specifying conditions or criteria, the auditor can generate directed or judgmental samples that can focus the fraud investigation. Directed sampling can significantly reduce the time and effort required to arrive at a conclusion concerning the allegations of fraud by pointing at a subset of the data, most likely to include fraudulent transactions, that can be manually checked and verified.

Example. A sample of 124 travel claims was selected to test the controls over the preauthorization process. The prosecution used the results to show that preauthorization was standard practice and that all employees followed this regulation, except the accused. This finding helped establish the case that it was fraud and not negligence.

Combining Techniques

Simply being aware of CAATTs will not be sufficient for the detection of fraud. Imagination, creativity, and a "what if" approach are needed. The best route combines knowledge of the business operation, the risks of fraud, the weaknesses in the controls, the data, the extraction and analysis software, and, most important, good auditor judgment.

Frauds will appear in many forms, and therefore the approach to fraud detection must be dynamic. A good understanding of the audit software's capabilities will give auditors and fraud investigators the ability to detect many different types of fraud. However, creativity and resourcefulness in detecting fraud is still the most effective tool.

The remainder of this chapter discusses various techniques, using case studies to illustrate how they can be used to assess the completeness, and to develop an understanding, of the data obtained or extracted. However, these same techniques also can be used to identify symptoms of possible fraud.

Assessing the Completeness of the Data

The need to ensure data integrity, of which completeness is an important aspect, is paramount to performing accurate analysis. When extracting and receiving data, the existence of control totals is an important step in ensuring the completeness. In particular, the auditor must verify that all of the extracted records have been successfully transferred, and are accessible to and have been properly interpreted by, data analysis software. As a first test of completeness, auditors should perform a simple count of the number of records and total of the control totals. Next, they should compare the first 100 records to the printout from the source system. The interpretation of the data by the analysis software should agree with the report produced by the source system.

A second aspect of completeness is ensuring that auditors have only the desired records. Several tests can be used to ensure that auditors have only the required records, and no extras; these tests include the use of filters, recalculating the data, checking for gaps, running statistics on key numeric fields, checking for duplicate records, and sorting the data on key fields. Each of these tests, while useful in ensuring the integrity and completeness of the data, also can identify potential fraudulent activity.

The remainder of this chapter presents approaches to ensuring the completeness of the data and illustrates fraud detection techniques that can identify incomplete or overly complete data.

Filter or Display Criteria

Filtering isolates those transactions that are of the most interest, and is perhaps the easiest of all the techniques discussed in this book, at least in concept. The difficulty arises in properly defining one's criteria before applying the filter. Why this is so important is precisely the reason that filtering is so powerful. Checking the data for completeness may not be a problem. For example, ensuring that the data received contains only records for fiscal year April 1, 2008, to March 31, 2009, simply requires the filter "date greater than or equal to April 1, 2008 and less than or equal to March 31, 2009." However, setting the criteria to identify potentially fraudulent transactions requires more practice and thought.

Reviewing a few thousand transactions manually is time consuming but possible. Manually reviewing the millions of records in today's corporate databases to locate the few that warrant follow-up is not. When using a computer to apply the criteria, auditors run the risk of ignoring relevant items or letting irrelevant ones clutter up the review. However, the computer is capable of selecting or filtering out records based on chosen criteria. The resulting data, a subset of the complete database, contains only those records that meet the specified criteria. (See Exhibit 5.1.)

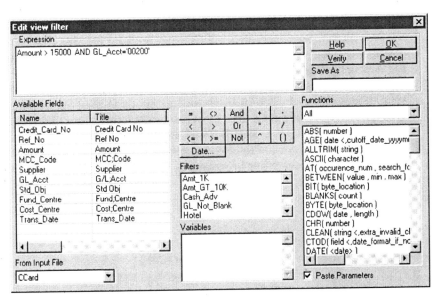

EXHIBIT 5.1 Filter Screen. ACL filter or display criteria for amount greater than 15,000 and GL account "00200".

Filters can be applied singly or in combination, using AND and OR logical expressions. The use of parentheses allows multiple conditions to be processed properly.

For example:

```
Quantity < 0
Value > 250,000 or Quantity > 200,000
(Location = '03' or Location = '22') AND Clerk = '0932'
```

By establishing criteria to identify the records that should be included in an analysis, auditors also can isolate those that should not be in the data. The records meeting the filter can easily be viewed, or extracted to a new data file, and a careful review can identify a range of problems, including fraud.

Case Study: Soaring Travel Costs

The company had entered into a three-year contract with a travel agency. All airline travel, hotels, and car rentals were booked through them. Under the terms of the contract, a fixed administration fee was charged for the first 100,000 bookings, after which a per-booking fee was charged. Management had expected travel administration costs to decline under the new consolidated arrangement, but was surprised when the administration fees were almost $300,000 more than expected for the first year. The auditors obtained a database containing all booking transactions and immediately set a filter to include only transactions that were from the first fiscal year. This isolated all transactions outside of the billing period and reduced the invoice amount by more than $210,000. Additional tests found other irregularities in the data used to calculate the invoice amount.

Scheme:	Inflated number of transactions—invoice based on dollars per transaction
Symptoms:	Transactions outside of billing period; duplicates; dummy transactions (no employee ID; no responsibility center)
Data Requirements:	Travel booking—passenger, transaction type, transaction date, cost

Expression/Equation

Part of verifying the completeness of the data includes ensuring that key fields are not blank and that the information is correct. Doing this often involves a recalculation of the data based on other fields. The computer is a perfect tool for performing calculations and comparing data. Auditors can easily verify information and calculations, and create new expressions. It is easy to build equations, such as quantity times unit price, to verify the cost of goods. The calculated amount can then be compared with the amount paid, as calculated by the system, to identify records where the recalculated amount disagrees with the amount in the system. The result can highlight both incomplete and incorrect data. (See Exhibit 5.2.)

By verifying key calculations, auditors can help to ensure the integrity and the completeness of the data received or downloaded. The ability to recalculate amounts and to compute averages across years also can be invaluable in reviewing the efficiency and effectiveness of operations. Calculating key figures such as inventory turnover rates, mean time to failure, and so on, can help auditors add value and detect fraudulent activities. For example, the use of audit software in an analytical review can detect inventory fraud by highlighting unexplained variances such as disproportionate increases in cost of goods relative to sales.[2]

	A	B	C	D	E	F	G
1	Vendor_No	Invoice_No	Product_No	Quantity	Unit_Cost	Amount	Recalc
2	11663	5981807	070104397	90	6.87	618.3	=D2*E2
3	13808	2275301	070104677	976	6.87	6705.12	
4	12433	6585673	070104657	1158	6.87	7955.46	
5	11663	5983947	070104327	709	6.87	4870.83	
6	12130	589134	070104377	1533	6.87	10531.71	
7	13411	49545947	030414313	122	47	5734	
8	12433	6585951	030414283	122	18	2196	
9	10721	123196	030412553	23	11.53	265.19	
10	12433	6585880	030412753	18	12.5	225	
11	13411	49540141	030412903	6	2.48	14.88	
12	10787	591533	030321683	828	1.47	1217.16	

EXHIBIT 5.2 Expression Screen. Using an Excel spreadsheet to recalculate Quantity times Unit Cost to compare with the provided Amount.

Auditors can also use the analysis software's calculation capabilities to verify key management reports. The report can be first saved to a file and then read by the analysis software as a data file. Auditors can then perform the calculations, and the results for each line, the subtotals and totals, can all be compared to the values on the report. Filtering will identify the discrepancies. These steps can be automated for recurring reports by building scripts, making such checks minimally disruptive to the reporting process. Although intentional misrepresentation in high-level reports may not be common, it can be all the more devastating when it occurs—look at what happened at Barings Bank.

Case Study: Missing Inventory

The fraud investigation team had been asked to conduct a review of the manufacturing plant for possible fraud. Part of the investigation reviewed the inventory that was used in the manufacturing process. Using the detailed inventory records, team members calculated the total cost of inventory for the first and the last six months of the current year. They also calculated the sales for the same period, adjusting for increases in sales prices. The analysis determined that the cost of goods sold had increased by 15.61 percent, whereas the adjusted sales had increased only by 8.74 percent. The difference was also reflected in a 2.31 percent decrease in the profit margin.

As a result of their analysis, team members focused their attention on the inventory area. Next they calculated the beginning inventory for the period, the amount purchased and used during the period, and the ending inventory. The calculated ending inventory levels for every product were compared with the actual inventory levels. This analysis identified inventory where the ending level was below the calculated amounts and led to the arrest of one of the inventory clerks who had been stealing inventory from the warehouse.

Scheme:	Items stolen from inventory
Symptoms:	The inventory at the beginning of the year plus purchases minus inventory used during the year is not equal to the inventory at the end of the year (Beginning + Purchased − Used < Ending).
Data Requirements:	Beginning inventory—product number, quantity. Ending inventory—product number, quantity. Transactions—product number, quantity purchased, quantity used.

Case Study: Cash Diverted

Since the recent downsizing, controls over the receipt of cash in the accounts receivable area were weak. The accounts receivable clerk often opened the mail and recorded the receipt of payment prior to crediting accounts. From time to time, especially when the customer paid in cash, the clerk would steal the payment. She would cover up the theft by adjusting the customer account by the amount of the theft.

The auditors were reviewing the controls and were concerned about the lack of separation of duties as well as the poor controls over the handling of payments. As part of the audit, they obtained a copy of the accounts receivable (A/R) database and calculated the total decrease in the accounts receivable. They compared this total with the total cash received. Since the clerk had been adjusting customer accounts without registering cash receipts, the total numbers did not balance.

The auditors presented the results of their analysis to the clerk. She had not considered that they might compare the two sets of data. When questioned about the growing discrepancies, she admitted to the theft of the payments.

Additional controls related to segregation of duties and handling of cash were put in place to prevent future frauds.

Scheme:	Theft of cash
Symptoms:	The amount at the beginning of the period plus purchases minus receipts is not equal to the balance (Beginning + Purchases − Receipts <> balance).
Data Requirements:	A/R—starting balance, customer number, receipt/sale, date, amount

Case Study: Invoicing Errors

The audit department at ABC Company received a phone call stating that John's Printing Supplies had been cheating ABC for years. The caller went on to suggest that the auditors review all the invoices from the printing supply company for the last two years. The vendor was a major provider of photocopy paper, toner, and other printing supplies. While concerned about the allegations, the audit manager had limited audit resources available to review the thousands of invoices. However, he decided to have a clerk scan the last six months' worth of invoices

(continued)

into the computer. When this was complete, the auditor imported the text file into the analysis software and performed tests to calculate the quantity times the unit price for each product and compare this with the corresponding value on the invoice. The calculated totals for each product were also summed and compared to the invoice total. Finally, because it was easy to do, the auditor performed a search for duplicate invoice numbers.

The results revealed that more than 10 percent of the invoices had errors in the product subtotals or the total invoice amount. Also, the auditor discovered three duplicate invoices. The audit manager immediately freed up additional resources to scan in all available invoices for the last three years. Since the auditor had created a script to perform the analysis of the first six months' worth of invoices, she simply ran this against the new file. This meant that once the invoices had been scanned, the rest of the analysis took less than two minutes to complete. The results showed that the error rate (10 percent) was consistent throughout the remaining invoices.

John's Printing Supplies—Errors in Invoice Amounts

Inv#	Qty	Unit	Invoice	Calc	Diff
4236	15	$22.97	384.55	344.55	40.00
4236	28	$27.32	794.96	764.96	30.00
4241	82	$43.12	3,785.84	3,535.84	250.00
...					
9201	47	$33.13	1,657.11	1,557.11	100.00

The auditors requested a meeting with the owner of John's Printing Supplies, and at first there was much confusion. The invoice amounts presented by the auditors did not agree with the accounts receivable figures at John's Printing. However, further investigation determined that one of the clerks in the invoicing department at John's and a clerk in the accounts payable section at ABC were working in collusion to defraud both companies. The clerk at John's Printing intercepted the correct invoices and substituted invoices that contained the overcharges. The clerk in the accounts payable section of ABC approved the invoices and sent the checks to John's Printing. The checks were cashed by the accounts receivable clerk, after which he wrote checks to pay the proper invoice amounts. The two clerks split the profits. This accounted for the fact that the A/R system at John's Printing disagreed with the audit data from ABC's accounts payable system. Both clerks were fired.

A further analysis of the A/R function at John's found a similar scheme being perpetrated by the A/R clerk on XYZ Company. This time, however, it did not involve collusion with the client's A/P clerk—just the fact that the invoices were not being checked for accuracy by XYZ before being paid.

Scheme:	Overcharging
Symptoms:	The total on the invoice is not equal to the quantity times the unit price (Total <> Quantity × Unit Price), or the addition of the subtotal lines does not agree with the grand total (Total of Subtotals <> Grand Total).
Data Requirements:	Invoices (text file)—name, date, invoice number, product number, quantity, unit price, subtotal, total

Case Study: Stamp Out Fraud

The company had centralized its administrative functions, creating a single unit to handle all administrative duties. The unit now performed many tasks, including word processing and mail delivery. Jim, a clerk in the new administrative section, was responsible for taking the postage meters to the post office and having them filled. However, he was exploiting a weakness in the controls. Using a company check for $3,000, he would obtain $2,500 on the postage meters and $500 in stamps. The receipt stated that he had purchased $3,000 in postage and did not break down the total. Jim then turned around and sold the stamps to friends and relatives, and kept the cash. Because the company mailed out lots of letters, he was able to repeat this scheme every month.

The auditor was concerned about the weaknesses in the controls for that area and performed an analysis as a proactive test for possible fraud. The auditor had joined three years of expenditure data together, creating a single file. She used this file to compare the expenditures for all general ledger accounts for the past three years, looking for trends. She calculated the percentage increase (or decrease) in the expenditures between Years 1 and 2, and Years 2 and 3. The 18 percent increase in the amount spent on postage over the last year was easily identified. Even after taking into account the increase in postal rates, the auditor felt that something was wrong and that it was worth investigating further. The auditor discovered a correspondence log that contained a record of every piece of correspondence. Every time a letter was received or sent out, the responsible clerk made an entry in the log. The auditor analyzed a copy of the log. Much of the correspondence was internal mail and did not require postage. Filtering the data on the zip code

(continued)

field, the auditor identified all correspondence in the last 18 months that required postage. However, the system did not indicate the type of correspondence (letter, parcel, etc). The auditor performed a manual review of the outgoing mail for a week and calculated that each piece of correspondence cost $0.56 on average. Using this figure, the auditor calculated the total postage cost per month and compared this figure with the postage expenses each month. The calculated cost was very close to the actual cost for the first 7 months. But there was a significant difference between the calculated and actual amounts starting 11 months ago, except for last July.

The auditor investigated further and found out that after the reorganization one year ago, Jim was given responsibility for filling the postage meter. She also determined that Jim had taken his vacation in the first two weeks of July and another employee had filled the meters for July. The auditor presented the results of her analysis to the manager of the administration section. After reviewing the calculation of the average cost per piece of correspondence and seeing the monthly comparison of estimated and actual postage costs, the manager was visibly upset. But this did not prove anything. Since the postage meters were due to be filled early next week, the manager asked the auditor to wait to question the suspected clerk. The following week, when Jim returned with the postage meters, the total on the meters were compared with the postage receipt and the fraud was obvious. When confronted, Jim confessed and full restitution was made. In addition, the manager instituted tighter controls over the postage meters and the expenditures reverted to a reasonable level.

Scheme: Clerk stealing stamps
Symptoms: Increase in postage—no corresponding increase in
                       amount of correspondence or postal rates
Data Requirements: Expenses—G/L code amount (three years).
                       Correspondence log—address, zip code, date (18
                       months).

Case Study: Telephone Bill Hang-ups

Telecommunication charges were increasing steadily, partially as a result of the increased use of cell phones, pagers, and Internet accounts. It was not surprising that, when the telecommunications budget more than doubled in three years, the VP of Informatics asked the internal audit department to identify inefficiencies and areas for cost savings.

The leader of the audit focused on possible inefficiencies in the use of long distance calls. Since head office was responsible for a significant portion of the billing increases, the audit team obtained detailed information for all calls made from head office. The data received from the phone company included the originating phone number, phone number called, date and time of call, and cost. The auditors calculated the call lengths and applied a filter to identify all long-distance calls of more than 60 minutes. The auditors were quite surprised to discover a number of calls that were exactly 999 minutes (over 16 hours) in length.

Analysis of Telecommunications Bill March Billing—Calls 999 Minutes in Length

Phone No.	Date	Start	End	Time
555–1234	18/03	08:32	01:11	999
555–1256	18/03	09:17	01:56	999
555–1385	19/03	12:08	04:47	999
555–2341	17/03	14:51	07:30	999
555–2348	26/03	16:04	08:43	999
. . .				
555–9745	06/03	12:42	05:21	999
555–9897	01/03	01:17	17:56	999

Note: Time can be calculated by creating an equation using start date and time and end date and time as follows: $(((24 \times (END\_DATE - STRT\_DATE) + END\_HR) \times 60 + END\_MIN) - (STRT\_HR \times 60 + STRT\_MIN))$

By performing a detailed review of the activity on these phone lines, the auditors found that other phone calls had been made from the same phone line during the same time period as that of the 999-minute call. None of the phones at head office had a feature that would allow the caller to make two calls at the same time. The auditor checked with the phone company and determined that a faulty communication switch had remained open after these persons had hung up the phone. The system failed to register the completion of the call, resulting in erroneous long-distance charges. The phone company's system had a maximum call length of 999 minutes; otherwise the call lengths would have been even higher. All charges related to the 999-minute calls were reversed by the phone company.

Next, the auditor noticed that in some of the cases where the calls were longer than 180 minutes, large data transfers were being performed between two sites. The auditors summarized the detailed billing

(continued)

information where data transfers were being conducted and determined that the usage was high enough to justify leasing a dedicated high-speed line, reducing the overall cost of the file transfers and improving the transmission speeds and reliability.

The next test centered on the identification of possible abuses of long-distance calling privileges. First, the auditors created display criteria to identify all long-distance calls made after regular working hours or during holiday periods. The auditor recommended controls over the ability to dial outside of the local area code after 6:00 p.m. and on weekends and holidays. Another test identified calls to long distance exchanges for pay-per-minute numbers (1–900, 1–976, etc.). Despite no serious evidence of abuse, the auditors recommended a simple change to the company's telecommunication switch software that blocked all access to the pay-per-minute exchanges.

The audit also reviewed the accuracy of the telephone bill and the efficiency and effectiveness of the use of leased lines. The audit team selected a sample set of bills for dedicated leased long-distance lines from a number of branch offices. Using the computer, they automatically generated confirmation letters that were sent to the appropriate branch offices. The letter asked the branch managers to verify the accuracy of the charges by ensuring that the line was still connected. The managers were also asked to review the justification for a dedicated line. In 10 percent of the cases, the lines were no longer required, but the service had never been canceled. In a further 5 percent of the cases, the lines were not even physically connected to a phone. Because of office redesigns, some telephone lines terminated in closets or were enclosed within the new walls. In some cases, dedicated lines—purchased to support data transfer requirements—were no longer connected to computer terminals, had been replaced by FTP capabilities, or the branch office had closed, but the service had not been canceled.

The use of data analysis software to generate confirmation letters, to analyze thousands of lines of detailed calling information, and to highlight anomalies or potential abuses greatly improved the effectiveness of the audit. The overall result was a 17 percent reduction in the total telecommunications bill.

Scheme:	Overbilling; abuse of long-distance lines; waste and inefficiency
Symptoms:	Overly long calls; pay-per-minute area codes; mismanagement
Data Requirements:	Call details—phone number, date, number called, start and end times, cost. Long-distance line billing—location, line number, date, amount.

Gaps

Although the completeness of the data is important for any fraud analysis, it can also be an indicator that a fraud has occurred. When searching for fraud, identifying what is not there can often be as important as identifying what is there. Auditors should look for expected items to ensure they do exist and follow up if they do not.

Exhibit 5.3 shows how IDEA can identify gaps in the Trans-id field.

The computer can review all transactions to ensure there are no missing items by examining the records for continuity and completeness, within the range of values. Missing items that can be symptoms of different types of fraud include:

- Missing accounts receivable payments
- Missing checks or invoices
- Purchase orders that have not been recorded
- Branch offices not reporting revenues
- Receipts missing for a given day
- Missing cash register tapes
- Water or electricity meter readings that are not recorded

Typically, when looking for gaps, the auditor can output a list of records that are missing, or the range of missing items. Exhibit 5.4 is an example of examining data for missing check numbers.

The auditor would want to follow-up on the missing checks to determine if they had been destroyed, are missing from the data for a valid reason, or are an indicator of a fraud.

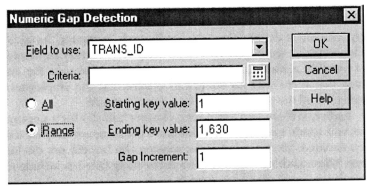

EXHIBIT 5.3 Gap Screen. Checking for gaps in a series of transactions using the IDEA Numeric Gap Detection routine.

Missing check number 12868
Missing the range of checks from 12878 to 12888
Missing check number 12953
Missing check number 12973

EXHIBIT 5.4 Analysis of Check Numbers (Search for Missing Checks).

In addition to finding gaps in a sequence, it can also be useful to find a sequence when none is expected to exist. Patterns in the data—either missing transactions where there should be a consistent pattern, or consecutive transactions where there should not be any—can prove fruitful for fraud detection.

Case Study: Long-Distance Honor System

Employees were permitted to use their office phones to make long-distance calls as long as they paid for the charges. From the employees' perspective, it was a good deal since the company had a special discounted rate with the telephone carrier. The person making the call was asked to complete a long-distance call slip detailing the date and time of each personal call. Each month, the employees returned the long-distance call slips and reimbursed the company for the personal calls. From the company's perspective, it was also a good deal. Employees liked the arrangement, and it increased the number of long-distance calls, allowing the company to negotiate a better long-distance discount rate.

At the end of the year, the auditors tested the controls over the reimbursement of long-distance charges. They found that each month Caroline in accounts payable properly reviewed the long-distance bill and identified noncompany numbers called. They found that she was very accurate at determining which calls were "company" long-distance calls and which were "personal" calls. They were equally impressed with the monthly recording and billing procedures. However, the auditors noted that there was no control to ensure that the employees were paying for all the personal calls they actually made.

Earlier, William had lost a long-distance call slip for a personal call and, as a result, inadvertently reimbursed the company only for the slips he submitted. Later, he found the missing slip but did not disclose the error. When nothing happened, he deliberately failed to include several long-distance call slips from time to time.

The auditors reviewed the reimbursement records looking for gaps in the call slip numbers. Since the long-distance call slips were prenumbered, the test easily identified 26 missing slips. The results were presented to Caroline, who matched the numbers from the missing slips to the carbon copies of the slips. William was identified as the culprit for 25 of the missing slips. When approached by the auditors, he admitted to neglecting to include all slips and said he would reimburse the company. In accordance with the strict company policy on fraud, he was fired.

Scheme:	An employee does not submit amount for long-distance bills
Symptoms:	Missing slips
Data Requirements:	Telephone slips—long-distance slip number, date, employee number, amount received

Case Study: Special Room Rate

The assistant to the president was required to accompany the president on many of her frequent business trips across the country. As a result, the auditors did not normally question the high travel expenditures of the president or her assistant. However, they had received an anonymous tip that the assistant was committing fraud.

During the initial fraud investigation of the assistant's hotel bills, they calculated her total travel costs by type and noticed that she had significantly higher accommodation expenditures than the president. The team leader, curious as to why this was the case, instructed his team to review all transactions related to her hotel expenditures. In particular, they examined the sequence of these expenses and checked for duplicates. As expected, there were no duplicates and the missing items check, run on the invoice number, revealed many gaps in the sequence of the hotel invoice numbers. This was not surprising since each hotel used its own invoice numbering series and had many clients, each receiving separate invoices. What surprised the auditors was that the analysis showed 10 bills from one hotel in the continuous sequence 20311 to 20320—even though the dates of the invoices spanned several months. The auditors checked with the hotel and discovered that the assistant had stayed at the hotel on the dates in question. However, the hotel manager told them that the invoice numbers were not part of their invoice sequence and could not have been issued by the hotel. The

(continued)

comparison of hotel bills for trips also taken by the president confirmed the invoice sequencing anomaly and the inflated prices.

The auditors brought the results of their analysis to the attention of the president and received permission to question the assistant. The assistant admitted to using her computer to scan in a real invoice from the hotel and then make copies, thereby falsifying her travel claims. She would inflate her hotel bill every time they stayed at that hotel. She had invented an invoice number and simply incremented it each time she generated a new invoice. By identifying an unexpected sequence in the data, the auditors found the altered invoices and discovered her scheme.

Even if she had varied the invoice number, a comparison of the president's hotel costs would still have revealed the fraud. Also, a ratio analysis on the room rate would have identified the inflated prices (see Chapter 10).

Scheme:	Assistant inflates bill by submitting falsified invoice
Symptoms:	Same hotel, same date as another employee, but different invoice number series and different amount
Data Requirements:	Travel expenses—employee number, hotel, invoice number, amount, date

Statistical Analysis

Another useful technique to test the completeness of the data is statistical analysis. In this case, the concern is that additional information is part of the data. For example, if auditors examine all payroll records for the current period, they want to be sure that payroll transactions from the previous period are not included in the extracted data.

Statistical analysis is used to obtain information about one or more numeric or date fields, including the average, standard deviation, and lowest and highest values in the file.

Statistical analysis is very useful for fraud work because, with a single command, the auditor can obtain an overview of all the values in a numeric or date field. This can help focus the detailed analysis on anomalies, such as negatives in a revenue field or unusually large or small values. (See Exhibit 5.5).

Statistical analysis provides this information about numeric fields:

■ Record counts, field totals, and average field values for all positive, negative, and zero-valued records, as well as all records in the file
■ Sum of the absolute values of all records

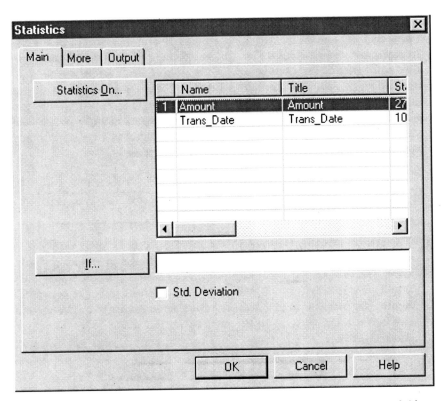

EXHIBIT 5.5 Statistics Screen. Preparing to calculate statistics on the Amount field using the ACL Statistics window.

- Range (maximum value minus minimum value)
- Standard deviation of the field
- Highest field values
- Lowest field values

Statistical analysis also can be used to examine a date field, providing the same information. A simple analysis of the possible values for a given numeric or date field often can highlight transactions of interest.

The auditor can:

- Quickly identify the highest and lowest dates.
- Determine if any transactions are outside the desired time frame.
- Identify blank or invalid dates.
- Understand the range of values for the given date field.

Statistical analysis also can be used to determine parameters for sampling, such as population size, and to establish ranges for stratified sampling. In particular, monetary or dollar unit sampling requires the auditor to know the total value of the population for the sample field before specifying an amount to be sampled. Further, a few very large or small values that can affect the entire population and impact the sampling approach are easily noted by reviewing the data's statistics. These can identify records with values outside of the usual range, and the auditor can choose to select a stratified sample or treat the unusual records separately.

Case Study: Missing Inventory

The auditors usually performed a standard inventory audit, comparing the manual count of the physical inventory with the inventory system's total. The size of the retail store inventory meant that ordinarily they could sample only a small percentage of the total number of inventory items. The fact that items from inventory were regularly in transit, and not in the warehouse or on the sales floor, also made the auditors' job more difficult.

   The manager wanted to ensure that when the auditors conducted their inventory audit next month, everything would balance. He was having a problem with shrinkage and had lost last year's bonus because of a similar problem. As a result, he was not eager to report the current problem and jeopardize his bonus again. He had planned to review the control framework and identify the source of the problem but had never gotten around to it. This year, instead of reporting the losses, he entered negative inventory transactions as he found out about them. For example, in the previous week, he recorded a receipt of −3 circular saws. This transaction was entered to make the inventory system value agree with the physical inventory. He felt confident that he could easily explain any other minor differences in the inventory figures. He was also sure that he could look at the controls later and see if theft was actually occurring, or if it was only an accounting problem.

   One of the auditors had just returned from a computer-assisted auditing course, where a copy of *Internal Audit: Efficiency through Automation* had been given to each participant. She felt that the inventory audit would be an ideal test for some of the techniques described in the book. Despite some reluctance from the programmer, she obtained a copy of the inventory transactions for the last year. The instructor had stressed the importance of gaining an overall understanding of the data before moving on to detailed analysis, so as a first step she ran a statistical analysis on several numeric fields, including the quantity received (Qty_Received) field. The results were:

Analysis of the Quantity Received
Field : Qty_Received

	Number	Total	Average
Positive:	11,820	591,048	50
Zeros:	1		
Negative:	180	−470	−3
Totals:	12,001	590,578	2
Abs Value:		591,518	
Range:		106	
Std. Dev.:		12.07	
Highest 5:	98 98 96 95 92		
Lowest 5:	−8 −6 −3 −3 −3		

The results were particularly unexpected, as there were records with negative values in the quantity-received field. At first she thought that she had not performed the analysis properly, but she confirmed the initial results by reviewing the analysis and running the statistics again. There was no doubt: 180 records had negative values.

Each record in the inventory system contained the user ID and the name of the employee entering the record. The auditor filtered the data to isolate the negative entries and totaled an expression that computed the value of the inventory (quantity received times the unit price) entered by each employee. The inventory manager had entered all of the negative receipt transactions.

Negative Receipt Transactions by Employee

Employee	Count	Total
Fredericks	180	−804,009.45
Total:	180	−804,009.45
180 of 2,001 met the criterion: Qty_Received<0		

The information was immediately brought to the attention of the audit team leader, and suddenly this was no longer a routine inventory audit. When questioned, the manager said that he knew there had been some losses but had not realized the full extent of the problem. He had

(continued)

always planned to look into the losses but never seemed to have time. The team leader dedicated a portion of the audit resources to the task of investigating the disappearing inventory. A detailed CAATTs-based analysis showed that more than $925,000 had been stolen in the last year.

The use of statistical analysis had allowed the audit team to quickly find the anomalies hidden in the detailed records. One advantage was that the auditor was not looking for a specific condition but simply reviewing the completeness of the quantity received. If the auditor had looked at the details without running a statistical analysis first, she might not have considered checking the detailed transaction file for negative values. A sample of inventory items would not have identified the problem either since the physical and system inventory values would have agreed.

Scheme:	Reduce inventory in system to agree with items on the shelf
Symptoms:	Negative entries by manager
Data Requirements:	Inventory—item, quantity received, user ID. Users—user ID, name.

Duplicates

In addition to checking for completeness in data, it is important to ensure that there are no duplicate records. The search for duplicates is a standard audit and fraud detection technique. Duplicates are defined as records where the key field, such as invoice number, is not unique. Audit software that tests for duplicates usually presorts the file and then checks for two or more consecutive records with the same value in the specified field. The search for duplicates can be on a single field or a combination of fields. (See Exhibit 5.6.)

Examples include:

- Duplicate direct deposit number
- Duplicate purchase order number
- Duplicate invoice number
- Same vendor number and date
- Same contract number and date
- Same vendor number, invoice number, and amount

In traditional auditing, with manual sampling, duplicates pose a dilemma. For example, in a database of a million transactions, the number

EXHIBIT 5.6 Duplicate Key Screen. The IDEA duplicate key detection routine allows the user to output the duplicates or all records without duplicates.

of duplicates may not be statistically significant if only 100 transactions are duplicates. The statistical probability of selecting even one duplicate record, in a sample of 200, would be less than 2 percent. However, since there was only one duplicate, the auditor would not know that it was a duplicate. The chances of having both halves of a duplication, and thus knowing that there is a duplication, are lower than 1 in several million. (Buy a lottery ticket; the odds are better.) Unfortunately, materiality may not be tied to the number of occurrences, and a small number of duplicate transactions can quickly add up to a sizable sum. The computer-assisted search solves this dilemma, as it performs a 100 percent check and lists all duplicate transactions.

Duplicate transactions are not necessarily indications of problems with data completeness or fraud. There may be a number of valid reasons to have duplicate records. As always, a sound understanding of the data is essential before drawing conclusions from results. For example, partial payments, each coded to the same invoice number, may appear as duplicate transactions; as might progress payments or payments split across different financial accounts. Similarly, auditors should check for adjusting or correcting entries, such as stop payment and credit transactions, when duplicates are found. All potential duplicate transactions should be carefully reviewed and verified.

Case Study: Duplicate Serial Numbers

The auditors were verifying the financial statements. Part of the review included calculating the value of the inventory on hand. After obtaining a copy of the inventory holdings and verifying the time period, they recalculated the inventory value (quantity times unit price) for each

(*continued*)

product. The figures agreed with the reported inventory value. However, the auditors performed one more test—they checked for duplicate serial numbers. The results revealed that the inventory manager had deliberately entered a number of high-value items twice to inflate the inventory value.

Scheme:	Overstatement of inventory
Symptoms:	Items counted more than once
Data Requirements:	Inventory—product number, product description, serial number, value

Case Study: Duplicate Payments

The president of Goodz Inc., a large supplier to X-treme Corp., called the audit manager at X-treme with a concern. The accounts receivable clerk at Goodz had received a call from X-treme's accounts payable department saying that an invoice had accidentally been paid twice, and requesting that Goodz send a refund. His concern was that this was the fifth time this had happened in the last month. The audit manager thanked him for the information and immediately launched a fraud investigation.

The invoice processing clerk for the A/P section at X-treme was well aware that the control over the payment of duplicate invoices relied on two fields. The A/P application would flag and reject any transaction where the combination of vendor number and invoice number was not unique. However, the clerk easily got around this control because there were no controls over the vendor table used to assign vendor numbers.

The clerk simply added vendor numbers for additional vendors using slightly different names and assigned a vendor number for each spelling:

Vendor Name	Vendor Number	Address
Goodz	N3450D12	101 Grey Rock
Goodz Inc	N5478X23	101 Grey Rock
Goodz Inc.	N5471C10	101 Grey Rock

This permitted the clerk to submit the same invoice for payment, without the A/P application controls detecting the duplicate. After the check was sent to the vendor, the clerk would call the vendor and say that the invoice was paid twice, request a refund check, and, when the check was returned, he would cash it himself.

The auditors routinely checked for duplicate payments when testing the controls to see if the same vendor number-invoice number combination had been paid more than once. The auditors never found any duplicate payments, despite the fact that the clerk was paying thousands of dollars in duplicate payments every month.

As part of the fraud investigation, they reviewed the vendor table, a key control over duplicate payments, and found the duplicate invoice control weakened by the presence of numerous vendors each with more than one vendor code. They modified the test for duplicate payments to look for identical invoice numbers and payment amount (ignoring the vendor number), identified the duplicate transactions paid to Goodz and other vendors, and uncovered the clerk's fraudulent scheme.

Scheme: A/P clerk pays invoices twice and requests a refund, which he cashes

Symptoms: Same invoice number and amount but different vendor numbers

Data Requirements: A/P—vendor, date, invoice number, amount, check number, user ID. Vendor—vendor number, vendor name, address, phone, user ID.

There are a number of possible variations to this scheme. The clerk might have also used the weakness in the vendor table controls to create new vendors with similar-sounding names and his address as the address of the vendor. In this manner, the duplicate check would be sent directly to the clerk's home. However, matching addresses on the vendor table with employee addresses would easily catch this scheme.

Other variations include sending the payment to a post office box or directing the payment to the clerk's bank account. In these cases, a test of the vendor table for duplicate post office boxes or bank deposit accounts would reveal different vendors with the same information (post office box or bank account)—a symptom of fraud.

In addition to the basic commands, software tools have many functions that may assist in detecting fraud. For example, searching for duplicate names in the vendor table—after removing special characters from the vendor name, including commas, dashes, slashes, asterisks, and so on—would identify the duplicate vendors. Additionally, summarizing the vendor table records on the field that shows the user ID of the person who created the duplicate vendor records would have identified the clerk.

Keep in mind that a match of vendor and employee addresses does not guarantee that a fraudulent transaction has been found. For example, an employee's spouse or child may be a valid vendor. However, cases where employee and vendor addresses match should always be examined. Particularly careful scrutiny should be given to matched addresses if the employee works in the invoice processing or contracting sections.

Case Study: Duplicate Check Numbers

Thomas, the clerk in the accounts payable section, "borrowed" a copy of a blank check, and used his computer to scan the check and save the image as a file. He later returned the check to the blank check storage. Every week, the clerk modified the computer file to create a check that he then cashed. At first he used the same check number each time, but, because he had an electronic copy of the company check, he finally realized that he could easily alter the check number and started doing so.

The audit manager was concerned about the controls in the accounts payable section and initiated a proactive fraud investigation. Until recently, verification of the A/P process had been minimally effective. The auditors selected a sample of 150 out of the 250,000 checks issued annually by the company. However, this year the auditors performed some automated testing of the A/P data. The analysis allowed them to review all the checks issued in less time than the usual manual testing required. As part of the investigation, the auditors obtained a file containing a list of all company checks that had been cashed and performed two tests: the first was a search for duplicates, and the second was a search for missing check numbers. Since the checks were prenumbered, the auditor expected to see only one occurrence of each check number and only check numbers from the current sequence.

The results were very effective in identifying problems in both test areas. The test for duplicates found that one check number had been used 18 times. In addition, the analysis for gaps identified check numbers that were not consistent with the company's stock of checks. The auditor obtained copies of the canceled checks that were either duplicates or not in the proper series, and found Thomas's name on each as the payee or endorsee. Thomas admitted to having stolen a blank check and making copies for his own use.

Scheme:	A/P clerk steals check—makes copies
Symptoms:	Duplicate and out-of-sequence check numbers
Data Requirements:	A/P—vendor, date, invoice number, check number, user ID

Case Study: Repurchased Equipment

The company purchased expensive, highly specialized equipment that was used in its manufacturing plants. All purchases were made centrally, and the equipment shipped to one of the plants when it was required. The company had recently implemented just-in-time inventory practices while maintaining a quick response time to orders from plant managers. These new inventory practices were saving the company millions of dollars per year, and the inventory manager was understandably proud of the inventory system. However, he had heard a few rumors about inventory theft. Although he was not personally aware of any problems, he asked audit to investigate.

The audit team conducted a thorough review of the controls and found only one area of concern: When items were shipped to a plant, they were automatically removed from the electronic inventory system. The receiving plant manager did not have to send any proof of receipt, so there was no sure way of knowing if the item had reached its final, correct destination. The inventory manager countered that if someone had ordered an item and did not receive it, he would certainly hear about it. He even produced a few e-mails where the recipient had questioned the status of deliveries that were only a day late. The audit team leader replied, "But what if they weren't expecting a delivery? Would they complain that it was late if they hadn't requested it?"

The audit team requested copies of all equipment purchases for the last year. The file included all equipment purchased, regardless of whether it had subsequently been shipped to the plants. The data was checked for duplicate serial numbers. The results revealed that 53 expensive items used in the manufacturing process had duplicate serial numbers. The company had purchased hundreds of thousands of dollars' worth of equipment it already owned. They determined that, while all equipment had supposedly been shipped to various manufacturing plants, none of the managers at the plants had placed an order for, or received, equipment. They also discovered that in each case, the shipping agent was the same person.

They started performing detailed reviews of all current shipments, and the first time the clerk in question prepared a shipment that included items the plant manager had not ordered, the auditor arranged for a private security company to follow the delivery truck. Instead of delivering the equipment to the plant specified on the shipping receipt, the unordered equipment was delivered to a warehouse in the city. Two days later, the inventory manager asked the clerk to place an order

(continued)

for the same model equipment that had been stolen. The clerk did so, and the security personnel followed the truck as it delivered the stolen equipment back to the company plant.

In the weeks that followed, audit was able to prove that the clerk was placing false orders for equipment and charging the inventory to phony projects. The equipment was delivered to a warehouse and held there until the company placed a purchase order for the same item. The clerk would then arrange for the equipment to be shipped to the company, in effect selling the company back its own inventory. The serial number had not been changed, so it would have been easily identified as a duplicate if the equipment had not been removed from the inventory system when it was shipped out the first time.

The clerk was fired and the serial numbers of all new equipment were compared to those of equipment that had previously been in inventory. Controls were also put in place to ensure that equipment was shipped to, and received by, project managers of valid projects.

Scheme:	Shipping clerk takes items out of inventory (supposedly shipped to a plant); these are stolen and then purchased again.
Symptoms:	Duplicate serial numbers
Data Requirements:	Inventory—serial number, date received at warehouse, amount, user ID. Items transferred from warehouse to plant—serial number, date shipped, location, user ID.

Sorting and Indexing

Ensuring completeness can be difficult if the transactions obtained are not in any particular order. If auditors had asked for all accounts between 0000001 and 9999999, how can they be sure that they received all of the required information? One of the easiest commands to understand is sorting. Sort can be used to test both the completeness of data and to look for fraud. Many frauds go undiscovered because they are lost in the volume of information that investigators must review. Manually testing for anomalies under these conditions usually means relying on some type of sampling of the transactions. If the sample is selected incorrectly, it might not be drawn evenly from the entire population, making the detection of anomalies even less likely. For example, randomly selecting numbers from one to ten thousand as a basis for selecting accounts numbered 1 to 10,000 would not select an account setup with an "A" at the beginning of the account number.

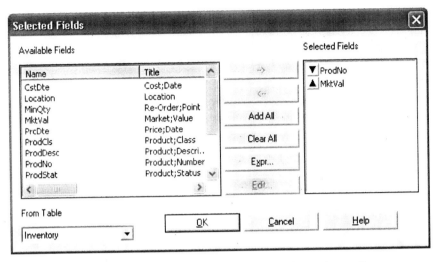

EXHIBIT 5.7 Sort Screen. Sorting using the ACL command. Too few auditors appreciate how easy it is to sort 100,000 accounts by account holder name or date last used, or the valuable information to be gleaned from such a sort.

However, with the application of CAATTs, electronic data can be sorted in any order, and the results quickly and easily reviewed for anomalies. (See Exhibit 5.7.)

The idea of sorting data on a field is not new to data analysis, yet the utility of this simple act is often overlooked. An electronic sort of the data can perform in seconds what would take days to accomplish manually. With data analysis software, the auditor need only specify the field on which the file is to be sorted, for example, on contract number, and the name of the sorted file.

Sorting the data will rearrange it into ascending or descending order, based on one or more key fields selected by the auditor. Depending on the software used, the sorted data can be saved in a new file that is physically arranged in the specified order or an index can be created that simply arranges the display of the data as viewed on the screen without creating a new physical data file.

Often the records at the beginning or end of a sorted file will prove to be of most interest to auditors or investigators. For example, sorting banking transactions by account number will easily highlight account numbers that are outside the range normally assigned to bank accounts. If the bank's standard numbering sequence specifies that accounts must start with the digits 0 to 9 and must be eight digits in length, a sorted file would quickly identify account numbers starting with the letters A to Z, or containing more or fewer than the required eight digits.

By focusing attention on the transactions at either end of the file, sorting improves the overall efficiency of the review process. It also serves to highlight possible symptoms of fraud or irregularities in the data, such as:

- Dates that are very old, or future dates
- Transaction values outside of the normal range for the field
- Payee or vendor names starting with blanks or unusual characters
- Records with blank field values
- Character data in numeric fields
- Numeric data in character fields

An alternative to sorting is to index the file on the key fields. Indexing does not physically reorganize the data or create a second data file but creates an index file that contains pointers to the original data in the specified order. Applying the index to the data file creates a logical view of the data such that the records are displayed in the desired order. (See Exhibit 5.8.)

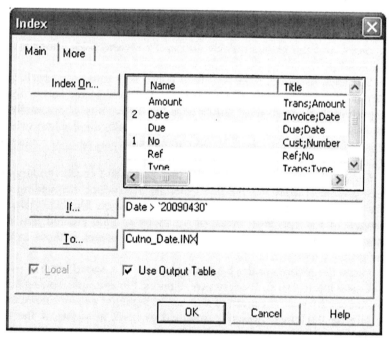

EXHIBIT 5.8 Index Screen. An index takes up less disk space than a sorted copy of the original data file, but the processing of an indexed file is much slower (ACL indexing window shown here).

When deciding whether to sort or index a file, the auditor should consider:

- The availability of disk space to sort and save the data file
- Whether a variety of analyses on the resulting data will be performed

---

Case Study: Fictitious Accounts

Reviews were always conducted by manually selecting a sample of insurance policies from the file cabinets. The results were sometimes surprising but rarely identified fraudulent activity. This year, one of the auditors decided to perform an initial review of the insurance information using CAATTs. The detailed insurance data was stored in chronological order, based on the date the policy was opened. The first step was to sort the insurance file data by policy number. This produced very interesting results. According to the company's numbering procedures, all policies used the year as the first four digits of the policy number. However, the sorted file of the current year's policies contained more than 50 policies starting with the letters "DC."

When the insurance policy manager was questioned about these anomalies, he sighed and opened his personal file cabinet. All of the "DC" policies were kept in his cabinet and, therefore, had never been manually reviewed by the auditors. He had been creating fictitious policies to cover shortfalls in targets to ensure that he received his bonuses. The previous audit teams were never even made aware of the existence of these policies since they were not kept in the main file cabinets. Given the thousands of policies, the manager felt sure that the auditors would never notice that a hundred files were missing. Even a statistical sample of policies was unlikely to select one of his "special" policyholders. Two years earlier the manager had needed only 17 more policies to make his quota for the year, and he thought he could catch up the policies in the new year. One year ago he created 26 fictitious policies, and in the current year it was 59. He thought that he was doing nothing wrong by inflating his numbers and honestly believed that the targets were unfairly high. Management had a different view and demanded that he repay the bonuses he had fraudulently received.

Scheme:	Fake policies with nonsequential or nonconforming policy numbers
Symptoms:	Fictitious policies to meet quotas; all processed by manager
Data Requirements:	Insurance policies—policy number, salesman, amount

Notes

1. ACL, Fraud Detection and Prevention: Transactional Analysis for Effective Fraud
   Detection, ACL Services Ltd., Vancouver, BC: 2006.
2. Joseph T. Wells, *Occupational Fraud and Abuse* (Austin, TX: Obsidian Publishing Co., 1997).

CHAPTER 6

Overview of the Data

Once the integrity and completeness of the data has been verified, auditors must get a better understanding of what it means. A good overview of the business meaning of the data will focus the investigation. This can also save a great deal of time and effort and improve the quality of the analyses performed at later stages.

Data analysis software makes it quick and easy to obtain an overview of the data. For example, a simple summarization by branch office can ensure that auditors have data from all branch offices, provide valuable information on the relative size of each office, and pinpoint invalid branch codes that may be a symptom of fraud. Stratifying the data on a numeric field will give additional information on numeric fields, telling auditors how many items fall within certain ranges of the data and allowing them to view items falling just below specific financial limits. A pivot table or cross tabulation, showing the use of general ledger (G/L) accounts by branch office, will help to ensure that the data contains all of the required branch offices and will highlight unusual G/L accounts, used by only one branch office, for example.

The commands used to verify completeness, such as statistical analysis and sort/index, also help auditors understand the data. Similarly, the commands discussed in the rest of this chapter can identify completeness concerns.

Summarization

Another important aspect of ensuring completeness is determining if information from all sources—all branch offices, all periods, all product classes, all types of transactions, and so on—has been included. In addition, auditors must gain an overview of the data. Both these objectives can be supported by the judicious use of summarization. As with all techniques discussed, summarization is also useful in detecting cases of fraud.

Summarizing the transactions will provide an overview of the data that enables auditors to gain a better understanding of the information system and conduct more informed analyses. For example, summarizing transactions by branch and totaling expenditures and revenues will help ensure that the data contains information for all valid branches and identify unknown or invalid branches. It will also allow auditors to compare each branch's revenues and expenditures, even providing the ability to calculate the ratio of expenditures to revenues for each branch. It is easy to use and yet provides auditors and fraud investigators with a wealth of information, including an overview of the data and the business operations.

Summarization can be used to total one or more numeric fields or expressions. For example, to determine the number and value of invoices paid per month, the auditor can summarize by month and accumulate the amount field. The result would identify all months included in the data and provide a total for the number of invoices processed as well as their total amount for each month, showing the cyclical trend of business activities. (See Exhibit 6.1.)

Summarization can also be used to verify the edit checks of an application. For example, if the field denoting sex is a key field for a health insurance claim system, summarizing on sex will identify all possible values of the field in the data. The presence of any values other than "M" and "F" indicates that the edit checks have failed.

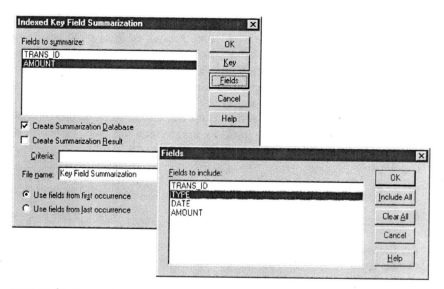

EXHIBIT 6.1 Summarization Screen. Summarize can be used to organize records into logical groupings and to accumulate numeric field values for each (IDEA key field window shown here).

Case Study: Vendor Address Changes

A review of the control framework had identified weakness in the accounts payable system. The area was often a source of fraud and the manipulation of the vendor table was a potential risk. As a result, once every quarter, the auditors reviewed the table to determine if vendors had changed addresses more than once—a red flag for fraud. All transactions that resulted in changes to vendor addresses were reviewed, and the total number of address changes for each vendor was determined.

This quarter several vendors showed 10 or more address changes, yet the current addresses of these vendors were the same as they were more than a year ago. The auditors extracted the detailed records for these vendors and found that all the address changes were to the same post office box and then back to the original vendor addresses the following day. The data was summarized to show the total number of address changes entered by each clerk. The results revealed that one clerk had recorded all of the address changes for the vendors that had had more than three changes of address. The clerk had manipulated the vendors' addresses in order to have checks delivered to him. A review of the canceled checks confirmed that the clerk had cashed them.

Scheme:	Clerk changes vendor address to send check to him- or herself
Symptoms:	High number of changes to vendor information
Data Requirements:	Vendor table transactions—vendor number, name, address, user ID

Case Study: Credit Card Processing Rates

The fraud investigation team was called to review the bank's retail credit card transaction processing. The vice president in charge of the credit card processing section had noticed a slight drop in the revenue generated from retail store credit card transactions. However, the total number of credit card transactions being processed had not decreased.

The fraud investigation team learned that the bank charged different percentages for processing different types of credit cards. They obtained

(*continued*)

the detailed transaction data, containing the credit card number, retail store number, amount of the purchase, and the code indicating the credit card type. They also obtained a description of all the credit card types from the manager of the programming department (01—Visa, 02—MasterCard, 03—American Express, etc.) and then totaled the credit card transactions by store and credit card type. The results showed that two stores had coded all of their transactions in the last six months to a test credit card type code. The code was used for testing only, and no bank processing rate was charged for transactions with that code. The two stores were very large, and several thousand transactions had been processed with a 0 percent processing charge, explaining the drop in revenue transactions.

The head programmer for the system told them that the test code was established so that the programmers could run test transactions through the system, without false revenue being generated. By running statistics on the transaction dates, the fraud investigators discovered that the stores had both started using the test code for their credit card transactions within one week of each other. Further inquiry established that the stores were both managed by the same person.

The next step was to try to connect someone in the bank, probably in the programming section, with the stores. Knowing it was a long shot, the investigators matched the store manager's home address with the personnel file. This identified a programmer, hired fewer than eight months ago, with the same address but a different name. Checking the information on her dependents, the investigators determined that she was the wife of the store manager and had worked on the credit card system less than a week before the stores started using the test codes. When confronted, she denied any knowledge of the credit card codes, but when shown the maintenance logs (which clearly proved that she had worked on the codes seven months earlier), she admitted to providing her husband with the test code. The bank fired the programmer, charged the store manager the full amount of the credit card transaction charges, and put procedures in place to ensure that all test codes were considered invalid when system testing was not occurring.

Scheme:	Process transaction against invalid card types
Symptoms:	Decrease in revenues, invalid card types
Data Requirements:	Credit card charges—card type, amount, store number, date, charge percentage. Card—card type, percentage. Human Resources—employee name, address, department, start and end date, dependents.

Case Study: Late Payments

Invoices were paid at approximately 100 invoice-processing offices across the country. The audit reviewed the invoice-processing procedures to find ways to reduce the interest costs being paid on overdue accounts. The auditors used the head office financial system to identify all invoices with late payment charges. Summarizing the data by office, they determined the total amount of interest paid by each invoice-processing office.

The analysis, sorted by the descending amount of interest charges, showed that the three top invoice-processing offices were responsible for 95 percent of the over $2.1 million in late payment charges. These offices warranted further audit review.

Payments on Overdue Accounts
(Offices with more than $10,000 in Late Payments)

Office	# Payments	Interest Charges
Chicago	21,281	980,241.52
Detroit	10,606	651,662.02
Boston	5,042	404,759.66
Los Angeles	1,257	60,610.74
Washington	1,001	34,508.00
San Francisco	1,006	12,144.52
Totals:	40,193	2,143,926.46

The auditors selected a sample of transactions handled by the Chicago, Detroit, and Boston offices and conducted an on-site review. The review lead to the discovery of inefficiencies in the invoice-processing procedures and also identified instances of over-/underpaid interest. It determined that all invoices were processed on a first-come, first-served basis. As a result, a large-dollar invoice could be processed later than small-dollar invoices, simply because the small-dollar invoices had been received first. By summing the interest charges by month, the auditors also determined that significant interest charges were being incurred at year-end.

The audit recommended that invoices over $50,000 be processed first and that less attention be expended on the low-dollar, low-risk invoices. The auditors also suggested that additional staff be hired during year-end, the peak invoice processing period. In addition, they

(continued)

recommended the development of regular reports on the amount of interest charges incurred by each invoice-processing office. As a result of the implementation of the audit recommendations, the invoice-processing time was improved. Interest charges on late payments were reduced by almost 70 percent in the first year and dropped a further 15 percent the following year. The savings in the first year more than paid for the audit costs, and the savings continued to be realized in future years.

Scheme:	Inefficiency
Symptoms:	Invoices paid late at certain offices
Data Requirements:	A/P—vendor, vendor number, amount, due date, date paid, amount, G/L account, office

Case Study: Set One Aside

The auditors received allegations of theft from the receiving dock. The manager making the claim said that he constantly had to e-mail the receiving dock because part of his order had not been delivered. He was convinced that it was not an accident and that someone was systematically stealing inventory.

In fact, the receiving clerk at the main warehouse had devised what he thought to be a fairly safe scheme for stealing inventory. When a multibox shipment arrived, he would simply remove one of the boxes and leave it on the loading dock, in plain view. The rest of the shipment would be forwarded to the manager who had placed the order. The clerk would wait several weeks to see if the missing box was noticed; if not, he would steal it. If the manager sent an e-mail asking about the missing item, the clerk would check around and "find" the missing box.

The auditors reviewed the e-mail messages related to reported shortage by importing the text into the data analysis software and treating it as data, thereby obtaining the contract number and the quantities of missing items. The reported shortages were then joined to the inventory receipt file containing the name of the receiving clerk that had processed the order. A simple summary, totaling the number of missing items reported, by clerk, discovered the fraud. Cameras were placed on the loading dock, and the clerk was caught in the act.

Scheme:	Ship partial shipment; if no complaint, steal remainder
Symptoms:	Clerk has a large number of "partial" shipment complaints via e-mail
Data Requirements:	E-mails—contract number, quantity missing. Inventory receipt—contract number, quantity ordered and received, receiving clerk.

Case Study: Unused Accounts

The accounts payable clerk was printing his own checks, using an electronic copy of a check he had scanned into his computer. The check amounts were then coded to an old account that he knew would not be reviewed by the account managers. He was confident his fraud would not be noticed as there were millions of checks produced every year, totaling billions of dollars.

The auditors were performing their yearly review of expenditures, and one analysis calculated the total expenditures by account. The summary by account was compared with last year's totals. This highlighted a number of accounts now active that had not been used for several years. When the auditors pulled the canceled checks, the clerk was easily identified as the person who had endorsed them, and the fraud was discovered.

Scheme:	Clerk processing checks against unused accounts
Symptoms:	Unused or invalid G/L accounts with new activity
Data Requirements:	A/P—amount, G/L account. G/L—G/L account, description.

Case Study: Wheeler and Dealer

The new manager of the company garage had been in the position for only one year but was already well liked. He and his assistant provided quick and efficient maintenance service for all the company cars. The garage also contained a gas pump and was considered a full-service station.

The garage manager was permitted to perform work on employee-owned vehicles, as long as the employees were charged the cost of the

(continued)

labor and parts used for the work performed. The company allowed employees to purchase automobile parts for their own cars at the company rates, which were well below retail. The employee would order the parts and the company would be invoiced at the discounted rate. The employees would then submit their payment to the parts manager. He would remit the money to the company, and the company would pay the vendor. However, the manager was "correcting" invoices to make it look like the parts had been used for maintaining company cars. He would keep the employee's payment and would pay the bill from the company's car maintenance budget.

The company maintained a fleet of cars for use by employees while on the job. A credit card was kept in the glove compartment of each car and was used when employees purchased gas at retail stations while on the road or obtained gas or had repair work done on the vehicle at the company garage. The credit card was used to track gas purchases and repair work by car. However, several employees, who were friends of the service manager, were bringing their personal cars into the company service garage and filling up with gas. The manager kept a list of credit cards and the cost of the gas was recorded against a company car's credit card. The service manager then charged the employees half the actual cost of the gas "purchased" and kept the cash he received.

Finally, the manager was also responsible for the disposal of vehicles no longer considered economical to maintain—many of which he sold to a friend at 65 percent of the book value. The friend then sold the vehicle for the book value and split the profits with the manager. The process called for sealed bids to be submitted by persons wishing to buy the vehicles. However, the manager would show prospective bidders a car in much worse shape than the one actually being sold, or would invent stories of accidents or mechanical troubles with the car. As a result, the bids from other buyers were usually lower than the friend's bid.

After the bidding process, vehicles were often equipped with new tires, mufflers, and other parts just prior to being sold to the manager's friend. This significantly increased the value of the vehicle to the point that sometimes the new parts were worth more than the purchase price of the car.

The auditors were performing the yearly review of the garage operations, and despite being unaware of the fraud being committed by the manager and his assistant, they still managed to uncover it.

The first analysis performed by the auditors was to total the repair work by vehicle. They were quite surprised by the total dollar value of the repairs performed on the company cars. A refinement to the analysis separated the vehicles by year of purchase. The manager's activities had been so extensive that even newly purchased cars were showing high levels of repair work. The auditors were particularly suspicious when invoices were paid for parts on cars that were still under the original warranty.

The analysis revealed that some cars that were less than one year old had undergone as much repair work in the last year as much older cars. The auditors calculated the total repairs by type of repair to determine the five repairs performed most often. Then the auditors totaled the number of repairs by year of purchase and vehicle number for these types of repairs: tire, muffler, alternator, tune-up, and battery. The analysis showed three cars that were less than one year old that had more than one new muffler and up to 12 new tires.

Cars Purchased in 2008 Repair Work by Type

Id Number	Repairs	Alternator	Tune-up	Battery	Muffler	Tire
A43665	9	1	2	1	4	12
A43666	4	0	1	2	2	0
A43667	5	1	1	1	2	8

As a separate task, the team leader instructed one of the auditors to review the controls over the sale of used vehicles. Twenty-four cars had been sold in the last year for a total of more than $68,000. The electronic purchasing data was summarized, and total dollar value of sales was calculated by purchaser. The results showed that Mr. Ford was the purchaser 18 times. What made this more disturbing was the fact that the average cost of purchase was $4,140 for the other six purchases but only $2,400 for the 18 purchases made by Mr. Ford.

Cars Sold in 2008 Average Purchase Price by Purchaser

Purchaser	Count	Sale Price	Avg Price
Mr. Black	1	4,125	4,125
Mr. Brown	1	4,200	4,200
Mr. Clarke	2	8,375	4,188
Mr. Ford	18	43,192	2,400
Mr. Jones	2	8,235	4,118
Total:	24	68,127	

The team leader thought it possible that the cars purchased by Mr. Ford were older models or were less mechanically sound and therefore

(continued)

were not worth as much. He asked the auditor to extract information about the 24 cars sold in the past year, including all repairs performed in the last year. He also asked for the report to show the information by vehicle and date of the repair work. The report indicated that the cars purchased by Mr. Ford were not any older than the other cars sold. However, it did show that they had undergone a significant amount of repair work. The team leader thought this might explain the difference in the purchase price—perhaps they were mechanically unsound cars—until the auditor pointed out that in every case, the cars had undergone repair work a week or two prior to them being sold to Mr. Ford. Most of the cars purchased by Mr. Ford were equipped with new tires, a muffler, and a battery less than five days before he picked up the cars. Only one of the cars sold to another purchaser had had any repair work done on it in the month prior to being sold. In addition, most of the repair work on cars purchased by Mr. Ford was performed after the closing date for the bids.

Using the Internet, the auditors obtained book value data from the American Automobile Association and compared it to the sale price of the vehicle. This analysis showed that cars of the same make, model, year, and mileage were being sold for significantly more than the purchase price paid by Mr. Ford. However, the six cars sold to other purchasers had been sold at prices that were comparable to the book value.

During the same time period, one of the new auditors was given responsibility for conducting a review of the controls over gasoline purchases. She was enjoying the sunny weather one lunchtime and happened to walk past the gas pumps—so that she was watching as an employee drove up, filled the car with gas, and handed some money to the assistant manager. She continued to watch as the assistant manager put the money in his pocket. This was highly unusual, as all gas purchases were supposed to be made using company credit cards. The auditor surmised that the purchases paid in cash were actually being charged to company credit cards. To test this hypothesis, she obtained an electronic copy of all gas purchase data from the company garage. This file contained a record of the number of gallons recorded against each car's credit card at the company garage. She also obtained a file containing credit card purchases for each company vehicle for gas purchased from retail gas stations. She totaled the gasoline consumption for each of the vehicles purchased in the last year. The gas consumption was divided by the total distance on the odometer for the new vehicles. This analysis showed that the cars purchased in the last year were only obtaining an average of 14 mpg. While not enough to prove any wrongdoing, it was sufficient to encourage further analysis and investigation.

Next the auditor did a search of the data for duplicate transactions—more than one gas purchase on the same day for the same vehicle. She discovered that numerous times in the past year, company cars had filled up at the company garage and at a retail gas station on the same day. She obtained the actual credit card receipts for the duplicates and found that in four cases, the retail station purchases were made in cities hundreds of miles away from the company garage. In one case the audit team leader had signed the credit card receipt. When she told him about the receipt and the date, he checked his personal calendar and noted that the purchase had occurred during a three-week audit of regional offices. He had been away the entire time, so it was not possible for the car to have been filled at the company gas station on the date in question.

The audit team leader reported his suspicions to the president, and a hidden camera was installed to monitor the gas pumps. The maintenance data was also reviewed daily, and a quick check was performed to determine if company cars were being repaired as stated. Within a week the camera captured evidence of the manager and his assistant filling up noncompany cars. Verification of the maintenance data also found several instances where the repairs had not been performed as stated. For example, the repair records showed that four new tires had been installed on a company car, but when the auditors checked the car in question, they found old tires. At first the manager claimed that he might have recorded the wrong credit card number, but he confessed to the entire scheme when shown the videotape of the gas purchases.

Scheme:	Garage manager—charging employees' car repair work to company cars; selling gas for cash and charging to company car, and selling cars for less than book value.
Symptoms:	High amount of repairs per vehicle (even new vehicles), sales for less than book value, repairs done on vehicles just before being sold, low gas mileage
Data Requirements:	Garage—employee number, credit card number, date, work performed, amount. Car sales—make, model, year, sale amount, purchaser, date of sale. Book value—make, model, year, value. Credit card transactions—credit card number, date, gallons purchased, amount, merchant.

Case Study: Last Bid Wins

XYZ Corp, one of the company's major vendors, sent a "brown envelope" to the auditors stating that after they had refused to provide "a little something extra" for Phil, one of the contracting officers, they had not won a single contract of any significant value. The auditors called XYZ's sales manager, and he said that he was convinced that they were losing contracts because the purchasing manager was fixing the bids.

The auditors decided to follow up on the allegation and selected a random sample of contracts. They found that the purchasing manager had selected the lowest bid in every contract they reviewed. At first glance, everything seemed to be in accordance with company policy. However, they continued their investigation with one auditor focusing on the control process while another analyzed the contracting database.

The contracting database contained details on all contracts raised by the company. It included information on contracting officer, vendor name, date of bid, date of contract award, and contract bid amount. The auditor created an expression to calculate the number of days between the bid date and the bid closing date. The auditor then summarized the data for each winning vendor—counting the number of contracts awarded and totaling the dollar value of the contracts and number of days the contract bids were submitted before bid closing date.

Winning Bids by Vendor

Vendor	Number	Total Value	Days
ABC Corp.	90	376,701.25	83
Brown Ltd.	16	61,567.68	41
Carleton Corp.	30	152,731.93	57
David & Co.	4	14,508.91	18
Everley Bros.	1	12,533.21	13
XYZ Corp.	5	9,405.12	19
Total	146	627,448.10	231

Using the results of this analysis, the auditor then calculated the average number of days between the contract bid submission and bid closing date (total days divided by number of contracts).

Winning Bids by Vendor

Vendor	Number	Total Value	Days	Avg Days
ABC Corp.	90	376,701.25	83	0.92
Brown Ltd.	16	61,567.68	41	2.56
Carleton Corp.	30	152,731.93	57	1.90
David & Co.	4	14,508.91	18	4.50
Everley Bros.	1	12,533.21	13	13.00
XYZ Corp.	5	9,405.12	19	3.80
Total	146	627,448.10	231	

This analysis showed that ABC had consistently submitted bids the day before or the day of the contract award date. A further analysis determined that whenever ABC submitted a bid within two days of the contract award date, it won the contract. The winning contracts were summarized for each vendor by contracting officer—totaling the contract amounts awarded. This analysis showed that Phil was the contracting officer for all of the contracts won by ABC.

The auditors discussed their analysis results with Phil, and he denied any wrongdoing. However, when the auditors approached the sales manager for ABC, he told them that they had gone along with the scheme because Phil had told him that "It was either that or never get any business." In exchange for bid information, ABC provided Phil with a kickback worth 5 percent of the contract value. This meant that Phil had received more than $18,800 from ABC in the last year. Phil finally admitted to the fraud when the sales manager provided the auditors with copies of the canceled checks bearing Phil's signature. His practice was to provide ABC with information on the lowest bid and then accept their bid after the closing date. In recording the result, he backdated the bid to just before the contract bid close date. He then said something that really bothered the auditors: "I realize now that I should have backdated the bid to a week before the close date. That would have made it harder for you to discover."

The audit team leader wondered about the validity of Phil's statement. It was true that their analysis of the average number of days between contract bid submission and bid closing date would not have identified ABC as a concern if Phil had backdated the bids by a week. However, the summary by vendor and contracting officer still would have identified Phil as the only contracting officer handling all the bids won by ABC. Also, the variance analysis, comparing the total value of

(continued)

contracts won by vendor for previous and current year, was always run. This variance analysis would have flagged ABC, because there had been a 200 percent increase in the value of contracts won by ABC over last year. The combination of the two analyses would have been enough to cause them to look into ABC's bids more closely. Plus, Phil had been sloppy, and had backdated one contract submission to a Sunday—another red flag.

Scheme: Collusion between contracting officer and vendor
                       (information on lowest bid)
Symptoms: Bid date is the same as the contract award date
                       (contract award minus bid date = 0 or close to it),
                       so the last bid wins
Data Requirements: Contract award—contract number, vendor, date of
                       bid, date of contract award or closing bid date,
                       contracting officer, bid amount, status

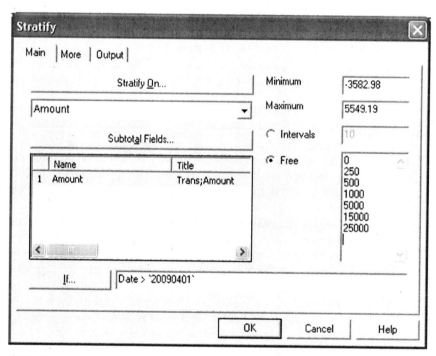

EXHIBIT 6.2 Stratify Screen. Stratification will allow you to choose specific ranges and total the transactions in each range (ACL Stratify window shown).

Stratification

Like statistical analysis, a stratification of a numeric field will give a high-level view of the data. Stratifying data will show how many records fall into ranges, or strata, of the selected numeric field. It allows auditors to total the value of one or more numeric fields for each of these ranges and can be used to get a profile of the data values for the specified field. For example, with contracting data, it will quickly determine how many contracts were raised in each of the default, or auditor-specified, ranges, such as all contract values. It can also be used to check numeric fields for reasonableness, quickly highlighting unusually large or small values. Used in combination with the aging of dates, it also can examine ranges of date fields. (See Exhibit 6.2.)

Case Study: Sole-Sourced Contracts

The auditors were reviewing the controls over the raising of contracts. One of the controls limited the total dollar value of contracts that could be raised without competition. Contracts under $25,000 could be sole-sourced, while contracts over $25,000 were subject to the competitive process. The auditors reviewed the contracting database and stratified the data by the contract amount, specifying a small range just below $25,000.

Analysis of Contract Amounts

Ranges of Contract Value	# of Contracts	% of Contracts	% of Amount	Total Contract Amount
$0–$24,490	1,738	88.09%	22.64%	1,795,052.52
$24,491–$25,000	216	10.95%	67.83%	5,378,027.37
>$25,000	19	0.96%	9.52%	755,030.11
Total	1,973	100.00%	100.00%	7,928,110.00

The analysis clearly showed that a substantial number of contracts were just under the $25,000 limit. A total of 216 contracts for $5,378,027 (67.8 percent of the total value of contracts raised) fell into this category, and the auditors decided to extract the details for these contracts.

The next phase of the analysis searched for duplicate transactions, using the vendor name and contract date as keys. A flag was set if one of the duplicates was within $1,000 of the $25,000 financial limit. This identified contracts with the same vendor, on the same day, where one

(continued)

of the contracts was just under the financial limit and the total exceeded the limit.

Search for Duplicates (based on Vendor and Date)

Vendor	Contract Date	Amount
CURRIE LIMITED	12/15/2008	24,970
CURRIE LIMITED	12/15/2008	21,508
DELANEY & SONS	07/28/2008	24,984
DELANEY & SONS	07/28/2008	7,296
FOWLER & EMERY	12/15/2008	24,990
FOWLER & EMERY	12/15/2008	24,575
...		
SEABY & MACLOUD	08/25/2008	24,901
SEABY & MACLOUD	08/25/2008	10,290
SEABY & MACLOUD	08/25/2008	16,238

A summary by contracting officer determined that Mark, one of the contracting officers, was responsible for 95 percent of the duplicates. A review of the statements of work, and contract deliverables for the contracts raised with the same vendor, on the same day, found that these transactions were split contracts. The work had been divided into two or more contracts to avoid the financial limits and the reporting requirements. In several cases the company could have suffered serious repercussions for failing to comply with government contracting regulations and legal requirements for full disclosure. In all cases, the sole-sourced contracts were at rates higher than would have been attained through the competitive process. Mark admitted to splitting contracts and directing them to certain firms in exchange for kickbacks.

Scheme:	Contracts just under the sole-source maximum $25,000 are directed to specific companies.
Symptoms:	High number of contracts just under maximum
Data Requirements:	Contracting—contract number, type of contract (competitive, sole source, standing offer agreement), amount, contracting officer, vendor, date

Case Study: Computer Logs

Computer logs were rarely reviewed during the audits of the data centers. However, the auditor decided to obtain and analyze an electronic copy of the log report. One of the analyses stratified the logon times recorded in the log. The auditor selected all logon transactions between 00:00 and 06:00 hours for one day. Stratifying by hour revealed that there was a significant jump in the number of logon requests between 03:00 and 04:00.

Logon Times

Hour	Count	Percentage
0 to 1	3	6.67%
1 to 2	2	4.44%
2 to 3	1	2.22%
3 to 4	37	82.22%
4 to 5	0	0.00%
5 to 6	2	4.44%
Total	45	100.00%

The auditor extracted the detailed records for the time frame in question, summarized the data, and found that the same user ID had been used 37 times, all with the message "Invalid password, logon failed." An analysis of the log files for the remainder of the week found a similar pattern.

The auditor informed his manager, and the head of security was alerted to the problem. The next night a trace was placed on the incoming calls, and they were able to identify the person who was attempting to use an employee's user ID to break into the data center system.

A follow-up to the audit reviewed the previous three months' data. The results determined that the technique employed by the auditor was sound and that his timing had been extremely lucky. No such problems appeared in the previous 100 days' records—during any other given week the review would have found nothing. However, given the ease of the analysis and the significance of the exposure, the head of corporate security asked that a script be created to run the same analysis every night. A report is now generated nightly and e-mailed to the data center manager each morning. Any usual increase in attempted logons are noted and checked. Further, the controls were tightened to lock user IDs after three failed logon attempts.

Scheme:	Attempted hacking
Symptoms:	Failed logons early in the morning
Data Requirements:	Computer log—user ID, date and time, status (successful, invalid password)

Cross Tabulation/Pivot Tables

Making sense of data often means finding the best way to look at it. Cross tabulation, or pivot tables, is a method of structuring the records to make it easier for auditors to view the data. Data is often more understandable when presented in a table format. The basic principle involves taking a series of records and creating a two-dimensional table or array.

To be suitable for cross tabulation, a data file must contain at least two character fields. Distinct values from one field will be the row values (y-axis), while the other field values will form the column headings (x-axis). For each cell (row/column combination), a selected numeric field will be totaled. The more distinct character values there are, the more rows and/or columns in the resulting table. (See Exhibit 6.3.)

Many people prefer to read data in a series of short rows instead of long rows. Consider, for example, a payroll file containing 1,000 employees who are paid in three categories: regular pay, overtime, and holiday pay. The total pay for each employee, by category, could be tabulated as three rows (regular pay, overtime, and holiday pay) with 1,000 columns (one per employee) or as 1,000 rows (one per employee) with three columns (regular pay, overtime, and holiday pay). If a character field has fewer unique values it is often better to use that field as the x-axis (column headings).

Cross tabulating character fields produces easy-to-use summaries that enable exploration of areas of potential concern by totaling specific numeric fields.

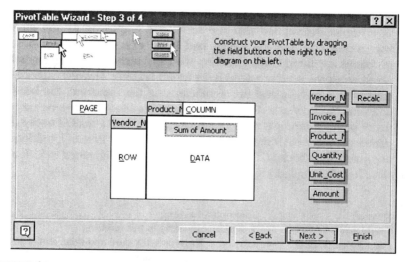

EXHIBIT 6.3 Pivot Table Screen. Cross tabulation lets you analyze character fields by setting them in rows and totaling numeric fields as your columns (Excel Wizard shown).

EXHIBIT 6.4   Detailed Salary Payments.

Emp #	GL	Amount
0123	0100	$2,000.00
0124	0100	$2,500.00
0125	0100	$1,700.00
...		
0978	0100	$1,000.00
0124	0110	$200.00
0124	0110	$100.00
0125	0110	$210.00
0124	0110	$250.00
0125	0110	$100.00
...		
0123	0190	$210.00
0124	0190	$250.00
0125	0190	$175.00

For example, given the pay records shown in Exhibits 6.4 and 6.5, an auditor might be interested in examining the total amounts paid to each employee by G/L account and determining if anyone is making more than 20 percent of their regular salary (GL 0100) in overtime (GL 0110) payments. A pivot table would present the data in a much simpler format to view and allow the auditor to conduct the required analysis.

Pivot tables or cross tabulation displays the data in a format that is easier to view and is more conducive to further analysis. The exhibits show all employees who are being paid overtime but have no regular salary. And a simple filter (GL_0100 equals 0 and GL_0110 greater than 0) is all that is required to identify them or to isolate employees making more than 20 percent of their salary in overtime (Pct Overtime greater than 20%). Without a pivot table, these filters would be much more difficult to construct.

Now it is clear that employee #0978 had $1,000.00 in overtime payments and $0.00 in regular salary. Auditors could go back to the detailed pay

EXHIBIT 6.5   Payroll Summary by Employee by GL Account.

Emp #	GL_0100	GL_0110	GL_0190
0123	$2,000.00	$0.00	$210.00
0124	$2,500.00	$550.00	$250.00
0125	$1,700.00	$310.00	$175.00
...			
0978	$0.00	$1,000.00	$0.00

transactions and isolate all transactions for this employee. They also can calculate the percentage of total overtime payments compared to the total salary for each employee (percentage overtime equals 100 times GL_0110 total divided by GL_0100 total). Filtering the records (percentage overtime greater than 20 percent) would show that employee #0124 had overtime payments ($550.00) equal to 22 percent of his regular salary ($2,500.00).

Pivot tables are also an excellent approach to identify control weaknesses such as vendor favoritism (cross tabulate by vendor [row], by contracting officer [column] and total amount paid) or lack of separation of duties (cross tabulate by user ID [row], by transaction type [column] and total the amount).

Case Study: Multiple User Authorities

The financial system supported several different profiles, or categories, of users. The profiles defined the actions the user could perform. The profiles were set up to ensure segregation of duties. For example, a user with an "auditor" profile could read all financial information but could not enter or approve transactions. A clerk could enter transactions into the system but could not approve transactions, and supervisors could approve transactions but could not perform the initial entry.

An auditor was assigned the task of verifying the internal controls for the financial system. As part of testing, the auditor decided to check the authorities in the financial system. The auditor obtained a user ID from one of the clerks and attempted to approve transactions. Then he obtained a user ID from a supervisor and attempted to enter new transactions. In both cases, the system correctly prevented him from completing any transactions.

Because there were thousands of users, and it would have taken too long to verify each user ID individually, the auditor ran a cross tab of the accounts payable data, by user ID, by transaction type—totaling the number of transactions. The auditor noticed an interesting fact immediately: Three different user IDs had both entered and approved transactions.

Financial System User ID Analysis

User ID	Entered Items	Approved Items
F109753	12,237	11,090
F115001	102	29,001
F118120	31,963	142

A review of the user IDs determined that the employee with user ID F109753 had been promoted from a clerk to a supervisor and retained the same user ID with a different profile. Thus, for the first part of the year she was entering transactions as a clerk, while for the second part of the year she was approving transactions as a supervisor. The auditor was told that there was no time during the year when she was using the same user ID to perform both functions. A simple sort of the data verified that all entry transactions were made before she was promoted to a supervisor and all approval transactions were made after the promotion. However, the auditor was concerned about the possibility that she had entered transactions while a clerk and then approved them while a supervisor. To determine if this had happened, the auditor reviewed the detailed transactions entered by the user during her last month as a clerk and found that she had not approved any of them when she was a supervisor. The auditor did recommend that a new policy be put in place to ensure that new user IDs were assigned when people were promoted.

The other two users were a different story. A review of the 102 transactions approved and entered by user F115001 and the 142 by user F118120 found that all 244 were fraudulent. A programmer had developed and assigned user profiles that were a modified profile—a hybrid authority—allowing the two users to enter *and* approve transactions. One would enter the transaction and the other would approve it for payment; then they would switch roles.

Without the use of CAATTs, it is doubtful that they would have been caught. The users had been processing an average of almost five fraudulent transactions a week, knowing that a random sample of transactions would be very unlikely to find any of the fraudulent transactions among the millions of records processed every year.

As a result of the audit, the programmer and the two clerks were fired, and additional controls placed on the security over the creation of new user profiles.

Scheme:	User makes unauthorized payments.
Symptoms:	User both entering and approving transactions
Data Requirements:	A/P—transaction number, date, amount, entered by, approved by. User ID—user ID, name, approval type (Enter, Approve, Change).

Case Study: False Claims

A clerk recently promoted to claims had previously worked in the policy administration section, entering policyholder information, including change-of-address data. Her manager did not realize that her user ID, which let her enter claims information for a policyholder, still allowed her to enter change-of-address data for the same policyholder. This allowed her to process claims for policyholders and change the address information so the check went to a friend's address.

As part of a routine check of user ID privileges, the auditors set up a counter for various types of transactions, including change-of-address transactions and claims entry information. They ran a job to produce a pivot table that showed the number of change-of-address transactions and the number of claims request transactions by user ID. Next, they filtered the records to highlight any user ID that had both change-of-address transactions and claims request transactions (testing that both fields were greater than zero). Since the former claims clerk was the only person with a user ID capable of doing both types of transactions, hers was the only one highlighted.

User ID Analysis

User ID	# Claims Requests	# Changes of Address
F207812	10,241	212

All claims requests processed by the clerk were extracted from the claims payment system, and the records were summarized by address. This highlighted 43 transactions that she had directed to her friend's house and 169 that had gone to a post office box. When they pulled the canceled checks, they found that the clerk had endorsed them all.

Scheme:	User processes phony claims, which are sent to her address, and cashes them.
Symptoms:	User can enter claims and make changes to policyholder information.
Data Requirements:	Policyholder—policy number, address, date, clerk. Claims—policy number, date, clerk, amount.

CHAPTER 7

Working with the Data

After ensuring data completeness and obtaining an overview of the data, the auditor can start working with the data to address specific audit objectives. This chapter discusses a variety of techniques that can assist in finding fraud symptoms in data. The techniques and cases are presented to illustrate how data analysis can be used to manipulate the data or combine files.

Aging

Aging the data calculates the number of days between two dates, and can provide auditors with valuable information in a variety of settings, such as when the timing of key events is critical to their validity and appropriateness. For example, the submission of all bids for a contract should be completed before the closing date, and goods should be received before the invoice date. Comparing the values in key date fields often can yield valuable information (see Exhibit 7.1).

The comparison of dates, or sometimes even the existence of an invalid date in a field, can be used to highlight fraud or wasteful practices. Computer-assisted audit tools and techniques (CAATTs), can analyze all transactions to pinpoint anomalies between what is expected and what is recorded in the application.

By aging data, one can calculate or highlight various items for further investigation, including:

- Overdue accounts receivable or accounts payable
- Favorable credit terms
- Inventory turnover rates
- Dormant accounts
- Records with future, blank, or otherwise invalid dates
- Items past a cutoff date

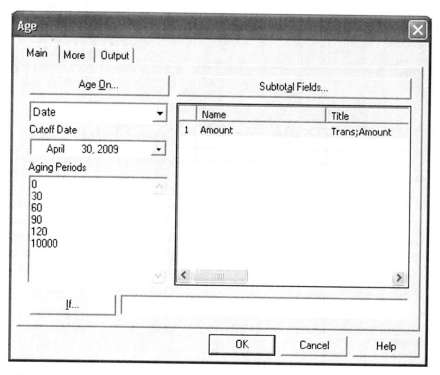

EXHIBIT 7.1 **Age Screen.** One type of aging is the comparison of one date with a second date. The second date value can be a date field, the system date, or an auditor-specified cutoff date, such as a fiscal or calendar year-end, as shown in this ACL Age window.

- Contracts awarded before contract closing date
- Bids accepted after the bid closing date
- Transactions outside of the billing period
- Mean time to failure for equipment
- Length in days of various activities

Sometimes auditors are primarily interested in cutoff dates, and the question they wish to answer may be: Did an event occur before a certain date? A simple filter to select all records where the date is before the cutoff date can answer the question. However, in other cases, auditors are concerned about the time lapse between two events, for example, the time between the delivery of goods to a customer and the receipt of the payment. Aging the data (payment received date minus delivery date) will determine the time between these events and the number of records falling within specified date ranges (age periods), such as 30, 60, 90, and 120 days. This type of analysis can be used to:

- Examine the timing of events for fraud.
- Check the efficiency of the accounts payable (A/P) and accounts receivable (A/R) processes.
- Calculate inventory turnover times, shelf life, and other critical date-related values.

An aged analysis of the accounts receivable transactions can identify inefficiencies in the A/R operations that result in cash flow problems and carrying costs. A similar type of analysis on the A/P transactions can test the efficiency of the system by determining the average number of days before payments are made on interest-bearing invoices. The efficient management of A/P can save the company thousands of dollars, whereas poor management practices can cost heavily.

Similarly, aging the data can highlight when invoices were paid within 30 days and early payment discounts were not received. This is a possible symptom of fraud: Someone may be processing the invoices early in exchange for kickbacks or may be paying the full amount of the invoice, requesting a refund check for the early payment discount amount, and cashing the check and keeping the money. In the A/R area, late payments not assessed an interest charge are also a possible symptom of fraud. In this scenario, the clerk may allow a customer to pay invoices late without penalty, in exchange for a kickback. Auditors have successfully used these types of analysis on A/R and A/P transactions. Naturally, before using this type of analysis, it is important to understand how the financial system handles interest charges and early payment discounts. Some financial systems will have a field to identify if a discount for early payment was taken, but other financial systems may record a discount as a separate transaction with a reference to the original transaction.

Similarly, aging the data has many uses in banking, retail, and a variety of industries, to detect fraudulent activities before they are fully operational. In particular, auditors can run an aging routine in the background to check for unusual activity involving dormant customer accounts.

Retail stores have an additional area of risk. They often offer their customers discounts for early payment or a special discounted price that may be in effect for a limited time. The controls over applying the discounted price may not be as effective as they should be. In some cases, clerks may be accidentally giving customers the discounted price when it is not applicable. In other cases, clerks may be giving the discounted price only to friends and family. Auditors can identify all sales that were at the discounted price after the end of the discount period. If the sales date is after the discount period, the customer should not have received the discounted price. These filters can identify such transactions:

```
AGE(Sales_Date,Discount_Date)<0 and Discount_Flag = 'Yes'
or
Sales_Date > Discount_Date and Discount_Flag = 'Yes'
```

If there is no discount flag field to indicate whether a discount was available, the auditor can use the purchase price and the full price to perform a similar test to verify if the sales date was after the discount period, and the purchase price was less than the full price. In this case, the filters would be:

```
AGE(Sales_Date,Discount_Date)<0 AND Purchase_Price
<Full_Price
or
Sales_Date > Discount_Date and Purchase_Price<Full_Price
```

A concern also exists when customers are charged the full price for purchases made within the discount period. These customers may be unhappy to find out later that they were overbilled. The next tests identify sales where the customers should have received a discounted price but did not:

```
AGE(Sales_Date,Discount_date)>0 and Discount Flag='N'
or
Age(Sales_Date,Disc_Date)>0 and Purchase_Price=Full_Price
```

Even where the error is an honest one, management may be interested in taking corrective action when customers did not receive the proper discount. These items should be reviewed to ensure that the full amount is not being charged to the customer, an adjusting entry made to the original transactions, and the difference being pocketed by the retail clerk.

Case Study: Still on the Payroll

The manager, Mr. Philip, was notoriously neglectful in preparing and submitting any type of paperwork. He even had to be reminded to complete month-end reports and yearly employee evaluations. His procrastination often resulted in delays in informing the payroll department when an employee left or was laid off. As a result, the payroll system continued to produce checks for former employees after they had departed.

In fact, far from being inept, the manager was splitting the overpayments with the ex-employees. This was a well-known practice, and terminated employees felt they were owed the additional money—considering it as a "retirement bonus."

Without being told about the terminated employees, the auditors were asked to investigate the payroll costs for Mr. Philip's area for possible fraud. The team leader had a series of tests he used to ensure the accuracy and completeness of the payroll transactions. One test performed was a simple comparison of the termination date, or departure from the company, with the pay period covered by the paycheck. A filter was established to extract all pay transactions for employees with a departure date prior to the date of the current pay period.

The results of the test revealed that several employees who had left the company were being paid after their departure dates. When contacted, they insisted that it was "standard procedures," and they had done nothing wrong. When asked to repay the amount, one fellow remarked, "Why should I have to repay the full amount, when the manager kept half?" The auditors reviewed transactions from previous payroll periods and determined the losses to be in the hundreds of thousands of dollars. The manager was fired. Whether senior management was initially aware of the exact nature of the fraud did not matter, because the audit program contained steps that searched for symptoms of fraud—and they had clearly proven their value.

Another approach to detect this type of problem would be to age the data and list all pay transactions where the difference between the pay period covered and the date of termination was a negative number. If the departure date is not one of the fields in the payroll system, the auditor can join the payroll and human resource data to create a file containing both the departure and payroll dates.

Before using these tests, the auditor must determine how the system handles employees who left the company and have subsequently been rehired. These employees may have a termination date that relates to their previous, rather than current, employment period. Where seasonal employees are involved, or employees have been laid off and called back, care must be taken to ensure that these employees are not wrongfully identified as cases of payroll fraud. In such cases, the previous test would incorrectly identify these records as possible fraudulent transactions. Requiring the departure or termination date to be greater than the current start date would refine the analysis and produce more accurate results. Employees who left and then were rehired would not be flagged as possible fraudulent transactions since their departure date would be prior to their current start date.

(continued)

Scheme:	Manager continues to pay employees who have left.
Symptoms:	Employees paid after they leave.
Data Requirements:	Payroll—employee number, pay date, gross pay.
	HR—employee number, termination date.

Case Study: Overdue Accounts Receivable

The company was having cash flow problems, and the vice president of finance had questions about the efficiency of the accounts receivable (A/R) department. The audit team leader knew that, because of cash shortages, the company would incur carrying charges on borrowed money if A/R had a large number of unpaid invoices beyond the standard 60 days. He also knew that an aging of the A/R transactions would quickly identify all invoices that were past the due date by 30, 60, 90 days, or any cutoff point he chose to specify. A simple aging confirmed the vice president's efficiency concerns, but the team leader decided to take the analysis a step further and calculated the average amount of time each account was past due for each branch office. In addition, he calculated the carrying cost of borrowing money to finance the shortfall in revenues.

This analysis determined that accounts at some branches were past due well beyond 60 days. The office in New York appeared to be the main source of late payments. In fact, a large invoice was 179 days past due. A review at the New York office identified inefficiencies resulting in long delays in cashing checks received.

The St. Louis office also had several accounts that were past due by more than 200 days, but their transactions presented another problem. The aged analysis identified 50 transactions that would not even be due for more than 100 days from the auditor-selected cutoff date. The team leader knew this to be a possible symptom of fraud—kickbacks from vendors in exchange for favorable credit terms.

New York Accounts Receivable

Days Overdue	Number	% of Number	% of Amount	Carrying Cost
0–29	981	51.58%	26.07%	103,430.06
30–59	602	31.58%	21.53%	85,428.58
60–89	110	5.79%	5.61%	22,259.33
90–120	190	10.00%	10.81%	42,873.09
>120	21	1.05%	35.97%	142,712.17
Total	1,904	100.00%	100.00%	396,703.23

A detailed analysis determined that all transactions not due for more than 100 days were processed by the same clerk, and were with only two firms. When presented with the analysis, the clerk admitted to accepting money from the firms in exchange for extending the due date.

The clerk at the St. Louis office was fired for accepting kickbacks, and after New York implemented the audit recommendations, its carrying charges were reduced by almost 60 percent in the first year and a further 18 percent the next year. The savings in the first year more than paid for the audit costs, and further savings continued to be realized in future years.

Scheme:	Clerk extends due date in exchange for kickbacks.
Symptoms:	Some branches have more overdue amounts; period between invoice date and due date more than 30 days; or invoices have negative days overdue.
Data Requirements:	A/R—invoice number, customer number, invoice date, due date, date received, amount, branch, user ID

Case Study: Unclaimed Early Payment Discounts

Despite management assurances that the accounts payable processing was both efficient and effective, the auditors had concerns. They had received information that some invoices were being paid immediately upon receipt, even if terms of payment specified otherwise, and that other payments were being made late. More recently, allegations of favorable treatment of vendors by the A/P department in exchange for kickbacks had surfaced.

As a first step in investigating the allegations, the auditors obtained the A/P transactions from the previous quarter and calculated the difference between the later of the receipt of goods or invoice date and the check date. They planned to highlight transactions that were paid within 15 days because, if the early payment discount of 1.5 percent was not claimed, these invoices were symptoms of possible fraud. This also represented a potential loss of interest on money, or a cost of borrowing money. The auditors were also interested in determining if the company was incurring late payment charges for invoices paid after the due date.

The analysis showed that only 4.6 percent of the transactions were paid within 15 days; however, this represented almost 31 percent of the total payments made. At the same time, 8.82 percent of the

(continued)

transactions were paid after 90 days, representing 14 percent of the total payments.

Accounts Payable Aging

Days Aged	Number of Invoices	% of Number	% of Amount	Amount Paid
0–14	48	4.60%	30.74%	1,125,187
15–29	228	21.86%	6.62%	242,123
30–59	451	43.24%	24.78%	906,662
60–89	224	21.48%	23.51%	860,241
>90	92	8.82%	14.35%	525,224
Total	1,043	100.00%	100.00%	3,659,437

The auditors reviewed the 48 transactions that were paid within 15 days and found that early payment discounts were claimed in only two cases. The other 46 invoices belonged to 13 vendors. The auditors also reviewed the 92 cases where payment was not made for at least 90 days. This revealed that the company was incurring significant interest charges on late payments.

The unclaimed early payment discounts were a monetary loss to the company, but they were also possible instances of fraud. The team leader had concerns about two possible fraud scenarios. In the first, the A/P clerk processes the original transaction for the full amount of the invoice and subsequently requests a credit from the vendor, for the early payment discount amount, keeping the credit. The second scheme involves deliberately paying invoices early, without claiming the early payment discount, and receiving a kickback from the vendor.

To identify the first type of fraud, the team leader sent out confirmation letters to the 13 vendors that had been paid early, requesting them to provide details on the terms and amount of the payment. All 13 vendors replied that they had initially been paid the full amount but had subsequently sent the company a check for the amount of the discount. The same clerk had processed all payments. The auditors asked the companies for copies of the canceled checks; all were endorsed by the same A/P clerk. The auditors expanded their review to include all invoices paid within 30 days of the due date.

Scheme:	Intercepting payment of discount
Symptoms:	Invoices paid early—no discount taken
Data Requirements:	A/P—receipt of goods date, receipt of invoice date, check date, invoice number, vendor, user ID, amount, discount amount

Case Study: Invoices Paid Too Early

As part of the audit of the accounts payable section at XYZ, the auditors reviewed the accuracy of the invoice-paying process. One of the tests was to see if credits were being applied to invoices when payment was made within the early payment period. The auditors aged the transactions to identify all payments made within 30 days of the invoice date. Typically, these invoices should have received a 1.5 percent discount for prompt payment.

The analysis identified thousands of invoices that had been paid within the 30-day period, totaling more than $92 million in expenditures. Some had been rushed through the system and paid within 7 days. Next the auditors matched the invoice numbers with all transactions that had received a prompt payment discount, leaving the unmatched records as invoices that were paid within 30 days without a prompt payment discount. The unmatched records totaled more than $10 million, representing over $150,000 in unclaimed discounts.

The auditors totaled these transactions by vendor and by invoice processing clerk. This determined that almost half of the payments ($4.72 million) had been paid to one vendor and all had been processed by the same clerk. The payments were all very large dollar progress payments on a $22 million contract. The clerk was questioned and finally admitted to rushing through payments for the vendor in question. At first, he had rushed through two large invoices as a favor because he had been told the vendor was experiencing cash flow problems. But after they sent him $1,000 to compensate him for his trouble, he rushed through all their payments. He had received a total of $11,500 over the last 10 months as a thank-you for paying the invoices promptly and not claiming the early payment discount.

He told the auditors that he had never thought about the fact that this practice was costing the company. He felt that if he had not paid the invoice early, they probably would not have been paid fast enough to qualify for the discount. He reasoned that he "wasn't hurting anyone" by doing this. However, the audit analysis proved that large-dollar invoices were paid within 30 days 89 percent of the time and the other invoice processing clerks were claiming discounts. His favors to the vendor had cost the company more than $70,000 in unclaimed discounts.

Scheme: Kickbacks for early payment
Symptoms: Invoices paid early—no discount taken
Data Requirements: A/P—receipt of goods date, receipt of invoice date, check date, invoice number, vendor, user ID, amount, discount amount

Case Study: Insurance Coverage Not Canceled

The review of the human resources department identified serious inefficiencies and control weaknesses. As with many companies in the high-tech industry, Dotcom Corp had a high employee turnover, and last month, a major downsizing initiative had resulted in the layoff of almost 1,300 employees. However, what also concerned the auditors was the length of time it took to process the termination notices. A review of payroll found no problem with ex-employees receiving pay beyond their departure/termination dates; however, the auditors were still concerned that the delays were costing the company money.

The termination file contained the departure/termination date for all employees who had left the company. The insurance file contained the dates of all medical insurance claims. The auditors joined the insurance claims file and the termination file to create a file containing the termination and the insurance claim dates for all employees. For each terminated employee, they highlighted all cases where the cancellation date was more recent than the employee's termination. These were cases where the company should not have paid for insurance coverage. Aging these records determined that employee insurance coverage was being maintained on terminated employees for up to three months after their termination date. Slow processing of termination data by the human resources department resulted in the company overpaying on its employee insurance coverage.

A second aging was performed to identify all claims where the difference between the termination date and the claim date was negative—in other words, a claim was made after the employee's termination date. Nearly 300 such insurance claims had been submitted after termination.

Armed with these findings, the auditors presented senior management with a strong case for timely reporting of employee terminations to the insurance provider.

Scheme:	Insurance claims paid after termination date
Symptoms:	Slow processing of termination
Data Requirements:	HR—employee number, date of termination, date processed. Insurance policies—employee number, date of claim, amount.

Case Study: Money-Laundering Scheme

The need for criminals to launder their illegal gains has generated many different schemes. An increasingly common method of laundering money is to purchase insurance policies with a cash-out clause. Such a policy may pay the policyholder up to 80 percent of the policy value if cashed out within one year. The purchase of millions of dollars in insurance policies and the subsequent cashing out of these policies can convert 80 percent of dirty money into "clean" money—a good return for the criminal element, a good deal for the insurance agent, and potentially profitable for the insurance company. However, the negative publicity that may result if the scheme is discovered outweighs the economic benefit.

At XYZ Insurance company, Bill was suddenly a top salesman, selling more policies in a single month than anyone in the company's 20-year history. In addition, few claims were being made against the policies he generated. He easily met his targets and received the maximum bonuses, plus incentives, such as trips and merchandise. XYZ management had never considered that Bill's policyholders might be using the insurance company to launder dirty money—until a police investigator came to their door with allegations against Bill.

The audit director of ABC Insurance Company read the newspaper headlines with concern. XYZ was under investigation because dirty money was being laundered through their insurance policies—was this happening at his company? The next day he initiated an audit of all insurance policies to look specifically for this problem. He met with the audit team leader and explained what had happened at XYZ Insurance. The team leader had also read the newspaper article and thought that this would be a perfect application for the new CAATTs software he had purchased recently. He explained that aging the data could be used to identify possible cases of money laundering.

The team obtained a copy of the policy file and calculated the time between the policy start and closing dates. Further, by summarizing the results of the aging by salesman, they were able to determine the average policy life attained by each salesman.

This analysis clearly highlighted potentially questionable sales practices and assisted the team leader in checking for money-laundering activities, whether knowingly or unknowingly abetted by the salesperson.

(continued)

Average Life of Policy

Salesperson	# Policies	Total Years	Avg Years
Paul	1,214	325	0.3
Mary	322	573	1.8
John	202	422	2.1
...			
Kate	202	601	3.0

The auditors reviewed the insurance claims raised by Paul and found that a large number of them were made in the name of only a few individuals, and that one person had opened 32 different policies, all of which had been canceled within two weeks. When confronted with the data, Paul admitted that he was helping to launder money and was fired. Because the company had been proactive in finding the fraud, it was able to correct the problem, keep the incident out of the media, and avoid adverse publicity.

Scheme:	Using payments from insurance policies to clean dirty money
Symptoms:	Policies closed early and 80 percent of value returned
Data Requirements:	Insurance policies—policy number, policy start and end dates, premiums, policy value, salesperson

Case Study: Activity on Dormant Accounts

A bank teller knew that some accounts were dormant—often for 10 years or more—and that several of these accounts contained considerable amounts of money. The teller easily justified the first few withdrawals as "short-term loans." The absence of any interest on his loan was a bonus, as was the fact that no approval was required. All he had to do was fill in a withdrawal slip for the amount desired and tell himself that he would repay the loan as soon as things turned around for him. But within one month he had withdrawn $10,000 from seven different dormant accounts.

He did not know that the auditors conducted a review of activities by account once a month. The date the account was last accessed was recorded for each account, and aging was used to calculate the time between this month's activity and the previous activity for each account. A dormant flag was set to "Yes" if the aged days was greater than 365 days. This flag identified all accounts with activity in the previous month that had also been dormant for the entire year prior to that. The details of all recent activity against the accounts with the Dormant Flag set to "Yes" were collected and reviewed. Typically, the file contained only one or two transactions, people who had suddenly started using their accounts again after a long period of inactivity. This month, however, there were 12 transactions all processed by the same teller. The auditors immediately interviewed the teller, and the fraud was ended within one month of the first fraudulent withdrawal.

Scheme: Teller withdraws money from dormant account.
Symptoms: Activity on previously dormant accounts
Data Requirements: Bank withdrawals—account number, amount, transaction date, teller

Case Study: Stolen Payments

Larry, a clerk at a retail store, accidentally stumbled on an interesting and profitable scheme. Payments made on customer accounts could be taken and the loss covered up by debiting another customer account. Larry had worked in the customer accounts section for years and knew the regular customers. He also had examined the accounts carefully and knew which were dormant. He took cash payments from customers and offset them by debits charged to the dormant customer accounts. The supervisor rarely reviewed the detailed reports, relying instead on the accounts receivable balance to serve as a check for the cash-on-hand total. By offsetting the cash taken with debits to unused accounts, Larry managed to ensure that, at the end of the day, the credits minus debits equaled the cash on hand.

Not being content with a single fraudulent activity, Larry also took advantage of a new store policy. All clerks were encouraged to keep a stack of store coupons by the cash. If a customer purchased a sale item that required a coupon, the clerk was supposed to make the customer aware of the sale price and offer a coupon. Larry used these coupons to his benefit rather than the customer's benefit. He would charge customers the full price for the item if they did not have a coupon.

(continued)

Later he would record a refund and then record a second sale with coupon, at the reduced sales price, taking the difference from the cash register. He tried not to use this method too often and would explain, if questioned about the series of transactions—sale, refund, discounted sale—that the customer produced the coupon after he had finished ringing in the sale.

In performing their quarterly review, the first item the auditors noticed was the increase in customer accounts that were not making the minimum monthly payments. They started by identifying the customer accounts that had failed to record a payment greater than or equal to the minimum, and totaled these balances by month. This showed that there was an increase in both the dollar value in these accounts and the number of accounts that had failed to make the minimum payment. However, the auditors knew that this could be related to many factors, including a recent economic downturn and a number of layoffs by firms in the immediate geographical area.

The next step was to determine if the layoffs and poor economy were the problem. If this was the case, the accounts would not have been in default before, and would show a normal pattern of purchases and payments up to the recent period. To test this hypothesis, the auditors calculated the number of days between the current and the previous transactions for each account. The analysis showed that a significant number of the defaulted accounts showed no activity in recent months. The increase in defaults was not due to changes among active customers, and also appeared unrelated to the economic downturn. For all accounts where the number of days of inactivity was greater than 200, confirmation letters were automatically produced and mailed out to the customers. In almost 80 percent of these cases, customers sent back a letter stating that they were no longer using their store charge card, or the confirmation memos were returned by the post office because the customer did not live at that address. This led the auditors to question the recent transactions recorded against the customers' accounts, and a quick review of the charges uncovered the scheme. The auditors totaled the charges to these accounts by clerk and found Larry's total to be higher than all other clerks combined.

Concerned that Larry was involved in additional fraudulent acts, the auditors reviewed all his transactions in more detail. One of the tests was a statistical analysis on the sale amount for his transactions. They found that Larry had processed more than 50 sales returns in the previous week. A review of the negative transactions and the transaction recorded immediately before and after each sales return revealed the scheme in which he had used store coupons to obtain cash. When confronted with the evidence, he admitted to the fraud.

Scheme:	Offset payments with charges on dormant accounts—steal payment, record sale, refund sale, record sale with discount coupon, pocket difference
Symptoms:	Charges against dormant accounts, and sale, refund, new sale series
Data Requirements:	Customer accounts—customer number, minimum due amount, due date, paid amount, date, purchases, date. Sales—transaction type, date, time, amount, clerk.

Join/Relation

Often the success of a fraud relies on the separation of two key pieces of information. It is, therefore, important to be able to link together key information, even if details are contained in separate files or different systems. As long as the right hand does not know what the left hand is doing, the criminal can get away with fraudulent activity. However, when the two pieces of information are viewed together, the crime may become obvious.

The time required to sort the information manually from two different sources and then match the records together can be overwhelming, especially when multiple files are involved. However, the computer is an ideal tool for matching information from two or more sources, making the time required trivial. (See Exhibit 7.2.)

Defining a relationship is even more powerful, allowing auditors to compare and contrast information from many different files. (See Exhibit 7.3.)

However, an even more important difference between joining and relating files is the way that duplicate records are handled. When relating files, child records without a parent will not be included in the resulting view. While Join can combine only two files (primary-secondary) at the same time, it offers a wider choice of options for the results, including:

- Unmatched primary records
- Unmatched secondary records
- Matched primary records
- Matched secondary records
- Both matched and unmatched primary and secondary records

Therefore, it is extremely important to understand the type of combination of the required files that will address objectives and how to accomplish the task with the analysis software being used, before attempting any join or relationship.

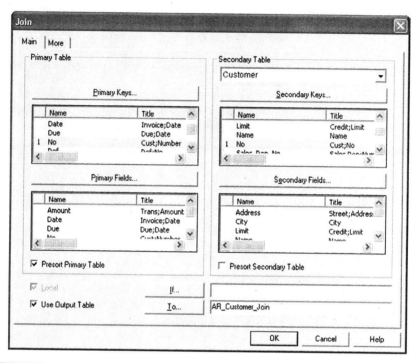

EXHIBIT 7.2 Join Screen. Joining data files allows auditors to create a single file from two separate files so that the data from the two sources can be compared (ACL Join Databases window).

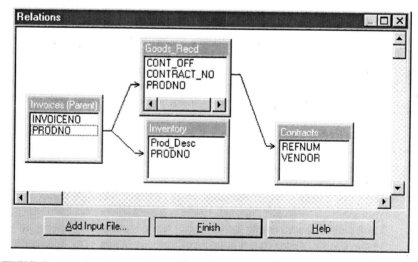

EXHIBIT 7.3 Relations Screen. The difference between joining files and relating files is that joining files creates a new file whereas relating files produces a logical view of the data from a number of files (ACL Relations window).

Case Study: Stolen Bank Deposits

Most of the staff just wanted to finish their shift and get home. Making the bank deposit just added more time to their shift and, even worse, it was risky. Everyone remembered the time a clerk was robbed; she was so frightened by the incident, it was almost two weeks before she would even leave her house. Dave, however, was more than willing to make the deposits and even picked up the empty bags from the bank once a week. It was not because he was particularly brave, but more that he believed he had an ingenious plan to make it worth his while.

The controls required one person to make up the deposit slip and another to check it before locking the deposit bag. Since he was taking the money to the bank, Dave said that he would check the accuracy of the deposit slips each night. But after checking the deposit slip, he would only pretend to lock the deposit bag. When he left the building, he would remove some of the cash from the bag and put in a new deposit slip, using deposit books he had picked up at the bank. When he picked up the empty bags, he would place the proper deposit slip back into the bag and remove the phony one. He had considered stealing a stamp from the bank but decided against it at the last minute. However, no one seemed to notice the absence of the bank's stamp on the deposit slips. At first it was fairly small amounts, a few dollars for taxi fare home—after all, he deserved it since he was going out of his way to make the deposit. But gradually the amount of his "withdrawals" increased.

There had never been a problem with the cash deposits before. The controls were sufficient, and the auditors did not expect to find any problem this time either. Usually the amounts differed by a few dollars at most. The auditors obtained copies of the deposit slips for the last six months and entered the deposit date, amount, and name of the person who had completed the receipt into a database. Then they obtained an electronic file from the bank containing all deposits. Using the deposit date, the two files were joined, and all deposits that did not agree with the bank records were highlighted.

There were not only more discrepancies, but in higher amounts than in previous years. One night the deposit had not even been made. A summary of the discrepancies (deposit slip amount versus bank amount), by person who completed the deposit slip, was produced. The employee with the highest discrepancy was Claire, who had signed the slip for the day the entire deposit was missing. However, a review of the employee schedule revealed that she was not even working that night. In fact, she had left the company a week prior to the incident to

(continued)

work for another company. A further examination showed that although her name was on the deposit slip, it was not the same as her signature on the personnel file. When the auditors looked at the dates, they noted that the discrepancies started around the time that Dave took over the bank deposit task.

The auditors talked to Dave and he freely admitted to having removed some of the cash to pay for his taxi rides home once in a while. He admitted to making the deposit the night that Claire was supposed to have signed the slip but denied keeping the deposit. He thought he could plead guilty to taking $10 here and there and get off with a slap on the wrist. It was not until much later that he realized that the auditors knew the full extent of his theft—an amount larger than even he had thought. By then the company had filed criminal charges.

Scheme: Employee steals portion of cash or entire deposit.
Symptoms: Discrepancies and missing deposits
Data Requirements: Bank deposits (Bank/Slip info)—date, deposit number, depositor, amount. Deposit slips—date, amount, completed by.

Case Study: Fictitious Vendors

Because of previous job responsibilities and the security officer's failure to update her user profile, the accounts payable supervisor still had access to the vendor file. This enabled her to set up a fictitious vendor called APS Limited and submit invoices for goods never delivered. When the invoices arrived, she approved them and the checks were sent to APS Limited for payment.

The auditors undertook a review of the accounts payable process. As part of this review, they checked the controls on the vendor file. One of the tests was looking for vendor addresses that matched employee addresses. The company had a strict policy stating that employees and their spouses could not be vendors unless specific written approval was obtained and kept on file.

The auditors joined the addresses from the personnel file with those on the vendor file. The results of the match identified a junior accounts payable clerk as having the same address as APS Limited. Since no approval was on file, the auditors extracted all invoices made out to APS Limited. Even though all the invoices had been approved for payment by the supervisor, the auditors ran an inquiry against the inventory system. The analysis found that there were no items in inventory for the given invoices. In fact, they were unable to find any evidence that the goods listed on the invoices had ever been received.

The date on the vendor table indicated that APS had been an approved vendor for five years. However, the auditors only had access to the current year's payments and thus were unable to fully quantify the loss. They questioned the clerk who told them that the A/P supervisor had being using his mailing address for several years. The supervisor had told him that the mailroom in her apartment was not very secure and that she had lost important letters in the past. After further investigation, it became clear that the fraud was the work of the supervisor, and the clerk had simply done as he was instructed.

Scheme: False payments sent to employee address.
Symptom: Vendor address matches employee address.
Data Requirements: A/P—vendor, date, amount, user ID. HR—employee number, address. User ID—employee number, name. Vendor master—vendor number, address, date created, user ID. Inventory transactions—invoice number, product number, quantity received, date, user ID.

Case Study: Goods Delivered?

Deliver First was a major vendor of ABC Limited for many years, and the companies had a good working relationship. There had never been a problem until one day the Deliver First accounts receivable manager accidentally sent out an invoice for a delivery that had been canceled by ABC Limited. A few days later, while reconciling the invoice file, the manager noticed his mistake and tried to call ABC Limited to tell them about it. Unfortunately, ABC had closed its offices early on that Friday for their annual picnic and Monday was a holiday. The manager meant to call first thing on Tuesday but completely forgot until one week later when ABC's check arrived in the mail.

The manager did not cash the check at first. However, he eventually did cash that check and others. "Deliver First is facing tough economic times and hundreds of people's jobs are at stake"—at least that was what the A/R manager told himself as he defrauded ABC over and over again. He told himself that he would "make it up to them later with some special discounts."

Believing ABC's controls to be poor, he devised several other fraudulent schemes. During the next three months, he occasionally sent goods and then invoiced ABC Limited for the items that they had not ordered. He also delivered quantities higher than requested on the contract and from time to time for goods not delivered. He would later submit

(continued)

invoices for the inflated quantities, and, from time to time, for goods not delivered at all.

The ABC auditors used the contract, accounts payable, and inventory files as part of a review of the accounts payable process. The purchasing regulations called for every purchase to be linked to a signed and approved contract. The A/P file was linked to the contract and inventory files by contract number. This gave the auditors a complete view of the history of each contract. They could now examine the contract date, price and quantity ordered, the quantity received into inventory, and the invoice quantity and payment amount. Armed with this information, the auditors reviewed the accuracy and completeness of the A/P transactions. In particular, it allowed them to identify all A/P transactions where:

- There was no match in the contract file.
- There was no corresponding record in the inventory system to show that the goods were received.
- The quantity received was greater than the quantity ordered on the contract.
- The quantity on the invoice did not agree with the contract or receipt quantities.

They had been running this test for several years and had never identified a serious problem. Nevertheless, the job was run every quarter, because the matching was done by a script and required very little audit time. Also, the audit director believed in taking a proactive approach to fraud prevention and detection, particularly in A/P, a high-risk area. This quarter, Deliver First showed up on the exception reports. Deliver First transactions failed to match contract amounts 11 times and did not match inventory amounts a further three times.

The vice president of Deliver First verified the audit findings, and the accounts receivable manager was fired. The A/P manager at ABC was given a refresher course on the importance of controls, and the auditors continued to run the test every quarter.

Scheme:	Vendor ships more than ordered and/or invoices for more than it sent.
Symptoms:	Quantity greater than ordered; paid amount greater than received amount; paid amount greater than contract amount; unit price times quantity not equal to amount.
Data Requirements:	Accounts payable—contract number, invoice number, date, amount, vendor, vendor number, clerk.
	Inventory—contract number, quantity received, date, amount, vendor, vendor number, clerk.
	Contract—contract number, order quantity, unit price.

Case Study: Short Delivery

It was a clear case of collusion; the controls were too tight to have permitted the fraud to work any other way. The driver, in collusion with the inventory manager, shorted the deliveries. The inventory manager recorded the delivery as complete, and the two split the proceeds of the sale of the stolen goods. It was a successful scheme under which everyone profited except the company paying for the shipment.

The auditors had been told that there was something going on in the receiving area. There were no specific allegations, just a hint of some type of impropriety. In previous years, the auditors had spent several days verifying the inventory system's quantities (for a sample of inventory items) with the physical inventory levels. This always gave the inventory manager time to order items where the physical inventory levels were short for the sampled items, ensuring that the auditors never found a problem. (See Exhibit 7.A.)

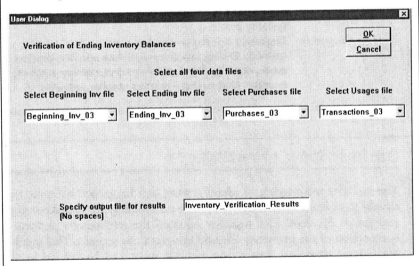

EXHIBIT 7.A Inventory Verification. A custom script can be written to perform annual verification of inventory balances (script shown is written in ACL).

However, this year they performed an electronic verification of 100 percent of the inventory levels and compared the inventory levels with the quantities purchased. The auditors obtained access to the inventory system, which contained the quantities on hand as well as the ending inventory values for last year. They also accessed the production

(continued)

database and calculated the inventory used in the last year. Next, they obtained a copy of the contracting database and calculated the total quantity purchased for every item.

By combining the four files by product number, a process that took only minutes to perform, they identified all items where the beginning inventory plus the purchased items minus the used inventory was greater than the ending inventory—that is, where the inventory was short.

The auditors then summarized all inventory records with shortages, first by vendor and then by the name of the employee who signed the receipt for the goods. They found only two vendors, and in both cases the inventory manager had processed a large number of the receipts. He admitted to the fraud and even told them that he had gotten away with it for years.

Scheme:	Inventory manager steals inventory.
Symptoms:	Previous ending quantity plus purchases minus inventory used is not equal to current inventory levels, but quantity ordered equals quantity received and equals quantity invoiced.
Data Requirements:	Beginning inventory—product number, product name, quantity. Ending inventory—product number, product name, quantity. Production—project, product number, quantity. Contracting—product number, quantity.

Case Study: Wrong Address Deliveries

The auditors were trying to identify what had happened to items that should have been in inventory but were not. Joining the goods received and goods invoiced files together allowed the auditors to perform a comparison of the inventory file and the purchase records. This quickly highlighted shortages, but it was unclear what had happened to the goods in question. An entire shipment of plywood and two shipments of fiberglass insulation were among the missing items.

Several techniques, such as summarizing by name for all employees signing for the receipt of the goods, had failed to shed any light on the matter. Finally, the auditors came up with another idea: Check the delivery location on the bill of lading. It turned out that the goods were never recorded in the inventory system because the vendor was delivering the goods to other locations. One of the auditors remembered an awards party that was held at one of the addresses—the home of the vice president for purchasing. The auditors reviewed all bills of lading for the vendor in question for the past two years and entered the delivery location into a database. They then looked for matches between the delivery location and employee addresses. This identified the locations of the remaining missing items as being the addresses of the purchasing manager, the accounts payable manager, and a clerk in receiving.

The simple matching of delivery addresses to employee addresses was all it took to uncover a fraudulent scheme involving personnel at various levels in the company.

Scheme: Inventory manager has items delivered to his home (inventory manager signs receipt of goods).

Symptoms: Shipped-to address matches employee address.

Data Requirements: Goods received—contract number, invoice number, product number, quantity. Goods invoiced—invoice number, product number, quantity, shipped to address. HR—employee number, title, home address.

Case Study: Construction Zone

The project manager responsible for a major construction project had a great deal of influence with the suppliers. It was early in the construction project, and millions of dollars worth of contracts were still up for grabs. It was no surprise to the auditors when they discovered that the project manager had arranged for several contractors to do work on his house and bill the cost of improvements to the company.

The audit director was curious about how the auditors had found the fraud so quickly. They had been at the construction site for only three days and had already uncovered more problems than any other team had found in audits lasting months or longer.

Anne, the team leader, explained the approach the audit team had taken. First, they obtained the time sheet file from each supplier, detailing the number of hours for each worker for the past month. They also obtained a copy of the pass control database for the past month—each contractor working on site was issued a day pass, and the information was recorded in the pass control database. Next, a join of the two files by contractor name and date was performed. This identified the hours claimed by the supplier that were not substantiated by the pass control data. The auditors thought the analysis had identified overbilling by

(continued)

suppliers. However, when one of the suppliers was questioned about the overbilling, he said the reason the workers did not show up on the pass control database was because they had been working off site that day. He had been told that all the hours worked, regardless of location, were to be billed to the project. They obtained the address from the supplier and checked it out—it was the project manager's house.

A further comparison of the invoiced materials with the contract quantities for several suppliers identified supplies that had been misdirected to the project manager's house. With the information in hand, the auditors questioned the project manager, and he confessed.

The auditors returned to the construction site to finish the remainder of the audit. The project called for the construction of several buildings. Each building was set up as its own project and had its own budget. However, the auditors discovered numerous instances where workers hired under one contract were recording their time against another contract. This was found by comparing the time sheet data with the contract data. The total hours by worker for each contract was compared with the total hours billed by contract. The detailed follow-up analysis identified a serious budget overrun on one of the projects. However, another project, which had been under budget, was being used to subsidize the first project. As a result, the second project, barely 2 percent completed, had already used up 26 percent of its budget. The manager responsible for the construction of both buildings had been hiding inefficiencies in the first building by charging them against construction of the second building. The same manager was scheduled to leave the job for a promotion elsewhere within the company, and his replacement would likely have been tainted by the budget problems if the auditors had not discovered them first.

The audit director was impressed with the audit work performed. A month ago, he had reluctantly let a few auditors attend a CAATTs training course and had purchased a copy of audit software. He had not expected to see the benefits so quickly or to have them be so obviously related to the use of CAATTs. The rest of the auditors were scheduled for the next available course, and more audit software was purchased.

Scheme:	Employees working off site (manager's home) and billing to on-site project; project costs coded to wrong project
Symptoms:	Time sheet data for days when no pass was assigned; hours billed to project does not match time worked on project or rates; overruns on a project charged to one that had not started yet

Data Requirements: Time sheet—contractor name, contractor number, date, start and end times, rate, project number, approved by (manager). Pass control—contractor name, contractor number, date, project. Contract labor hours—contractor number, rate, project number. Project—project number, project name, start and end date, total labor cost, manager. Invoice—project, contractor number, rate, hours, amount, invoice number, date.

CHAPTER 8

Analyzing Trends in the Data

The use of audit software to join files together or to establish relationships between normally separate data files allows auditors to examine trends and find problem areas and anomalies. This is especially useful in the area of fraud detection. It also allows auditors to check the logic of an application system independently by comparing the application's results with that of the audit software.

Trend Analysis

The search for fraud does not have to rely on manual audit methods or even a single snapshot of the data at a point in time. Auditors often perform similar audits year after year or perform similar audits at different branch offices. Even with the first audit in a specific area, historical figures may be available that will allow the auditor to look at trends in the data. A review of a single year, or single operational area may not be very telling, but by combining that with other data, the auditor can determine if there is anything unusual.

People who commit fraud often use very simple means to accomplish their task. They may do very little to hide the fraud, assuming that it will be lost in the details. They hope that the individual transactions will not stand out and that the fraud will succeed. However, comparing the set of transactions with previous data or to data from other locations can highlight the fraudulent acts.

Trend analysis can help to find fraud in many areas, even when the criminal hides the theft. For example, the principal method of detecting omitted credits, such as skimming cash receipts, is trend analysis.[1] The analysis can be used to identify decreases in profits that are equal to the cost of goods or services stolen. There may also be an unexplained increase in the cost of goods sold. Shrinkage or unexplained decreases in inventory do not occur when sales of services are taken but do occur when sales of goods are stolen. Some level of shrinkage may be expected because of inferior goods or losses due to damage or spoilage, but high levels of shrinkage may be an indicator of fraud.[2] Therefore, shrinkage rates and trends must be carefully monitored and reviewed.

Case Study: Lots of Parking

The company owned 12 parking lots in the downtown area of the city. All the lots charged a fixed daily price for parking, regardless of the actual time patrons parked their cars.

The attendants gave each patron a prenumbered ticket when they entered the lot. The number of tickets issued was used as a check on the revenue collected by the attendant for the day. Deposits were made each night and compared with the number of tickets issued. As an additional control, the attendants were moved from lot to lot each week.

The auditors analyzed daily revenues generated by each lot, by attendant. The analysis allowed them to compare and contrast revenue collected.

Analysis of Lot Revenue by Attendant

Attendant	Lot 1	Lot 2	...	Lot 12
John	$3,245	$3,623		$2,156
Bill	$3,423	$3,751		$2,078
Paul	$3,303	$3,812		$2,097
Mary	$3,772	$3,698		$2,149
...				
Pat	$3,001	$3,313		$1,903
Kate	$3,404	$3,818		$2,221

The analysis showed that Pat's daily deposits for each of the 12 lots were close to 10 percent lower than the revenue collected by the other attendants. The auditors staked out the lot where Pat was working that week and watched as he failed to give tickets to several patrons. Since he did not give them a ticket, there was no evidence that they had parked there, and he pocketed the cash. The auditors captured the transactions on camera and obtained statements from customers who had paid for parking but had not been issued a ticket. Pat laughed when presented with the evidence, saying he was surprised they had taken so long to catch him.

Scheme:	Attendant does not give out ticket, pockets cash.
Symptoms:	One attendant's receipts are less than all other attendants at every lot.
Data Requirements:	Parking—amount, date, lot number (1–12), attendant

Case Study: Inflated Prices

The auditors were reviewing various purchases to determine if the company had been receiving the best value for its money. For each item purchased, an expression was created to calculate the average purchase price. This calculation was done for each of the last three years. The results were joined to create a single file showing the average purchase price per item for the last three years. The auditors then identified all items where the purchase price had increased by more than 5 percent over the last three years. These records were extracted to a file for further analysis.

Analysis of Average Prices

Item	Average Yr 2	Average Yr 1	Average Curr Yr
Paper	1.93	2.12	2.97
Toner	32.43	36.41	41.45
. . .			
Fuser Pads	1.07	2.48	3.01

A total by vendor determined that 83 percent of the items that had increased in price over the past three years had been purchased from only two vendors. The remaining 17 percent of the items were purchased from more than 20 vendors.

The auditors felt that the two vendors in question, ABC Corp. and Great Co., might have been overcharging, but more work was required to prove or disprove this theory. The auditors obtained pricing data for the past three years from four competitors of the two vendors. Then the auditors compared the prices in the file with the pricing data from the four competitors. On average, the prices charged by ABC and Great Co. were almost 26 percent higher than those of the competitors, for the same products.

(continued)

Summary by Vendor

	Count	% of Count	% of Amount	Amount
ABC CORP	25,007	26.57%	41.83%	4,137,692.98
ACME LTD	1,712	1.87%	3.92%	388,019.52
GREAT CO	32,318	34.33%	41.58%	4,112,757.78
INC LTD	924	0.98%	4.68%	463,015.82
JANE & CO	566	0.60%	0.24%	24,034.97
KATE INC	731	0.78%	0.43%	42,517.90
...				
QUEENS LTD	372	0.40%	0.25%	25,208.67
RUSTICAN	905	0.96%	0.35%	34,416.75
TELEFORM	121	0.13%	0.71%	70,157.28
UNIVERSE	212	0.23%	0.79%	78,340.00
VITAMES	607	0.64%	0.50%	49,530.00
Total	94,127	100.00%	100.00%	9,891,169.67

The company employed eight full-time purchasing agents. In order to help determine if there had been any collusion between the vendors and a purchasing agent, the next analysis calculated the total dollars by purchasing agent on items purchased from the two vendors. This analysis revealed that one purchasing agent, Lindsay, had initiated more than 72 percent of the transactions with the higher-than-average purchase price. A second purchasing agent, Jennifer, accounted for 27 percent of the total. No other purchasing agent had bought more than $12,000 worth of goods from the vendors in the last three years.

The two agents were questioned separately. Lindsay was adamant that she always tried to get the best deal from all the vendors. If ABC Corp. or Great Co. had increased their prices, she was still sure that their prices were lower than other companies. She said that she used the same two vendors more often than other vendors because of faster delivery times and more selection. Jennifer was to be questioned second, but the auditors told her that her statement was not really required because Lindsay had "told them everything they needed to know." Suddenly Jennifer burst out, "I don't care what she said, it was all her idea in the first place." This surprised the auditors because they had believed Lindsay and were not even going to question Jennifer. Jennifer then told the auditors that Lindsay had arranged the scheme with the vendor and that they received "gifts" for accepting the excessive prices. She even had kept an e-mail Lindsay had sent her, telling her which goods to order from ABC and which to order from Great Co.

Scheme:	Order higher-priced goods for kickbacks
Symptoms:	Higher prices for the same items available from another supplier
Data Requirements:	Contract—contracting officer, date, quantity, unit price, amount, product number, vendor number

Note: a variation of the ratio analysis test (see Chapter 10) would also have identified this type of problem.

Case Study: Inferior Goods

Burns Ltd. always purchased combustible materials, such as coal and gas, from Com_Bust Inc. They had a long-standing relationship and never had experienced any problems with either the quantity or quality of the products purchased. So the auditors were surprised to get a call from the purchasing manager. He wanted them to conduct an immediate investigation of all purchases from Com_Bust Inc.

Once a week Com_Bust delivered gasoline to eight Burns company gas stations across the state. From there the gasoline was pumped directly into company cars. The auditors decided to start with a review of the controls over the delivery of the gasoline. At each station, the amount of gas in the underground storage tank was measured before and after the delivery and the difference recorded in a logbook. One of Burns's employees at each gas station took the readings, and when the auditors did an early-morning spot check at each gas station, they confirmed the starting figures. The auditors returned later in the day to calculate the starting value, minus the amount in the tank, plus the amount sold during the morning. They compared this result with the amount purchased from Com_Bust Inc. and found a measurable difference. The gas station manager and the auditors were at a loss to explain why. The pumps had been calibrated recently, and the seal on them was not broken, so there should not have been any significant difference in the volumes. The auditors went to the other seven gas stations and found similar unexplained discrepancies.

The auditors also reviewed the gas usage data for all company cars and compared this to previous years' consumption. Data for the past three years was used to determine the total volume of gasoline purchased. The volume had increased despite a reduction in the number

(continued)

of company cars and the territory covered by its salespeople. The auditors also used the gasoline data to calculate the average miles-per-gallon rating of the company cars for the past three years. They found that this had increased slightly last year but had dropped significantly this year.

The auditors reported their interim findings to the purchasing manager and the company vice president. The manager said he was not at all surprised by the findings but wanted to know why. The vice president, however, was sure that Com_Bust Inc. was not the problem. He was worried that the underground storage tanks were leaking and that Burns would be facing large environmental damage costs. He was so sure about the integrity of Com_Bust that, when he received a call from the vice president of sales for Com_Bust, he told him about the unexplained variance in yesterday afternoon's delivery.

The vice president of Com_Bust was confused, since they always made Burns's deliveries Wednesday morning, not in the afternoon.

The auditor checked the delivery schedule and found that up until 13 months ago, all deliveries were made in the morning. Since then the deliveries had been made in the afternoon. The auditor, with the approval of the Com_Bust vice president, followed the delivery truck on the next Wednesday. Instead of going to the first Burns company gas station, the driver drove to a warehouse parking lot.

The auditor, accompanied by security personnel from Com_Bust, went back to the warehouse. They found several workmen emptying gas from the truck. After removing gasoline from the tanker, the workers were replacing it with cheaper kerosene. The resulting mixture had a lower octane level, explaining the poorer miles-per-gallon averages. Further, since the tanker was sitting out in the sun all morning, the gasoline was warm and expanded. This caused the reading of the volume to be overstated.

The truck driver was fired and controls were put in place to establish and monitor a delivery timetable. In addition, a lock was placed on the tanker so that only Burns employees could unlock the pumping mechanism.

Scheme:	Theft of gasoline
Symptoms:	Poor gas mileage; variance in amounts
Data Requirements:	Company car—license plate number, gallons, mileage, car, date. Gas station—gallons purchased, date.

Regression Analysis

Regression analysis is a statistical method for examining a series of records to determine if the values are appropriate. It can be used to assess the reasonableness of the values in one or more numeric fields based on a "driver." A mathematical relationship is established between the driver and the dependent variable (the field being assessed). Using the mathematical relationship, an auditor can estimate the value of the dependent variable. For example, the amount of heating fuel used is dependent on the temperature: The colder it gets, the more heating fuel used. Using regression analysis, an auditor can estimate how much heating fuel will be used for a given temperature. Auditors and fraud investigators can use regression analysis to compare actual values with predicted values. For example, the actual gallons of heating fuel used for any given day can be compared with the statistically predicted value to identify anomalies. (See Exhibit 8.7.)

The relationship between the two variables can be linear or nonlinear. In a linear relationship, the variables are related by a constant. They are in strict

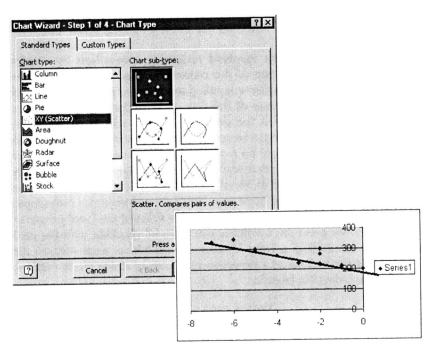

EXHIBIT 8.7 Trend Analysis. This Excel Chart Wizard allows an auditor to graph a wide variety of linear and nonlinear relationships, to detect anomalies.

proportion to one another. A nonlinear relationship occurs when the two variables are related, but in a nonconstant way. One may be proportional to the square of the other, for example. The advantage of regression analysis lies in the ability to estimate values even when the relationship is not linear and therefore not intuitively obvious.

Case Study: Stolen Credit Cards

The bank was losing millions of dollars to fraudulent purchases made using stolen credit cards. The audit director had been asked to find a way to identify inappropriate purchases as early as possible, even if the card had not yet been reported as stolen. During a brainstorming session with the auditors, regression analysis and two other tests were suggested.

Regression analysis was used to compare each transaction for each cardholder to their normal purchasing pattern. Anomalies were identified and cardholders were called to determine if they had made the purchase. The results were amazing. After several months of refining the program, transactions were being selected in many cases where the cards had been stolen, detecting the fraud after only a few purchases had been made.

The second analysis involved reviewing transactions by vendor. Vendors not normally part of the customer's purchasing pattern were flagged, and the cardholder was called to verify the purchase. The third analysis was a comparison of the date and locations of the purchase. Two purchases made on the same day, but in widely separated zip codes, would cause a flag to be set. The rationale was that it was unlikely that two purchases would be made in different parts of the country on the same day, so verification was obtained from the cardholder. Finally, analysis was performed to identify even amounts and purchases from the same vendor on the same day. While these sometimes erroneously flagged transactions as potential frauds, the value of the fraud prevented greatly outweighed the administrative costs of checking with the cardholders. In addition, a large number of cardholders were pleased that the company had taken a proactive approach to stolen credit cards—a valuable, intangible benefit.

Scheme:	Theft of credit cards
Symptoms:	Unusual patterns in the data (same vendor same day, even amounts, split purchases, abnormal amounts); unusual vendors
Data Requirements:	Credit card—card number, date, amount, merchant, merchant address

Case Study: Heating Things Up

The heating plant manager figured he was set for life and might even be able to retire early. Four months ago, he arranged for a friend to arrive at the plant late at night, every Wednesday, and together they siphoned a few hundred gallons of heating oil. There was little chance of being caught. The plant supplied the heat for all buildings on the campus and used thousands of gallons of heating fuel. On top of that, there were always problems with spillage. "As long as we don't get too greedy, we can get away with this for years," he told his friend. They sold the heating oil to friends at discounted prices and were doing quite well.

This year, when the auditors performed a yearly audit of the heating plant, they noted that the fuel usage had increased, despite a mild winter. They decided to analyze the daily heating oil usage figures. They knew that the number of gallons used would vary depending on the temperature, so they obtained a file of the nighttime lows from a local weather station. Next, using regression analysis, they plotted the number of gallons used each day against the temperature. Sixteen readings were significantly outside of the expected values. The auditors' interest was raised a notch when they extracted the data for the 16 records and noted that it was always the same day of the week (Wednesday). The next Wednesday, they set up a surveillance team and caught the plant manager and his friend in the act of stealing the heating fuel.

Scheme:	Heating plant manager siphons fuel.
Symptoms:	Fuel consumption inconsistent with expected consumption based on temperature
Data Requirements:	Fuel—date, gallons used. Temperature—date, low.

Case Study: No Vacancy

The manager of a large apartment complex in the city always had a 5 to 10 percent vacancy rate—at least that was what he claimed. The rate was not significantly higher than any of the other buildings owned by the company. However, he was in fact renting out apartments to friends and relatives without having them sign a lease. They paid him a nominal sum each month, and he kept the cash. Since they did not sign a lease, the owners of the complex thought the apartments were empty.

(continued)

The auditors were reviewing the leases for all the buildings owned by the company. They had enough data to use regression analysis to predict the number of people living in a building based on the electricity, water, and heat usage. The predicted number of tenants was then compared with the number of people listed on the leases. Everything checked out within acceptable limits until they came to this complex. The analysis estimated that there should be approximately 1,200 tenants, but the leases only accounted for 1,137. A careful review of all apartments found 58 people living in 18 apartments that the manager had rented without a signed lease.

Scheme:	Manager is renting apartments without leases and keeping rent payments.
Symptoms:	Water, heat, and electricity usage trends different at one building.
Data Requirements:	Lease—building address, apartment number, number of people, lease start and end dates. Utilities—water, heat, electricity usage by building.

Parallel Simulation

Parallel simulation is a technique that can be used to verify the programming logic of an application system. Auditors can use CAATTs to test the accuracy of the program by simulating part of the application program. The input data is read and manipulated by the analysis software and the results are compared to those obtained by the application.

There is an urban legend of a programmer responsible for maintaining a program that calculated the interest on savings accounts. He changed the program to collect fractions of a penny in round-off errors from each account every month,—amassing thousands of dollars in a short time. This is a perfect example of how parallel simulation can be used to detect fraud. Analysis software can be used to perform the same calculations, and then compare the results to the application's calculations. This would detect any error in the application's program logic.

Case Study: Recalculating Move Costs

ABC Inc. had almost 100,000 employees at branch offices spread throughout the world, and they were frequently transferred between offices. This meant packing up the employee's household goods and moving the employee and family to the new location. A contract with Moves International, a large multinational moving company, had been in effect for three years and was under negotiation for renewal.

The auditors reviewed various aspects of the contract and noted that the moving company had supplied ABC with software to coordinate the thousands of moves every year. The software even calculated the move costs and the insurance rates. When the initial contract was established, ABC hoped to achieve a decrease in the cost of moving employees to their new work locations. However, when the auditors reviewed the costs for the previous three years, the total cost had not decreased significantly. In fact, they noted that the cost of insuring goods in transit had actually increased despite a lower overall insurance rate.

One of the auditors wanted to manually calculate and compare the cost of the move, and its insurance costs, for a sample of moves from last year. The team leader had a better idea: Use parallel simulation to calculate the costs for every move and compare the auditor-calculated cost to the amount calculated by the contractor software. The auditors reviewed the contract to determine how moving and insurance costs were calculated. Next, they obtained raw data from the moves database and used audit software to calculate the moving and insurance costs. Comparing their calculated costs with the actual costs charged by the contractor revealed that the moving costs were 6 percent higher and the insurance costs were almost 12 percent higher than expected.

A detailed review of the Moves International software determined that the weight of the employee's car (when it was transported separately) was also being included in the total weight of the household goods. Since the weight was a key cost driver, the total costs were being overstated. Insurance costs were also based on the total weight of the household goods and thus were also overstated. The auditors contacted XYZ, another company using Moves International software, and found that the version of the software ABC was using was different from the version used by XYZ. Moves International was eager to cooperate, especially when they found that the amount being charged to ABC Inc. was more than was being recorded by the accounts receivable department at Moves International. With assistance from Moves International fraud investigators, the auditors determined that a programmer and an accounts receivable clerk at Moves International, in collusion with a clerk at ABC, had made changes to the software and were splitting the overcharges.

(continued)

Scheme:	Programming error—double counts weight of cars
Symptoms:	Weight of vehicles counted in weight of household goods as well as separately as vehicles
Data Requirements:	Moves—move number, total weight of household goods (perishable plus fragile plus other), vehicle weight, total other weight, insurance rate, insurance amount

Because parallel simulation uses the actual data from the system as input and compares the auditor-calculated results to the system-generated results, 100 percent analysis is possible. In addition, modern audit software, with built-in financial and other functions, often can perform the simulation easily—requiring little or no programmer involvement. Finally, when saved as a script, the analysis can be used to verify newer versions of the application software and run periodically to test for fraud.

Notes

1. Joseph T. Wells, *Occupational Fraud and Abuse* (Austin, TX: Obsidian Publishing Co., 1997), 73.
2. Ibid., 120.

CHAPTER 9

Known Symptoms of Fraud

The detection of fraud may call for a search for duplicates, a comparison across years, a recalculation of the total price, a search for anomalies (such as labor costs with no labor hours recorded), or other techniques. Data analysis software allows the auditor to interact freely with the data, moving from one task to the next, but the software cannot determine what to look for. The analysis software is simply a tool, while the auditor remains the key ingredient in the detection of fraud. In other words, knowing the symptoms of fraud is not enough; having a powerful tool is not enough; both are required for success.

The value of computer-assisted audit tools and techniques (CAATTs) is in their flexibility and power. Flexibility is necessary in order for auditors or fraud investigators to be effective, especially when dealing with many possible fraud scenarios. The software used should permit auditors to pose iterative questions of the data and examine the results before posing the next question. This will allow auditors to approach a single problem from many different angles. The power of CAATTs also lies in repetition and speed of operation. For example, scripts can make it easy to run the same query again and again, even for thousands or millions of records. The ideal is analysis software that permits auditors to employ a number of different techniques and to be creative in their approach while being able to crunch through large, repetitive tasks with ease.

Many of the examples of fraud in this book have focused on one technique, such as a search for duplicates. In truth, while a single technique can and often does have utility, and is often successful in detecting fraud, combinations of techniques are essential. Also, flexibility and inquisitiveness in the use of analysis software and in the auditor's approach are vital since the same fraud can be manifested in many different forms. A specific computer technique may identify possible fraud in one case and completely miss it in the next case. Auditors and fraud investigators must endeavor to understand the data, to interact with it, and to test a variety of hypotheses. They should consider possible control weaknesses, hypothesize on the possible effects of fraudulent scenarios on the data, and run tests to search for evidence of the fraud. It is not necessary to run a job and wait hours for the printout; filters can be set and applied, equations and calculated fields created and displayed, files joined together showing unmatched records, and a variety of other techniques used interactively and immediately.

An auditor's greatest asset is the ability to effect change. Doing this requires him or her to review information critically, determine cause and effect, and arrive at objective recommendations that can be implemented to address the problem at hand, not simply the symptoms. The recommendations flowing from the audit can improve the control framework of the organization or its systems. Because CAATTs save time in performing an analysis, thus allowing auditors more time for critical thought, they contribute directly to the auditors' ability to effect change. Auditors bogged down with manual and nonproductive tasks—such as manual comparisons of two sources of information, using adding machines to calculate trial balances, and so on—have little time left to reflect on the information and isolate the significant issues. Combining techniques in an innovative way can help auditors and fraud investigators not only to detect serious fraud, but also to provide a higher level of assurance and coverage while saving time and energy.

Finally, data analysis software is not only a powerful investigative and fraud prevention tool. It can also have significant value in the area of criminal prosecution. Auditors and fraud investigators must recognize the full range of the tools and techniques available to them. Too often, the tools and techniques are narrowly defined, reducing their usefulness.

In particular, when we combine database software and audit software, the total is greater than the sum of the parts. Auditors and fraud investigators must be creative in their pursuit of criminals and in their use of technology. The symptoms of fraud are in the data; it just needs to be mined.

Known and Unknown Symptoms

The use of data analysis in audit can be very easy when the auditor is looking for something that is well understood and defined. For example, given an audit of accounts payable—with the objective of verifying that the company is not paying the same invoice twice—auditors can easily define the criteria required to search through millions of transactions and highlight the potential duplicates. Looking for records with the same invoice number, same vendor, and same amount will quickly identify transactions for review. Here auditors are dealing with known symptoms, cases where they can define the criteria and use data analysis to highlight all transactions meeting the criteria.

However, even with known symptoms, the criteria can be difficult to determine. Sometimes the criteria are less obvious and require more thought and experimentation. Take, for example, an audit where auditors are trying to assess whether corporate purchase cards are being used to make personal purchases. What might the symptoms look like in the data? The answer will depend on the data captured by the system, system edit checks, and other factors, such as corporate policies and procedures.

There are also times when auditors will not know what the symptoms look like until they find the fraud. Is data analysis still applicable? In many cases, the answer is yes, because the data itself will reveal the anomalies. The identification of outliers is a common example of unknown symptoms. Auditors do not know what an outlier looks like until they have examined the entire population; then it is quite obvious. Another technique to identify unknown symptoms of fraud is to look for trends in the data, such as comparing one year to another or one operational area to another. Auditors can also look for patterns in the data itself, including frequently occurring amounts, unusual combinations of digits in a numeric field, and so on.

The rest of this chapter discusses how known symptoms can be used to find fraud in various functional areas. (Chapter 10 deals with unknowns.) Payroll and purchasing have been singled out for a more indepth discussion because they exist in most organizations and have a higher level of fraudulent activity. Detecting fraudulent schemes in these areas usually demands a combination of audit techniques. The techniques presented are not exhaustive; they are a sample of useful tools for detecting payroll and purchasing frauds.

Appendix B also describes how fraud can be detected by the application of analysis techniques.

Auditors and fraud investigators must apply the power of data analysis software to the unique fraud prevention and detection requirements of each functional area. Each functional area has its own risks and fraud symptoms. Therefore, it is important to consider not only the capabilities of the software—the commands and functions—but also the possible exposures of the functional area. Typically, doing this will demand the application of a combination of techniques and fraud detection approaches.

Fraud in the Payroll Area

The increasing use of electronic applications in payroll is a double-edged sword for audit. It makes the review of the controls somewhat more complex, while it also provides auditors with automated techniques to address the risk areas.

Because of the high volume of transactions, the complexity of the computer systems, and the number of personnel involved in the process, payroll remains one of the major areas for fraud. The pay process is designed to "pay people," making it easier for someone to obtain cash fraudulently. By allowing auditors to examine all payroll transactions to look for anomalies, such as duplicate direct deposit account numbers or invalid Social Security numbers, audit software can give them the advantage in detecting payroll fraud.

The most common payroll fraud is still the creation of ghost employees, where fictitious employees are entered into the payroll system. The embezzler then receives and cashes the resulting payroll checks. Another scheme is to keep terminated employees on the payroll for several pay periods after they have left. The embezzler then cashes the paycheck for the terminated employee. Duplicate payroll checks for the exact amount of the legitimate check are also common. Another kind of payroll fraud is an overpayment scheme involving higher pay rates, inflated hours or days, or unauthorized bonuses. Each of these schemes is discussed and the symptoms identified in more detail in the pages that follow.

Ghost Employees

A "ghost employee" is a fictitious employee entered in the payroll system. Since these employees are not real, these types of frauds tend to stand out. Rarely does the perpetrator of this fraud follow all the rules and regulations that would be followed for actual employees. Audit software can be used to search for the resulting anomalies. For example, bona fide employees will have valid Social Security numbers; bank accounts for electronic payment, or home addresses; work telephone numbers; appropriate wage levels for the given classifications; and tax, pension, and benefits deductions. Further, real employees will take holidays and sick leave, and will have previous employment data and employee evaluations on their personnel file. However, ghost employees will often only be receiving a check every two weeks—no deductions, no work telephone number, and no vacation or sick leave.

The next entries list ways in which personnel and payroll files can be used to identify possible symptoms of ghost employees. Not all the tests will be valid in every organization, and other tests may be appropriate for a specific company. The aim is not to provide an exhaustive list of all possible approaches but to encourage auditors to explore various lines of inquiry to identify ghost employees. As with all tests for the symptoms of fraud, auditors must first review the control framework to make themselves aware of the specific exposures and available information sources in their company. They then must develop tests for the specific symptoms of the possible frauds.

SOCIAL SECURITY NUMBERS   An employer is required to report the salary and wages paid to every employee for taxation purposes. For this reason, each employee should have a valid Social Security number (SSN). A simple audit check for ghost employees is to search for the existence of invalid or blank SSNs. Lists of valid SSNs can be purchased from many companies, and tests for valid SSNs are available from some government sites for free. A simple join of payroll to the list of valid SSNs will highlight unmatched (invalid) SSNs. An additional test is to check for duplicate SSNs, since only under special circumstances should one person be receiving two payroll checks.

DUPLICATE DIRECT DEPOSIT NUMBERS   More and more payroll systems are using direct deposit as a means of paying employees. Instead of producing a check, the pay is deposited directly into the employee's bank account. A useful test is a search for duplicate bank account numbers for direct deposit. Two scenarios could be symptoms of fraud. The first scenario is where more than one employee has the same direct deposit account. The second is where an employee has more than one direct deposit account. These could be symptoms of an employee diverting pay from a terminated or ghost employee to his or her account. Auditors must keep in mind that the company may employ more than one family member, and they may have a single bank account. Also, some firms allow employees to split their check and deposit portions into multiple accounts. As always, auditors must carefully check and verify the results of all analyses before making accusations of fraud.

DUPLICATE HOME ADDRESSES   Duplicate home addresses can also be located easily. Again, auditors must be aware that more than one family member may be an employee.

P.O. BOX ADDRESSES   Another test is to search for addresses containing post office boxes. Fraudulently obtained payroll or vendor checks may use P.O. boxes as a mailing address. However, in rural areas, P.O. box addresses are more common, resulting in more false positives, and making this type of analysis less easy to use effectively.

WORK PHONE NUMBERS   In many businesses, employees each have an office phone number. Matching the payroll file with the company phone data will identify all employees without a valid telephone number. However, auditors must take care with the assumption that all employees have a work phone number and must ensure the telephone data is current. If only certain types of employees have a phone number, auditors can run the test for these employees and use another test for the other employees. A further enhancement to this test would be to check phone records to see if the phones in question are actually sending and receiving calls. The person committing fraud may have arranged for a discontinued phone to be associated with the ghost employee.

WORK LOCATION At a summary level, auditors can calculate the number of people at an office, plant, or location based on both the personnel and pay systems. Where they disagree, a more focused approach can be taken. Many personnel systems contain information on each employee's work location or "address." In some cases, the work location is sufficient to identify the actual workstation or desk of each employee. Matching the payroll data with the work location data will highlight all employees without a valid work location. Additionally, a test for duplicate work locations can be performed on the matched data. This will identify locations where there is more than one employee. In organizations with "job sharing" or a high level of employee turnover, duplicate work location analysis will be less meaningful.

WAGE LEVEL Where there are clearly defined job classifications with salary levels, a ghost employee can be easily identified if the rate is not appropriate for the classification. This could occur because the ghost employee did not receive an across-the-board salary increase or was being paid at an incorrect rate from the beginning. Stratifying the data to analyze salary levels by classification may pinpoint the fraudulent employee.

This type of analysis will highlight cases where the ghost employee is not being paid an amount appropriate for the job classification and level. For example, a Programmer Level 3 being paid $1,800 per week when the pay levels are $1,500, $1,600 and $1,650, might indicate a ghost employee. An exception would be employees who have changed job classifications involuntarily. They may be "salary protected," being paid at their previous classification's rate. (See Exhibit 9.1.)

Another test is to identify all persons whose salary did not increase after an across-the-board pay raise. The ghost employee may be set up in the

EXHIBIT 9.1   Weekly Salary Analysis for Level 3 Programmers.

Salary Level	Number of Employees	% Number Employees	% of Amount	Total Amount
1500	509	49.85%	47.98%	763,500
1600	341	33.40%	34.28%	545,600
1650	170	16.65%	17.63%	280,500
1800	1	0.10%	0.11%	1,800
Total	1,021	100.00%	100.00%	1,591,400

pay system in a nonstandard manner and would therefore not automatically receive pay increases. In addition, auditors can look for unexplained increases in pay, from one period to another, when no salary increases were granted and the person was not promoted or did not change jobs.

DEDUCTIONS A ghost employee may be receiving a regular paycheck without any of the usual deductions for tax, pension, health insurance, and so on. Audit software can be used to calculate and verify the accuracy of the deductions or to identify payroll records that have no deductions. There may also be discrepancies between tax monies remitted to the government and recorded salary expenditure.

VACATION AND SICK LEAVE Employees usually take vacation and sick leave at some point during the year; ghost employees often do not. In general, a failure to take vacation is considered to be a red flag for fraud. A test for ghost employees is to match the payroll records with the leave database. Unmatched records will identify all persons on the payroll with no vacation or sick leave recorded.

PERSONNEL HISTORY Matching the payroll file to the personnel file will identify all employees on the payroll who have no previous employment history, no previous positions, no performance evaluations, and so on. This will identify all new employees, but will also assist to identify potential payroll fraud.

A combination of these tests can assist auditors in identifying ghost employees, but additional tests specific to the company might also need to be developed. The tests can be saved as queries or scripts and run periodically. A review of the employees identified will help to ensure that ghost employees are not on the payroll. Running a series of tests will reveal persons identified by more than one of these symptoms; their pay should be carefully investigated.

Terminated Employees

The retention of terminated employees on the payroll after they have left their job is a common payroll fraud. The embezzler then receives the paycheck for the terminated employee and either cashes it or splits it with the terminated employee. A principal technique for identifying this type of activity is the comparison of the payroll file to other sources of information on "active" employees.

PERSONNEL FILE   The payroll transactions can be matched with the personnel file. Records where the pay period date is after the departure date can be identified with a filter:

```
AGE(Pay_Period_Date,Departure_Date) < 0
or
Pay_Period_Date > Departure_Date
```

These will identify employees who have departed prior to the current pay period. A variation on this scheme is to pay a new employee for the period prior to the start of employment.

```
AGE(Pay_Period_Date,Start_Date) > 0
or
Pay_Period_Date < Start_Date
```

ACTIVE EMPLOYEE FILE   Matching the payroll file and the active employee file can identify employees on the payroll who no longer work for the company. A match of the payroll with the "active" employee file can identify the unmatched payroll records. These records represent individuals not in the personnel file but who are receiving a paycheck.

Auditors and fraud investigators must have a sound understanding of the payroll and personnel files to use these types of tests. In particular, it is important that the payroll, personnel, and active employee files are up to date and concurrent. Differences in when the files are updated can wrongly identify records as possible frauds. One solution to the timing problem is to choose the most recent point when the files were concurrent and work forward from there. The results of such a comparison must be carefully evaluated before using them as the basis for any investigation of possible or suspected fraud.

At the same time, differences in the timing of the updates of the information on these files can present opportunities to commit a fraud. Any such difference should be considered as an exposure and treated accordingly.

Overpayment

The essence of overpayment fraud is the receipt of more money than the individual is entitled to receive. Overpayments involve actual employees rather than ghost employees. In these cases, the perpetrators simply attempt

EXHIBIT 9.2   Analysis of Bonus Payments (Actual Not Equal to Calculated).

ID	Date	Calculated Bonus	Actual Bonus
A0785412	03/25/98	1,825.00	1,450.00

1 of 1021 met the criterion: CAL_BONUS <> ACT_BONUS

to receive unearned bonuses and commissions, or payments at higher pay rates, for longer hours, or more days than they actually worked.

INAPPROPRIATE BONUSES   Most often, a bonus is tied to meeting a specified target so that the person receiving it must achieve a given sales level or production quantity. The bonus may also be awarded based on a sliding scale, with a larger bonus received for reaching a higher target. Bonuses that are higher than authorized can occur if the bonus rates are not properly calculated. Audit software can be used to create an expression that calculates the amounts of the bonus based on the target and actual levels. The calculated bonus can then be compared to the bonus paid and transactions with a difference between these two amounts highlighted for further investigation. (See Exhibit 9.2.)

Since bonuses are tied to achieving production or sales targets, the manipulation of these levels is a frequent source of fraud. The most common type of manipulation is overstating the levels achieved. This can be accomplished in many ways, such as generating fictitious sales or producing inferior goods at a faster rate.

An audit technique for detecting inappropriate bonuses for the target levels is to examine the types of transactions after the end of the bonus period. In sales, there may be an increase in the number of returns; in manufacturing there may be an increase in the number of defective items. (See Exhibit 9.3.)

The data may show that sales, or production, is high for the month the bonus is calculated (July) and that the return or defect rates increase substantially the following month (August). Also, the sales and production levels may decrease the month prior (June) to the month in which the bonus is calculated. This may be a sign of "saving" sales/production until the next month. Auditors must be aware of the targets used to calculate bonuses and review the controls over the measurement of the target amounts. A bonus system based on annual number is less easy to abuse, but the converse problem of "rushing" sales before year-end will occur, somewhat distorting sales trends.

The next examples illustrate how audit software and analysis techniques can be used to highlight cases where employees have managed to obtain

EXHIBIT 9.3   Sales Return and Production and Defect Levels.

Sales Return Level			Production and Defect Levels		
Month	Sales	Returns	Month	Production	Defects
Jan	134	6	Jan	15,623	16
Feb	132	7	Feb	15,712	17
Mar	134	5	Mar	15,124	14
Apr	137	5	Apr	15,733	19
May	138	6	May	15,689	15
Jun	121	4	Jun	15,031	11
*Jul	152	6	*Jul	16,319	7
Aug	136	21	Aug	15,101	72
Sep	131	8	Sep	15,619	16
Oct	124	7	Oct	15,558	19
Nov	123	6	Nov	15,663	15
Dec	119	5	Dec	15,644	18

*Bonuses are calculated in July

pay at higher rates. In one case, simple rounding up to the next quarter hour produced a significant increase in the payroll costs, when accumulated over the entire year.

Case Study: Error of Commission

In accordance with the company compensation policy, sales staff were paid on salary plus commission. The previous November, a special contest was held for all sales staff. November was traditionally a poor month for sales, and management wanted to shake things up a bit. The top five salespeople in the month received an extra 5 percent commission. Last year was the first year that the special commission was offered, and management felt that the program had been a modest success, with November sales increasing by 14 percent.

However, the audit director had concerns about the compensation program. He felt that the financial incentive could create pressure on the staff to produce sales in November, no matter what, and he saw this as a potential fraud exposure. As a result, he asked an audit team to review the program.

The team performed several different analyses of the sales data. First, the auditors examined the total sales for September through November for the last four years. The results showed that there had been no significant increase in the total sales for the three months last year as a result of the November contest. This led them to question management's belief that the program had been a success. Fred (the team leader) reasoned that if the overall sales had not increased, perhaps October sales were lower than normal. He feared that some sales representatives might have delayed some October sales activity and reported it in November. This would make their November figures look better but not affect the overall sales for the period September to November.

To test this hypothesis, the team totaled the sales by month for the past four years. In the previous years, September and October sales had been fairly consistent. However, with the introduction of the special commission, the sales figures dropped in October. This increased Fred's fear about the accurate reporting of the timing of the sales orders.

Next, the audit team totaled the sales by each sales rep in September, October, and November. The auditors found that the sales for October were extremely low for two sales reps in particular. Further, the analysis showed that their November volumes were extremely high in comparison. Looking at the sales orders by day, the auditors found that the two sales reps had no sales in the last two weeks of October and that the first three days of November accounted for close to 25 percent of their total November sales. This seemed to confirm Fred's suspicion that the sales were actually from October, and they had just delayed reporting them until November, to be eligible for the contest. Confirmation letters sent to the customers established that the orders had been placed in October. One customer even stated that he was told the delivery would be delayed for several weeks because a new computer system was being installed. But the confirmation letters revealed another problem: A number of letters were returned as "Addressee Unknown."

The next step was to examine the number of returns in December. The auditors totaled the returns by salesperson and, again, the two salespeople who had delayed October sales also had a higher returns percentage in December.

The use of audit software to examine the trends in sales levels over four years and to review the figures by month, by day, and by salesperson helped the auditors confirm their suspicions. The salespeople, when presented with the detailed analysis and confirmation letters, admitted to fabricating and delaying sales to make their November figures look good. In addition, the auditors were able to demonstrate to management that the results for the November contest did not justify the additional 5 percent commission. The program was canceled, to the relief of most of the salespeople, who felt that many customers considered November a welcome downtime before the December rush.

(continued)

Scheme:	Obtaining bonuses by shifting sales to contest month; creating fictitious policies
Symptoms:	Decreased sales prior to contest, then increased in contest month; large number of sales canceled in next month
Data Requirements:	Sales (four years of data)—salesperson, transaction type, amount, date. Customer—customer number, address.

Case Study: Higher Pay Rates

The plant manager was left pretty much on his own. The plant had been profitable for many years, and head office management did not bother to drop by very often—not even once in the last three years. There was a small matter of a routine audit every year, but that was more of an inconvenience than a worry. About one year earlier, the manager decided that everyone needed a raise; they had worked particularly long hours during a rush special order. But corporate office had complete jurisdiction over all pay increases and did not agree with the manager's recommendation. The manager already had enough years in that he could retire with full pension; and he did not really care if he got caught, so he went ahead and authorized higher pay increases than provided for by head office.

Shortly after the auditor arrived at the plant, she performed a quick analysis to compare the cost of production to previous years. She found that the cost of manufacturing goods had decreased slightly. However, this was not as favorable as it might sound since the other four plants she had visited on the audit had shown significantly larger decreases in production costs. An in-depth review of the cost data determined that there had been a 21 percent decrease in the raw materials, but this was largely offset by an increase in labor costs.

The auditor did a quick calculation of the average salary by employee category and compared this with the other plants. The results showed that the plant was paying its workers almost 12 percent more on average. The auditor also compared the average pay rates with previous years. This clearly showed that there had been an 11 percent increase over last year's rates. She knew that head office had given out pay increases last year, but the maximum increase had been 3.5 percent. When she talked to the manager, he admitted that he had given everyone an unauthorized raise, in addition to the amount set by head office. He had not expected the auditor to notice because the overall cost of production had decreased. But he did not realize that the auditor would or even could compare his production cost data with the other plants.

Management was in a tough spot. It was one thing to grant only a small raise; at least this was seen by the employees as something positive. It was another thing to take away a pay increase, even if it was unauthorized in the first place. Management decided to allow the workers to keep the pay increase but eliminate future increases to bring them back in line with the other plants.

Scheme:	Manager overpays employees despite HQ cap on salaries.
Symptoms:	All plants show a decrease in cost of goods manufactured, but one plant has less of a decrease than the others. Salary rates for employees in same classification increased by more than allowable amount.
Data Requirements:	Cost of goods—plant, raw material, labor costs—four years. Salary data—employee, classification, gross pay.

Case Study: Rounding Up Hours

All employees working overtime were required to punch in at the start of their shift and punch out at the end. Overtime was paid based on the nearest quarter hour; therefore, if the worker put in an extra 67 minutes, overtime was calculated at 60 minutes. However, if a worker put in an extra 68 minutes, overtime was calculated based on 75 minutes. Management figured that over the course of the year, the time would all even out, and no one would be unfairly treated.

The auditors were examining the overtime pay and noted that there had been an increase over the previous year. The manager agreed but was at a loss to explain why. He did not feel that there had been a corresponding increase in the workload or production. The auditors' review of the production levels agreed with the manager's feelings; although the difference was not alarming, only a matter of a percent or two, the increase in the overtime hours did not correlate with greater output.

One of the auditors manually reviewed several dozen overtime transactions, looking for signatures and prior approvals, and thought that the hours worked were being rounded up too often. He obtained a copy of the time reporting data and analyzed the overtime hours worked. First he calculated the difference between the starting and ending times to obtain the minutes of overtime worked. Next, he stratified the minutes and examined the point at which individuals clocked out by taking the

(continued)

modulus 15 of the time worked; this gave him the remainder after dividing the minutes by 15. If the modulus 15 of the minutes worked was greater than 7, then the minutes were rounded up to the next quarter hour; if 7 or less, then the minutes were rounded down. For example:

**Calculation of Overtime Minutes Paid
Based on the Quarter Hour**

Time Worked (minutes)	Time (Mod 15)	Paid Overtime (minutes)
1	1	0
7	7	0
8	8	15
9	9	15
22	7	15
23	8	30
37	7	30
38	8	45
52	7	45
53	8	60
67	7	60
68	8	75

The work was such that, if workers were simply signing out after they finished their job, the modulus 15 of the minutes worked should be random. This would mean that all values between 0 and 14 would occur with the same frequency. But when the overtime minutes were analyzed, the results showed something different. The auditor totaled the number of times each employee's modulus of the overtime minutes worked equaled 8 or more, and compared this to the total number of times the employee worked overtime. The results were sorted to determine the employees who were working 8+ minutes the most often.

**Analysis of Overtime Hours
(Using Mod 15 of the Hours Worked)**

Employee	# Times O/T Worked	# Times Mod 15 > 7	% of Times Mod 15 > 7
Jones	142	142	100.00
Black	127	127	100.00
Smith	141	140	99.29
...			
Coderre	115	65	56.52
Currie	114	56	49.12

The plant was large, with more than 200 employees on the shop floor, and typically there were two or three days with significant overtime each week. The analysis showed that a majority of the employees typically worked 8 minutes or more—resulting in their overtime hours being rounded up. In particular, some employees almost always worked 8 minutes or more. A further analysis was performed on these employees to get a detailed breakdown of the actual hours worked.

Analysis of Overtime Hours
(Details of Mod 15 of the Hours Worked)

Mod 15	Jones	Smith	Black
1	0	0	0
2	0	0	0
3	0	0	0
...			
7	0	0	0
8	142	140	126
9	0	0	1
...			
15	0	0	0

The auditors were surprised to discover that many employees consistently worked minutes equaling 8, which was rounded up and calculated as 15 minutes of overtime. A manual review of their time cards revealed that employees were putting their cards in upside down (often several times) and waiting until the time clock registered 8 minutes. By recording 8 minutes, the employees ensured they were paid for 15. Spread across hundreds of employees and dozens of overtime days, this small unearned increment was enough to change the results for the year. Equally important, it was clear that some employees were simply standing around, waiting to punch their cards, rather than working during the 8 minutes.

Scheme:	Employees are punching out at 8 minutes so that overtime is rounded up to the next quarter hour.
Symptoms:	Overtime increased by 2 percent over last year
Data Requirements:	Overtime—employee number, date, hours worked, start and stop times

Fraud in the Purchasing Area

For many organizations, the purchasing function is another area that is particularly vulnerable to fraudulent activity. It often has the most contact between employees and external agents, and can be the primary area of risk for misappropriation, both by employees and by outsiders.

Common types of fraud in the purchasing area are payments to a fictitious company and payments for goods not received. These frauds can be carried out by employees, by vendors, or by employees and vendors working together.

Employee Activities

Individual employees can commit fraud without colluding with a vendor or other employees. If the controls over segregation of duties are weak, a single employee can create a vendor, submit a fake invoice, certify the receipt of goods, submit the invoice for payment, and cash the resulting check. In other cases, more than one employee may be involved in the verification of the receipt of goods and the approval of the invoice for payment. For example, one employee could establish a fake company and have the company registered as a legitimate vendor. The other employee could then submit fake invoices for payment. Depending on the internal controls, such as separation of duties, the scheme may or may not require the perpetrator to have responsibility for authorizing payment. Also, it may or may not require collusion between various employees, such as receiving and accounts payable personnel. A comparison of vendor and employee addresses and/or phone numbers, matching of user names with vendor names, and determining who has authority for creating vendors, can identify problems in this area. Another test is to examine the number of accounts payable (A/P) clerks processing payments for each vendor. Unless the A/P area is organized such that the same clerk always handles the same vendor, vendors with multiple payments should be processed by more than one A/P clerk. Thus, vendors with many payments, all entered by the same clerk, would be a symptom of possible fraud. Finally, the matching of contract, inventory, and invoice data may prove useful in detecting various kinds of schemes.

Vendor Action and Employee Inaction

Often the employee is not actively involved in the fraud and does not even benefit from the fraud. For these types of fraud to succeed, the vendor relies on the employee *not* doing something. For example, a vendor in good standing submits a fake invoice for goods that were not received. If the controls are weak and the vendor regularly sells to the company, the invoice may be certified and submitted for payment, simply because of a lack of action by the employee responsible for verifying invoices. Often the initial action by the vendor is accidental, the invoice is canceled, and the money is returned by the vendor when it discovers the mistake.

However, even when an invoice is submitted by accident and a payment is received, a vendor or someone in the accounts receivable area may note the weakness in the system and decide to keep the overpayment. The vendor or person may then start taking advantage of the weakness in the controls by deliberately submitting more unsupported invoices.

Collusion between Vendor and Employee

Several possibilities for fraud exist when the vendor and an employee conspire against the company, such as when a valid vendor submits an invoice for payment, even though the goods were not delivered. The employee bypasses or falsifies the receipt of the goods and submits the invoice for payment. A simple test for this type of fraud is a three-way match of the contract detailing the goods to be delivered, the receipt causing an increase in inventory levels, and the invoice showing the payment for the goods. Invoice amounts with no matching contract amounts or no corresponding increase in inventory levels may be symptoms of fraud.

A second fraud scenario involves overpaying the vendor for goods received. This includes paying for more items than were received, paying a higher price than normal, or paying full price for inferior goods. Once again, an effective means of detecting this type of fraud is the matching of contract, inventory, and invoice data. The inventory levels would be less than the invoice amounts or the price paid would be higher than on the contract. Inferior goods should show a higher defect or failure rate.

A third type of purchasing fraud involves the payment of more than one invoice for the same receipt of goods and services. The vendor submits two invoices for the same item, and the employee processes both invoices for payment. A simple search for duplicate invoices is a good starting point for this type of fraud. Totaling the goods ordered, received, and invoiced—by contract number—would also highlight the existence of duplicate payments, even if the vendor had more than one vendor number.

Symptoms of Purchasing Fraud

Not all symptoms of fraud are readily visible when using CAATTs, but CAATTs are the most effective weapon in finding fraud. Exhibit 9.4 shows an example of purchasing fraud symptoms.

Kickbacks

A "kickback" is the receipt of monetary or other payment by an employee from a vendor in exchange for directing business to that vendor. It is a

EXHIBIT 9.4   Purchasing Fraud Symptoms.

Concern	Symptom
Photocopied invoices	Searching for the same invoice number or the same list of goods as well as verifying that the goods have been received and comparing the amount on the invoice with the contract amount. (This can highlight invoices that are photocopied.)
Altered invoices	Invoices that have been tampered with, such as sections that have been whited out and typed over, can be highlighted by searching for duplicate invoice numbers, comparing the amount of the invoice with the contract file, and checking for invoice numbers that do not follow the vendor's usual numbering pattern.
Vendors not doing business with anyone else	These can be found by searching for consecutive invoice numbers from the same vendor. Keep in mind that small, specialized vendors may have legitimate reasons for issuing sequential invoices to one customer.
Inconsistent invoice numbers from the same vendors	These can be found by sorting on vendor number and invoice number, and examining the first and last few invoice numbers for each vendor. Typically these would involve different numbers of digits. A change in the vendor's accounting system can also lead to a false positive.
Contracts that fall just below the threshold for review or approval	These cases can be found by stratifying the contract amount and setting intervals or ranges to identify contracts just under key financial limits. Specific instances can be found by filtering records based on the contract amount.
Splitting of contracts to avoid financial limits	Isolate cases by searching for multiple contracts raised with the same vendor on the same day, where the total contract amount is greater than key financial limits.
More than one vendor with the same address and phone number	Identify these by searching for duplicate vendors based on address, zip code (postal code), or phone number.
Fictitious vendors	Tests for fictitious vendors include: • Searching for post office boxes as addresses by setting a filter to identify records with "P.O. Box" or "Post Office Box" in the address field. • Joining records from the vendor table and employee file to search for a match between vendor and employee addresses

EXHIBIT 9.4 *(Continued)*

Concern	Symptom
	• Searching for vendor names such as "Mr.," "Mrs.," ".," "Cash," "The Bearer," or any name that can be easily altered to make the check payable to someone else.
	• Isolating vendors and employees with the same phone number, by matching the vendor table and employee file on the phone number field.
	• Searching for 'phonetically' duplicate vendor names—vendors with similar sounding names but slightly different spellings.
	• Isolating vendors with no phone number.
	• Setting up a filter 'if contact name is blank' to find vendors with no contact name.
	• Searching for common generic company names like Acme Ltd or ABC Corp.
	• Searching for vendors only serviced by one contracting officer or A/P clerk.

common type of fraud in the purchasing area. The kickback can be paid for any number of activities, including:

- Fixing the bids so the same vendor usually wins.
- Certifying receipt of goods never received.
- Approving payment of duplicate invoices.
- Permitting the substitution of items of lower quality than the ones billed.
- Granting favorable credit terms.
- Paying higher-than-required prices for goods received.
- Paying bills early without obtaining early payment discounts.
- Purchasing more items than required.

The symptoms of kickback activity may include:

- The purchasing agent handles all matters related to a vendor even though it might be outside or below his or her normal duties.
- Only one contracting officer or A/P clerk handles all transactions for the vendor.
- A vendor receives an inordinate amount of business from the company for no apparent business reason.
- A vendor salesperson makes frequent, unexplained visits to the purchasing personnel.
- Management receives tips or complaints from employees or vendors.

A kickback occurs directly between the employee and the vendor, so such payments will not be found on the company's financial system. Evidence of this type of unusual income may exist only in the details of the individual's personal life. For this reason, proof of the existence of kickbacks may be difficult for internal auditors to obtain, and they may have to rely on evidence of favorable treatment to a vendor. However, if the auditor has access to the suspected employee's bank account or can obtain copies of canceled checks, the proof may be more readily available. Regardless of the difficulty of locating such evidence, auditors should be aware of the symptoms of kickbacks, and investigators must follow up where this activity is suspected. Some typical red flags include indications that an employee's lifestyle is higher than usual for the salary, such as the purchase of expensive clothing, jewelry, or vacation trips, excessive gambling, and so on. This may signal either an existing flow of illicit cash or tastes and commitments that create financial pressures that can lead to the commitment of fraudulent acts.

Fixed Bidding

Fixed bidding includes a number of activities designed to favor one contractor over the others, including:

- Key contracts being awarded without a formal bidding process—check for contract type (competitive, standing offer, purchase order, sole-sourced) using summarization.
- Raising contracts that are just below the financial limits for the competitive bidding process, so they can be sole-sourced to a particular contractor—check the range of contract amounts using stratification.
- Contracts being sole-sourced without adequate justification—check summarization by vendor and contracting officer.
- Splitting contracts in order to avoid financial limits that would result in them being subject to the competitive bidding process—check the contract date by vendor to find duplicates where the total is above the financial limit.
- Ensuring that one vendor wins most bids—summarize contract amount by vendor, and compare vendor summaries for several years.
- Arranging so that the last bidder consistently wins the contract—calculate the days between the close for bids and the contract submission date, by vendor.

In addition to fixed bidding, there are other variations of purchasing fraud, each with recognizable symptoms.

Goods Not Received

Tests to indicate that goods were not received include:

- Purchase quantities are not in agreement with the contract quantities—filter/display criteria.
- No change in inventory levels—trend analysis.
- Inventory system levels do not agree with the contract and invoiced levels—join and filter/display criteria.

Duplicate Invoices

Standardize or normalize the invoice number by removing slashes, dashes, blanks, and special characters, and run tests, including:

- Duplicate invoice numbers
- Duplicate date and invoice amounts

Inflated Prices

Tests for inflated prices include:

- Prices from a particular vendor are unreasonably high, when compared to others for the same products—ratio analysis
- An increase in production costs compared to previous years or other plants—trend analysis

Inferior Quality

Tests for inferior quality include:

- Low quality of goods, or services, received from a vendor—higher number of defects
- A higher-than-normal rate of returns or defects—summarization by vendor

Excess Quantities

Tests for excessive quantities include:

- Unexplained increases in inventory—trend analysis
- The purchase quantities for raw materials are not appropriate for production levels—expression/equation
- Increases in quantity ordered compared to previous contracts, years, or plants—trend analysis

CHAPTER 10

Unknown Symptoms of Fraud
(Using Digital Analysis)

B asic techniques, such as the use of filters to find phantom vendors or questionable invoices, can be used to identify many types of exposures or symptoms of fraud in functional areas. In fact, many fraud detection techniques require auditors to look only for known symptoms—that is, items in the data corresponding to a specific kind of fraud risk. A simple application of this technique is the search for duplicate transactions, where the symptoms would be the same invoice number and vendor number. (See Exhibit 10.1.)

Ordinarily, invoice number-vendor number combinations should be unique. Auditors use the known pattern in the data (i.e., same vendor number and invoice number and amount), to highlight possible instances of fraud that should be examined. Auditors must keep in mind that fraud symptoms are only that—symptoms—and should take care to investigate the transactions properly before jumping to conclusions. For example, transactions that look like duplicates may simply be progress payments or equal billing of monthly charges. A more detailed discussion of this technique is offered in the section "Assessing the Completeness of the Data" in Chapter 5.

However, more and more, fraud prevention and detection experts are examining broader patterns in the actual data. This innovative approach is called *digital analysis*. It expands on the previously discussed techniques by identifying suspicious patterns in the data rather than looking for known symptoms of fraud. The rationale is that unexpected patterns can be unknown symptoms of possible fraud. Three advanced techniques for the detection of unknown symptoms are data profiling, ratio analysis, and Benford's Law.

EXHIBIT 10.1   Duplicate Transactions.

Invoice Number	Vendor Number	Amount
129304	A543891	$1,035.71
129304	A543891	$1,035.71

Data Profiling

Data profiling is a series of analysis techniques that examines key numeric fields to identify anomalies (values that fall outside of the norm) and focus attention on specific transactions. For example, a review of corporate purchase card transactions might focus only on large-dollar transactions. Data profiling would help to identify other concerns, such as payments to unusual vendors, purchases for even dollar amounts, bypassing of financial limits, and credit card theft. Data profiling techniques examine 100 percent of transactions and highlight the few that have a higher risk of being fraudulent.

Many data analysis techniques search for specific types of exceptions in the data. We looked at more than a dozen techniques in earlier chapters. However, advanced techniques such as data profiling search for unsuspected symptoms of fraud. Combining several of these techniques can be even more powerful.

Not all data profiling tests can be run using the techniques described in previous chapters, and some will require special scripts to be developed. The techniques should be designed to profile the unique data and be customized to the specific environment. In addition, they should be run on a regular basis in areas of high risk, to detect fraud early, and thereby reduce the amount of the losses.

For example, if auditors are reviewing corporate purchase card transactions, they can profile the transaction amount field to identify:

- The minimum, maximum, average, highest, and lowest 10 transactions
- Ranges of purchase card transaction amounts (0 to 99.99, 100.00 to 299.99, 300.00 to 499.99, etc.)
- The most often recorded amount of purchase card purchases
- Transactions for even dollar amounts ($2,000.00, $7,000.00, etc.)
- The most and least often used vendors or card numbers

Best of all, running data profiling tests regularly makes it possible to reduce losses by detecting fraud in the early stages. An advanced use of data profiling includes the development of a fraud analysis template, allowing the auditor to select the data file to be reviewed, the numeric field to be profiled, and the tests to be run. (See Exhibit 10.2.)

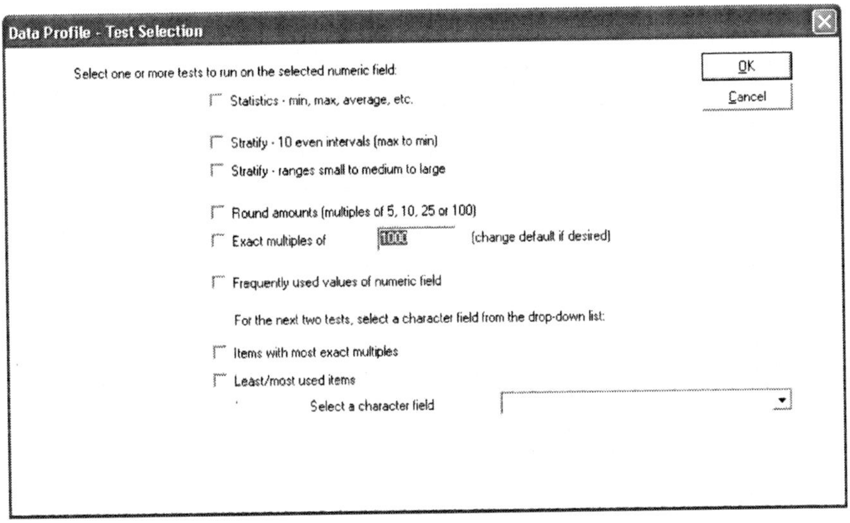

EXHIBIT 10.2 Custom Data Profiling Script.
Source: David Coderre, *Fraud Analysis Techniques Using ACL* (Hoboken, NJ: John Wiley & Sons, 2009). Reprinted with permission.

A more detailed discussion of each data-profiling technique is presented next.

Statistical Analysis

The first test provides a range of basic statistical information and can quickly detect anomalies in numeric fields. It will help to establish a direction for additional audit tests, and so should be run first if possible. The standard statistics command in IDEA or ACL provides details including average value; absolute value; highest and lowest values; number of negative, zero, and positive values; and so on, for any given numeric field. This may quickly highlight possible fraud. One of the advantages of data profiling is that it does not require the auditor to know in advance to look for specific transaction types (e.g., negative inventory receipt values). The statistics test simply reviews and reports on all values of the selected numeric field.

Stratification

Stratification can be used to highlight unknown symptoms by examining all possible ranges, or strata, of key numeric fields. Stratification will report the number of records falling into specified strata, or intervals of the values

EXHIBIT 10.3   Contract Values Analysis.

Amount	Count	Count %	Amount %	Amount
0.00–9,999.99	11,248	97.96%	74.25%	17,175,349.53
10,000.00–19,999.99	124	1.08%	7.65%	1,769,660.28
20,000.00–29,999.99	64	0.56%	6.37%	1,473,722.52
30,000.00–39,999.99	20	0.17%	3.12%	720,991.80
40,000.00–49,999.99	8	0.07%	1.58%	365,092.00
50,000.00–59,999.99	0	0.00%	0.00%	0.00
60,000.00–69,999.99	4	0.03%	1.16%	268,960.00
70,000.00–79,999.99	4	0.03%	1.30%	300,012.11
80,000.00–89,999.99	8	0.07%	2.93%	676,692.56
90,000.00–100,000.00	4	0.03%	1.65%	381,760.00
Total	11,484	100.00%	100.00%	23,132,239.80

of a numeric field, and total the value of one or more numeric fields for each of the strata. For example, stratifying on the field "Contract Amount" will provide the auditor with a summarized view of the different levels of contracts raised. Auditors use this technique to focus their examination on transactions of high materiality, but it can also be used to identify possible symptoms of fraud, such as transactions exceeding a person's financial authority limit, or a high number of returns. (See Exhibit 10.3.)

Given the results in Exhibit 10.3, the auditor might review the contracts with values over $30,000. These 48 contracts represent only 0.40 percent of all contracts raised but account for close to 12 percent of the total value of all contracts. In addition, if the financial limit for sole-sourcing is $50,000, then the 20 contracts for more than this amount would be of particular interest to auditors. The use of a stratification of amounts can highlight anomalies as well as values just over, or under, key financial limits.

Frequently Used Values

The next technique used when profiling a numeric field is to identify values that occur most often. There may be reasons for certain numbers to occur more often than others, such as price breaks, multiple purchases of the same item, and so on. Apart from such reasons, the frequency distribution of the values of the numeric field (such as purchase card amounts) should be random. However, persons creating fraudulent transactions are often lazy, or not very creative, when making up the amounts for the fraudulent transactions. Often they will use the same amounts over and over again. Thus, frequently used values may be a symptom of possible fraud. (See Exhibit 10.4.)

```
┌─────────────────────────────────────────────────────────────────────┐
│ Data Profile - Frequently Used Values Results                    [X]  │
│                                                                       │
│                                              ┌──────────────────┐     │
│                                              │       OK         │     │
│                                              └──────────────────┘     │
│                                              ┌──────────────────┐     │
│                                              │     Cancel       │     │
│                                              └──────────────────┘     │
│                                                                       │
│    A file, Freq_Used_Num, has been created containing:                │
│                                                                       │
│                                          ┌──────────────────────────┐ │
│         Frequently used values for       │ Order_Qty                │ │
│                                          └──────────────────────────┘ │
│                                                                       │
│                                          ┌──────────────────────────┐ │
│              Most-often-used value       │          4045            │ │
│                                          └──────────────────────────┘ │
│                                                                       │
│                                          ┌──────────────────────────┐ │
│              Number of times used        │           6              │ │
│                                          └──────────────────────────┘ │
│                                                                       │
└─────────────────────────────────────────────────────────────────────┘
```

EXHIBIT 10.4 Frequently Used Value. This custom test result scripted in ACL is similar to the search for duplicate transactions but has a broader application.

This data profiling technique will determine the most frequently used numeric values for the selected field, making it easy to examine, for example, the 78 transactions for $3,140.00 to determine whether they are appropriate. The next step might be to summarize these transactions by general ledger (G/L) account or by vendor to determine if a pattern exists for the 78 transactions. Auditors should also review the second, and third most used values, and so on.

Values that occur infrequently are also potential anomalies. A valuable expansion to this test is to determine the first, second, and third least used values, and so on. The overall results can be used to determine the average number of times values are used and to determine what anomalies should be reviewed.

Even Amounts and Rounding

The next data profiling technique is to identify even dollar amounts, representing numbers that have been rounded up, such as $200.00 or $5,000.00.

The existence of even amounts may be a symptom of possible fraud and should be examined. For example, travel expenses consistently rounded up to the daily maximums deserve audit attention.

The modulus or MOD() function can easily identify these types of even numbers. For example: MOD(Amount,100) = 0 will identify transactions that are a multiple of 100, such as $300.00 and $700.00, and also $1,200 and $25,000, but would not identify transactions with amounts of $200.23, or $1250.00. MOD(Amount,1000) = 0 will identify transactions with amounts that are multiples of 1,000, such as $27,000, but would not identify transactions with amounts of $500.00 or $22,100.00. Keep in mind that certain types of goods and services (such as consulting fees) are normally rounded. So rounding by itself is not a definite indicator of fraud. The key is to find rounding where it is not expected.

Case Study: Maxed-Out Meals

Travel expenses had always been a concern for the auditors as the controls were weak. Employees had a maximum per diem rate when traveling but had to submit actual receipts to cover the expenses. Maximums were also established for meals: Breakfast $10, Lunch $20, and Dinner $30, and $150 for Hotels. The auditors identified transactions that were multiples of $10 and compared them to the manual receipts to ensure that the amounts expensed were appropriate. The manual review determined that some people were charging the maximum rates for meals and hotels even though the receipts did not justify the amounts.

Scheme:	Overcharge on travel claims
Symptoms:	Always claims the maximum; claim twice on same day
Data Requirements:	Travel Expenses—employee number, amount, type (breakfast, lunch, dinner)

Note: A variation would be to find the percentage of expenses that were at their maximums and review employees with the largest percentage.

Least/Most Used Categories

The last data profiling technique to be discussed here is the identification of the least/most used category. For example, in accounts payable, it is easy to identify the least- and most-used vendor accounts. The aim is to highlight frequently and infrequently used expense categories.

Data Profile - Least/Most Used Results ☒

A file, Freq_Used_Character, has been created containing:

[OK]

[Cancel]

Least/most used | Vendor

Least used   Most used

| Alternative Life Styles Shop | | General Office Supplies |

Number of times used   Number of times used

| 1 | | 1,425 |

EXHIBIT 10.5 Frequently Used Character.

Using a purchase card example, it is easy to determine the most and least often used suppliers. A review of the suppliers at either end of the spectrum (least used—most used) can often be very revealing. In addition, running the test each month allows the auditor to establish trends (normal patterns) in the data, making anomalies even easier to identify.

In a very large file of accounts, there may be thousands of suppliers that have only ever been used once. This is normal, as most organizations have a variety of one-time needs during the course of a year. However, this fact may also attract a fraudster looking for ways to conceal a phony transaction. The test does not take long to run, and the results can be reviewed quite quickly. (See Exhibit 10.5.)

In the screenshot in Exhibit 10.5, one might have expected General Office Supplies to be a commonly used supplier when examining purchase card expenses. However, 7,740 times is enough that perhaps the company should be requesting volume discounts from General Office Supplies. Meanwhile, the two transactions at Alternative Life Styles Shop might not be for office supplies, and should be reviewed to ensure that they are valid expenses.

Ratio/Variance Analysis

When auditors want to assess a company's performance over time or compare a company to others like it, a favored strategy is the use of financial ratios like debt to equity, inventory turnover, or return on investment. These give indications about the relative health of the company and any upward or downward trends.

A fraud detection ratio is a similar kind of tool. As with financial ratios, it is used to search for sudden changes or disturbing trends. One critical difference is that fraud ratios are often built from a single data source, such as an accounts payable file, rather than from separate data files. Ratio analysis is perhaps the single most powerful analytical technique in fraud detection because it can highlight anomalies in files containing millions of records. Four commonly employed ratios are:

1. Highest value to lowest value (max/min)
2. Highest value to next highest (max/max2)
3. Current year to previous year (yr1/yr2)
4. One business area to another (area1/area2)

Maximum/Minimum

The existence of a high ratio for a given organizational unit can pinpoint a fraud. For example, auditors concerned about prices paid for a product could calculate the ratio of the maximum sales price (unit cost) to the minimum sales price for each product number. If the ratio is close to 1, then they can be sure that there is not much variance between the highest and lowest prices.

However, if the ratio is large, this could be an indication that a customer was charged too much or too little for that product. Simply comparing the normal sales price to the transactions for the highest and lowest charges will determine if a customer was overcharged (largest sales price was greater than the normal price) or a customer was undercharged (lowest sales price was less than the normal price). (See Exhibit 10.6.)

Product 1 has a large difference in the unit price between the maximum and minimum (ratio of 1.85), whereas Product 2 has a smaller variance in the prices (ratio of 1.01). Audit should review the transactions for the customers charged $235 and $127 for Product 1 to ensure the proper payments were made.

EXHIBIT 10.6   Product Maximum/Minimum Ratios.

Product Line	Max	Min	Ratio
Product 1	235	127	1.85
Product 2	289	285	1.01

EXHIBIT 10.7   Customer Max/Max2 Ratios.

Customer	Max	2nd Highest	Ratio	Count
XYZ Corp.	$100,080	$16,068	6.23	203
ABC Corp.	$103,429	$101,210	1.02	481

Charging less than the standard sales price may be a symptom of favorable treatment of a customer for kickbacks. Overcharges may be frauds committed to cover the losses in another area or to benefit the organization and "earn" a sales bonus.

A similar analysis could be performed on the prices paid for products. Paying abnormally high unit prices for products may be a symptom of kickbacks in the contracting area.

Maximum/Second Highest

The expected ratio values will vary depending on the field analyzed. While ratios for price variations for a product should be low, ratios in the accounts receivable area for the maximum/minimum customer invoice amounts may easily be 10.0 or higher. In this case, the ratio maximum to the second highest value may be more revealing.

The ratio of the maximum to the second-highest value (max/max2) can also highlight possible frauds. For example, examining the pattern of payments made to vendors can be revealing. In this case, a large ratio could indicate an anomaly in the data. (See Exhibit 10.7.)

A large ratio indicates that the maximum value is significantly larger than the second highest value. Max/Max2 ratios of 5.0 and higher would likely be of interest to auditors and fraud investigators, as they represent significant deviations from the norm. Unexplained deviations could be symptoms of fraud. In the last example, 202 invoices from XYZ were for an amount less than or equal to $16,068 and only one was for more ($100,080).

Current/Previous

The third technique calculates the ratio of one year to another (yr1/yr2). Again, unexplained variances can be symptoms of waste, abuse, or fraud. For example, G/L accounts that are no longer used will be revealed if charges are suddenly coded to them. This may be a symptom of a fraud that is being hidden in dormant or infrequently used accounts. (See Exhibit 10.8.)

The closer the ratio is to 1.000, the less variance there is between the amounts coded to the G/L account in the two years. Accounts showing large

EXHIBIT 10.8   G/L Account: Previous/Current Year Ratio.

G/L Account	FY 2002	Fy 2003	Ratio for FY02/FY03
Bonuses	$12,885	$125	103.080
Travel	$50,012	$52,190	0.983
Spec Purpose	$16	$14,081	0.001

or small ratios should be examined to discover the cause. For example, the low ratio of fiscal year (FY) 2002/FY 2003 (0.001) for the G/L—Special Purpose indicates that FY 2003 has significantly more charges to that G/L than FY 2002. The high ratio (103.080) for G/L—Bonuses indicates that the amount charged was much higher in FY 2002 than in FY 2003.

Choosing a context for current/previous analysis can be important. If activities are highly seasonal and trending upward, it may be more helpful to compare a quarter's worth of data to the same quarter in the previous year.

One Business Area/Another

The ratio of two operational areas can also highlight anomalies that may be symptoms of fraud. For example, the ratios of two manufacturing plants would be of interest if one or more of the ratios were significantly different from the other ratios.

In Exhibit 10.9, the high ratio of prepaid expenses (4.34) and the low result for receivables (1.16) should be reviewed by auditors to determine the cause.

Even if an auditor has never run a ratio analysis before, the results will be immediately useful. The technique allows auditors to focus on anomalies without having to establish predetermined or historical cutoffs. The power of ratio analysis lies in the ability of computer-assisted audit tools and techniques (CAATTs) to perform the many calculations necessary to determine

EXHIBIT 10.9   Comparison of Operational Areas.

Account	Plant 1	Plant 2	Ratio
Prepaid Expenses	127,643	29,407	4.34
Receivables	344,775	297,217	1.16
Inventories	901,417	492,920	1.83
Investment	8,217	4,124	1.99
Cash	156,062	77,497	2.01
Prop/Plant/Equip	634,849	343,446	1.85
Other Def Charges	4,221	2,099	2.01

the required ratios for every customer, vendor, or product. The anomaly is identified because it is different for the other values for the given entity (customer, vendor, or product). However, ratio analysis becomes increasingly effective when it is repeated over long periods. Against an established historical background, sudden changes in ratios will stand out more clearly. Knowledge of historical trends will speed up the identification of important anomalies.

The calculation of all four ratios—max/min, max/max2, yr1/yr2, and area1/area2, all for the same file—gives an additional level of refinement to the analysis, helping to focus attention on areas of even higher risk.

Case Study: Doctored Bills

The auditors reviewed the patient billing system to determine if the appropriate charges were being assessed to the patient's healthcare providers. Although there was no fixed price per procedure, it was expected that the billed prices would not vary too much.

An initial analysis of the data was performed to calculate the ratio of the highest and lowest charges for each procedure. The auditing standards required that procedures with a ratio of highest to lowest (max/min) greater than 1.30 be noted and further reviewed. During this particular quarter, three procedures had ratios that were higher, the highest being 1.42.

A filter was set to identify the records related to the three procedures, and additional analysis was performed. This quickly determined that one doctor was charging significantly more than the other doctors for the same procedures. However, a comparison of the charges from the billing system with the payments recorded in the accounts receivable system revealed that the amount recorded in the receivable system was in line with the usual billing amount for the procedures. The doctor was unable to justify the higher prices or explain the difference in the billing and the receivable systems. Finally, the doctor admitted to skimming some of the payment received.

Scheme:	Overbilling
Symptoms:	Higher rates for certain procedures
Data Requirements:	Medical bills—patient, date, procedure, doctor, amount. Accounts receivable—invoice number, patient, procedure, doctor, amount.

Case Study: Contracting Kickbacks

Johnathan, one of the contracting officers, had devised a great scheme. It benefited him and the companies that were willing to do business under his conditions. Companies that were not willing to provide him with a little extra would not get the contract.

The auditors decided to use digital analysis as part of their review of the contracting section. One of the analyses calculated the total contract amount by vendor for each of the past two years. A ratio of current year to previous year (yr1/yr2) was calculated for each vendor, and statistical analysis was used to look at the minimum, maximum, average, and highest and lowest five ratios. While the average was close to 1.0, the highest and lowest five values showed that some companies had significant decreases in business while others had experienced significant increases.

The auditors reviewed the details for all companies that had a previous year to current year ratio of less than 0.7 or more than 1.30. The detailed records were extracted to a file, and totals were summarized by contracting officer. For companies that had seen an increase in business, the results revealed that Johnathan had raised many of the contracts. In comparison, he had raised no contracts with the companies that had seen a decrease in business. The auditors learned of Johnathan's kickback scheme when they interviewed salespeople from the companies that had ratios less than 0.7. Interviews with salespeople from the firms that had increased sales by 1.30 or more added credence to the fraud accusations. Neither group of firms liked the arrangement, so they were happy to cooperate with auditors during their investigation.

Scheme:	Kickbacks
Symptoms:	Increases in business over three years—same contracting officer
Data Requirements:	A/P—three years—vendor, date, amount, contracting officer

Case Study: Dormant but Not Forgotten

The teller thought that no one would notice a few small withdrawals from accounts that had been dormant for years. He figured that the owners of the accounts had either forgotten about the money or had died—either way, they wouldn't miss it. So one week he removed a few hundred dollars from seven previously dormant accounts. Given that the bank had over 12,000 savings accounts and an even greater number of checking accounts, a manual review of the month's transactions was out of the question. What the teller did not realize was that the auditors were using data analysis to monitor these accounts. The application of CAATTs allowed the auditors to find all accounts with no activity in the previous month but activity in the current month.

The monthly ratio analysis compared the total withdrawals for the current and previous month for all accounts in which the total of the current month's withdrawals was also greater than $0.00. Then all accounts with a ratio (previous_month/current_month) equal to 0.00 were reviewed in detail. Truly dormant accounts would be filtered out, since the current month's withdrawals would be 0.00. However, since the accounts the teller was taking money from had been dormant, the ratio (previous/current) was always 0.00. For example, if he took $125.00 from one account, the ratio would be $0/125 = 0$; and if he took $75 from another account, the ratio would be $0.00/75.00 = 0$. All accounts with a ratio of 0 were flagged and the date of the last activity determined. Thanks to the vigilance of the auditors, the teller was caught at the end of the first month of his scheme.

Scheme:	Theft from dormant accounts
Symptoms:	Activity on dormant accounts
Data Requirements:	Bank withdrawals—account number, date, amount, teller

Benford's Law

More advanced techniques take data analysis to another level, examining the actual frequency of the digits in the data. Benford's Law, proposed by Frank Benford in 1938, makes predictions on the occurrence of digits in the data. Benford's Law concludes that the first digit of each transaction in a large number of transactions (10,000 plus) will be a "1" more often than a "2"; and "2" more often than a "3." In fact, the likelihood of the first digit taking on a value decreases as the value of the digit increases. Benford calculated that the first digit will be a "1" about 30 percent of the time, whereas "9" has an expected frequency of less than 5 percent as the first digit.[1]

Benford's Law calculates the expected frequencies (rounded to three decimal places) for first and second digits as shown in Exhibit 10.10.

EXHIBIT 10.10   Benford's Law: First- and Second-Digit Frequencies.

Digit	Frequency (First Digit)	Frequency (Second Digit)
0	–	0.120
1	0.301	0.114
2	0.176	0.109
3	0.125	0.104
4	0.097	0.100
5	0.079	0.097
6	0.067	0.093
7	0.058	0.090
8	0.051	0.088
9	0.046	0.085

However, not all data will have distributions as predicted by Benford's Law. Sometimes there are valid reasons for certain numbers occurring more frequently than expected. For example, if a company sends a large of amount of correspondence via courier, and the cost is a standard rate ($6.12) for sending a package of under one pound, then the first digit "6" or the first two digits "61" may occur more often than predicted by Benford's Law. Guidelines for deciding whether the data will comply with the law include:

- There should be no set maximum or minimum (although a minimum of zero is acceptable).
- There should be no price break points, such as $6.12 for all packages under one pound, and $7.13 for between one and two pounds.
- The numbers should not be assigned, such as policy numbers, Social Security numbers, or telephone numbers.
- The more diverse the data, the better (e.g., rent checks paid to a large real estate company will not have as wide a range of values as the company's full accounts payable file).

Given Benford's Law, valid, unaltered data is expected to follow the predicted frequencies. Data that meets the listed criteria but fails to follow the expected frequencies may include fraudulent amounts.[2]

An analysis of the frequency distribution of the first or second digits can detect abnormal patterns in the data and may identify possible frauds. An even more focused test uses the frequency distribution of the first two digits (FTD). The formula for the expected frequencies is:

$$\text{Expected FTD Frequency} = \log(1 + 1/\text{FTD})$$

Therefore, the expected frequency of "13" is log(1 + 1/13). The expected frequencies range from 0.041 for "10" to 0.004 for "99."

Analyzing data for significant variance from Benford's predicted values can highlight many types of fraud. Take a simple case where the fraudster is manipulating amounts by changing the first digit of the amount from a "1" to a "4" or "7" or "9." This will increase the value of the transaction and so benefit the fraudster. However, in each case, the digit "1" is being changed to a digit that occurs less frequently according to Benford's Law. (See Exhibits 10.11 and 10.12.)

Case Study: Signing Authority

The auditors were investigating possible fraud in the contracting section, where thousands of contracts were raised every month. They used Benford's Law to examine the first two digits of the contract amount. The results of their analysis revealed that the initial digits "49" appeared in the data more often than expected.

A summary by contracting officer, for all contracts with "49" as the first two digits determined that the contracting manager was raising contracts for amounts in the range $49,000 to $49,999 to avoid contracting regulations. Contracts under $50,000 could be sole-sourced; contracts $50,000 or higher had to be submitted to the competitive bidding process. He was raising contracts just under the financial limit and directing them to a company owned by his wife.

Schemes:	Contracting officer bypasses limits and directs contracts.
Symptoms:	Amounts just under financial limits
Data Requirements:	Contracting—vendor, date, amount, contracting officer

---

Digital analysis is an advanced application of data analysis for auditors and fraud investigators interested in preventing and detecting fraud. In fact, using digital analysis, fraud symptoms are easier to find when there are millions of transactions than where there are only a few thousand transactions. The patterns in the data become more obvious and focus added attention on the fraud. Investigators can use these data patterns to develop a "fraud profile" early in their review of operations. Through the identification and understanding of these patterns, fraud can be discovered. The patterns can function as auditor-specified criteria; and transactions identified by the

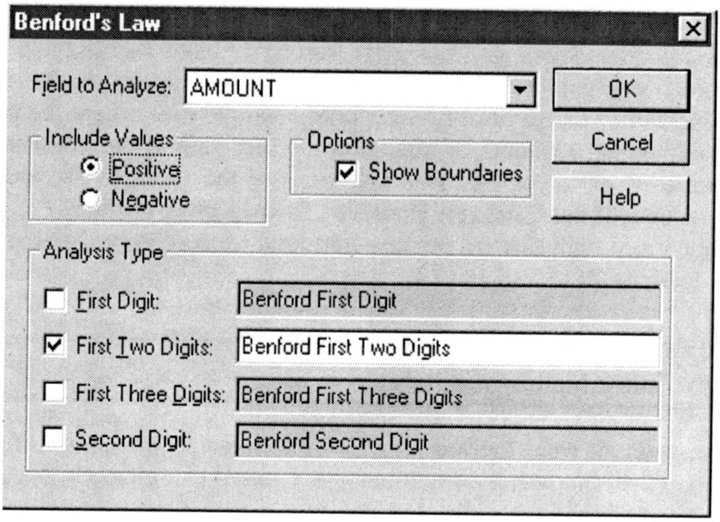

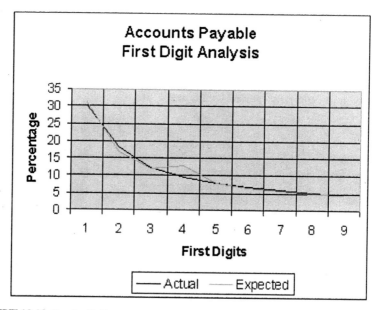

EXHIBIT 10.11 Benford's Law.

EXHIBIT 10.12 Benford's Law: Accounts Payable.

Note: Both IDEA and ACL have a Benford analysis command that will calculate the actual frequency distributions and compare these to the Benford-predicted frequencies. Note that Benford's Law applies to all currencies.

fraud profile can trigger auditor reviews. The profiles and user-defined criteria permit the investigator to focus the review on higher-risk areas. Systems can even be built to monitor transactions on an ongoing basis, as a proactive approach to the early detection of fraud.

Notes

1. Ted Hill, "The First-Digit Phenomenon," *American Scientist* (July-August 1998): 358–363.
2. Mark J. Nigrini, *Digital Analysis Using Benford's Law* (Vancouver, BC: Global Audit Publications, 2000).

CHAPTER 11

Automating the Detection Process

The ability to analyze data and find anomalies makes the computer ideally suited to the detection of fraud, but data analysis software affords other benefits that contribute to the decision to implement computer-assisted audit tools and techniques (CAATTs). In particular, specific analyses that work well and are useful to auditors can be saved in a script and run when desired. This can save the auditor time and ensure that the very same analysis is performed again. Scripts can be used to analyze similar information at different times or at different locations. The use of saved routines can make the investigation process faster and more efficient—given that the same set of commands can be issued during the next investigation or used to proactively look for fraud in other areas.

Further, scripts allow auditors to share their analysis techniques, increasing the efficiency and effectiveness of the entire audit department and ensuring consistency of analysis.

Scripts can also be designed to be interactive, where the user of the script is prompted for information that will complete the processing of the routine. For example, a script testing for duplicates may prompt for the name of the input file, and the field to be used to test for duplicate records. (See Exhibit 11.1.)

The results of the tests can be saved in a file, output to the screen, or both.

Scripts are a powerful method of using CAATTs in a controlled environment, to ensure consistency of application. In addition, running the same script helps to ensure the integrity of the results.

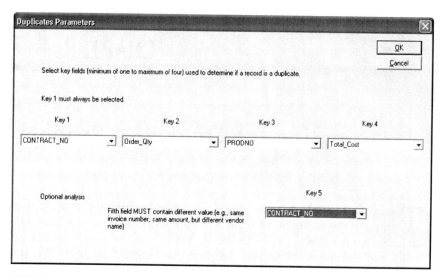

EXHIBIT 11.1 Duplicate Parameters. Since interactive scripts can be developed to prompt the user for each required input, users with limited knowledge of analysis software still can perform useful tests.

Source: David Coderre, *Fraud Analysis Techniques Using ACL*, (Hoboken, NJ: John Wiley and Sons, 2009). Reprinted with permission.

Case Study: Ex-Employees Still Paid

The company was going through a period of rapid growth, coupled with high turnover of staff. This meant that every month there were hundreds of new employees being added to the payroll and almost as many employees leaving. The auditors had reviewed the controls to ensure that ex-employees were no longer being paid and that new employees received their proper rate of pay. The review indicated that the volume of people being added and removed from the payroll system created a risk of continuing to pay ex-employees or paying new employees for periods prior to their actual employment date.

The auditors had performed a detailed review almost one year ago, creating tests to compare the personnel system and the payroll system to identify instances of improper payment. The tests were saved in a script and were now run every quarter. The analysis had successfully identified both types of payroll errors—with limited work being required from the auditors. The payroll supervisor was so impressed that she asked to have access to the test so she could run it every pay period, before the checks were released. This meant that erroneous checks could be removed from the system before they were mailed out.

Scheme: Timing issues in HR/Payroll systems
Symptoms: Employees paid before start or after end date
Data Requirements: Payroll—employee number, date, rate, amount.
                       HR—employee number, start date, end date,
                       rate, amount.

Fraud Applications or Templates

Scripts can also be used to develop fraud templates, in effect small self-contained applications, to carry out tests for fraud. These scripts can be run proactively to prevent fraud or detect it early. Scripts that analyze the corporate data for specific symptoms of fraud, and are run periodically, can help focus audit or investigative resources.

Symptoms based on exposures can be developed for each functional area, such as payroll, asset management, and so on. (See Exhibit 11.2.)

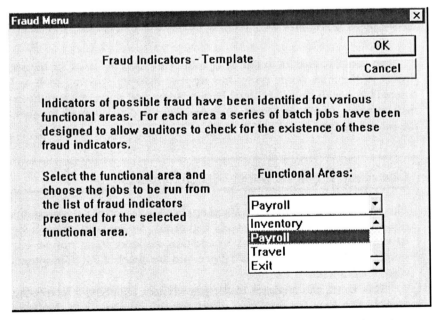

EXHIBIT 11.2 Fraud Menu. Auditors and fraud investigators can select the scripts to be run and test for the existence of fraud symptoms. This example is from a custom template written using ACL.

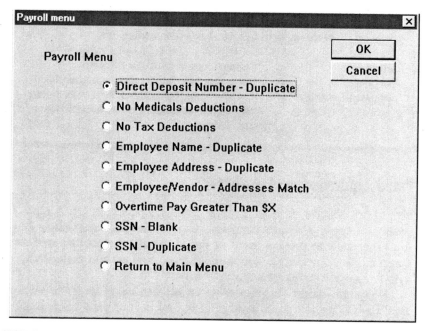

EXHIBIT 11.3 Payroll Menu. A template can then direct the auditor to a menu of tests relating to the specific area (from the same custom ACL template as in Exhibit 11.2).

The identification of fraud symptoms can then be used to trigger a review of the area. Some symptoms may be industry specific, such as incompatible health claims, such as hysterectomy and male; other symptoms may be more generic in nature, such as duplicate direct deposit number in the payroll system. (See Exhibit 11.3.)

Case Study: Duplicate Direct Deposit Numbers

The auditors had developed a fraud application for several departments of the company to monitor areas of higher risk. Scripts were run weekly to identify symptoms of fraud. In addition, auditors could run ad hoc queries against the data and drill down into the details if fraud symptoms were encountered.

This week, the analyses in the payroll area highlighted interesting results. The tests for duplicate direct deposit numbers and duplicate employee addresses had identified a potential problem. A programmer in the payroll department, responsible for the benefits system, had been identified by the duplicate test. The additional review determined that while he should not have had access to the payroll system, he was able to create three ghost employees and direct their pay to his bank account.

A stop payment was issued immediately and the employee was questioned. The proactive use of CAATTs to look for fraud symptoms meant that the auditors were able to detect, and even prevent, the fraud.

Scheme:	Programmer creates employees and directs their pay to his account.
Symptoms:	Duplicate direct deposit numbers
Data Requirements:	Payroll—employee number, date, rate, amount, direct deposit number. HR—employee number, address, start date, end date, rate, amount.

Case Study: Purchase Cards

The use of purchase cards in ABC Corp. was seen to be a positive move toward decentralization for small purchases and an improvement in efficiency in the accounts payable (A/P) area. However, the introduction of purchase cards brought a different set of risks that needed to be considered. Two main things happened to cause internal auditors to become concerned. The first was a front-page news story about the abuses of purchase cards by municipal employees in the city where ABC's headquarters was located. The second was specific allegations of improper purchase card use within ABC Corp. These two things resulted in both management and internal audit having concerns about the controls over the use of purchase cards. Additionally, internal audit was interested in assessing the degree to which the use of purchase cards had been effectively encouraged as a cost-saving and efficiency issue in the A/P area.

A quick review of appropriate policies and the control framework highlighted the fact that there was only limited monitoring being performed by management. Further, since the monitoring was being performed in 10 different divisions, even when applied, it was inconsistent. The review was often of only a small sample of transactions or a manual review of purchase card statements, to look for unusual merchants—a sign of a potential inappropriate purchase.

The auditors identified the main control weaknesses and the areas of highest risk. Next they worked with management to determine the

(continued)

best method to obtain the monthly detailed transaction file from the two banks that issued the purchase cards. Finally, the auditors developed a series of scripts to review purchase card transactions. They also ensured that the scripts could be used by both the national card coordinator and the divisional card coordinators, to perform continual monitoring of purchase card transactions after the investigation was completed.

Some of the tests were run monthly—for example, cash advances, because of the higher inherent risk—while others were run on a quarterly basis. (See Exhibit 11.A.)

Purchase Card Tests	✕
Purchase Card Menu	OK
	Cancel
☐ Transportation expenses	☐ High credit amounts
☐ Hotel expenses	☐ Split purchases
☐ Questionable expenses	☐ Duplicate purchases
☐ Weekend purchases	☐ Even multiples
☐ Top 10 amounts	☐ Invalid card number
☐ Purchase great than limit	☐ Cardholer not an emplyee
☑ Execute all tests	

EXHIBIT 11.A Purchase Card Tests. Interactive scripts make it easy to import the current month's detailed transactions for each card, transform the multiple-record-type text file into a usable database, and select which tests are to be run.

The tests searched for high-risk transactions including potential personal expenses (food, entertainment, jewelry, etc); car rentals; hotels; airlines; gasoline and car maintenance; purchases on the weekend; and so on. There was also a test that looked for duplicate transactions and another that searched for possible split transactions to avoid financial limits. In addition, the auditors also examined the span of control (number of cards per approving authority) and percentage utilization of purchase cards (compared to invoices), and tested for cards being used by persons who had left the organization.

A number of the tests for high-risk transactions used the merchant category code that is assigned to each merchant by the credit card companies. Other tests used the day of week, statistical analysis, and trends or advanced digital analysis techniques. The output of the high-risk tests was individual files by cardholder that were forwarded via e-mail to the cardholders. Each cardholder was asked to provide sufficient documentation to justify the highlighted purchases.

The introduction of an automated series of tests greatly improved the control framework and reduced the risks involved in operating a purchase card system. Further, the development of scripts to monitor purchase cards removed a significant manual review burden and provided for easy monitoring across all divisions. It also formed an important control to ensure the proper and effective use of purchase cards as the preferred method of payment for amounts under $5,000. Finally, ABC Corp. now has a consistent, easy-to-use method for monitoring purchase card expenses for compliance and for known and unknown risks. The scripts continue to be refined as additional areas of risk are identified, tests are improved, and the number of false positives are reduced.

Scheme:	Inappropriate transactions using corporate purchase cards
Symptoms:	Unusual vendors, split purchases, duplicates, weekend purchases, and so on
Data Requirements:	Purchase card—card number, cardholder, transaction date, merchant, merchant category code, amount

Fraud Application Development

Several steps should be taken when developing a fraud template, or fraud application, including:

- Analyze the control framework to identify areas of greatest risk.
- Review the list of possible risks, including SAS 99, *Consideration of Fraud in a Financial Statement*, and SIAS 3, *Deterrence, Detection, Investigation and Reporting of Fraud*.
- Identify the symptoms related to these risks—how would possible frauds be recorded in the data.

* Develop scripts to test for symptoms of fraud.
* Crate a template to control the running of the individual tests.
* Determine a frequency schedule for the running of the scripts.
* Run the tests and review the results.
* Verify to source.

Fraud templates are an extension of the script concept, developed to provide additional control and management over the submission of analysis jobs.

In conclusion, we all face more challenges because of the changing business environment and the increased use of technology. But these same factors provide new tools and techniques. To combat fraud, everyone should consider the applicability of data analysis software as another tool to be carried in his or her toolbox.

CHAPTER 12

Verifying the Results

Fraud investigations are much more damaging to people's reputations than audits. With an audit, the client has an opportunity to comment on the accuracy of the findings before the report is released. However, if the results of a fraud investigation are not carefully guarded, the allegations can ruin a person's reputation and open the organization to possible lawsuits. The analysis of data to identify symptoms of fraud does just that—identifies symptoms of fraud. It is important to drill down into the data and examine the details. Wherever possible, auditors should obtain and safeguard the original source documentation.

The data will tell investigators where to look; the source documentation will provide the evidence. The canceled check with the perpetrator's signature, the phony invoice, the shipping bill with the inventory manager's address, even the fingerprints on the hotel receipts are the evidence that can make a case.

Confirmation Letters

It is a common technique to send letters or e-mails to customers, policy-holders, and so on, asking them to confirm the information contained in the corporate information system. In the past, this usually required the auditor to obtain a printout of the details for each customer, manually prepare a letter with the detailed information, and address it to the customer. Modern audit software automates this time-consuming task by extracting all the re-quired information and creating and addressing the confirmation letters. A confirmation letter or e-mail, individualized for each customer, with proper salutation, address, and account details—even including the mailing labels or printed envelopes—can be produced by audit software with minimal auditor time or effort. The process can be further automated by saving the required commands in a script that can be run again and again.

Information, such as name, address, and outstanding balance, is exported to a Word or WordPerfect file. Next, the word processing software is used to create the primary file and to merge it with the primary file with the detailed customer information. Some audit software can also automatically create and send e-mail messages, with the account details contained in an attachment.

Case Study: Credit Cards

Audit had set up a program to record credit card transactions for accounts that had not been used for two or more years prior to the current transaction period. The rationale for the surveillance of these accounts was that if the customer had not used a store account for two years, the current transaction had a high likelihood of being fraudulent. There were three possible scenarios:

1. Someone in the store's credit department was fraudulently charging items to dormant accounts.
2. The customer's card had been stolen and was being fraudulently used.
3. The customer had resumed using the credit card.

The details for these transactions were extracted from the credit card transactions database on a daily basis and combined with the customer master file. Audit software was then used to create personalized confirmation letters and envelopes, addressed to each of the cardholders. In cases where the customer had internal accounts, an e-mail was created. The letter or e-mail contained detailed information about the credit card transactions, including the date, store location, description, and amount of the purchases.

Two weeks after starting to run the credit card verification report for dormant accounts, several confirmation letters came back "Addressee unknown," and one came back with a note from the customer stating that she had not used her credit card for some time. The auditors reviewed the details for these transactions and discovered that the same clerk had processed them all. The clerk worked in the credit section but was also a part-time cashier. When interviewed, he admitted to charging items to dormant customer accounts, but claimed that he had planned to pay for the items as soon as his vacation pay arrived. Management used his vacation pay for that purpose and part of his severance check as well. Audit continued to verify charges against dormant accounts as a deterrent against fraud and theft.

Scheme: Theft from dormant accounts
Symptoms: Sudden activity on dormant accounts
Data Requirements: Transactions—account number, date, amount, clerk.
                         Customer—account number, customer name, address.

Case Study: Accounts Received?

Ivy, the accounts receivable (A/R) clerk of a retail store, had a great deal of responsibility and authority. Not only was she responsible for the receipt and proper coding of customer payments, but she had the authority to write off accounts that had failed to make the proper payments. She also mailed out all of the customer statements and believed that she was terribly underpaid. To compensate for her "meager" salary, she started cashing customer payments.

She devised several schemes to skim money from customer account payments. Most customers did not send cash in the mail, but if they did, she simply took the cash and did not record the payment against the account. When customers paid by check, she used one of two methods. The first method was take the customer check, cash it, and not record the payment. In these cases, she would create a new customer monthly statement to make it look like the payments had been credited to the accounts. The accounting system would still show an account balance higher than the balance reflected on the statement she prepared, but the customer would not know that. The second method was to cash the customer's check and hide the theft by crediting the customer account with the payment—meanwhile debiting a fictitious account she had set up. This meant that the receipts balanced, and the valid customer accounts were correct. Sometime later, she would write off the fictitious account as a bad debt.

The A/R manager had received complaints from customers that their balances were incorrect and decided to ask the auditors to conduct a review. The auditors examined the controls in the A/R department and had serious concerns over the lack of separation of duties, the handling of payments, and other issues. They talked with the manager, and he agreed that an investigation should be undertaken.

(continued)

The auditors followed up with the customers who had complained about incorrect account balances. They determined that close to 60 percent thought they had made a payment but were not sure. Of the remaining 40 percent, 34 percent had sent cash in the mail. The other 6 percent told the auditors that the balance on their statement did not agree with the balance they obtained from the new automated account status system the store had implemented. The system allowed customers to phone in and get their current balance directly, by keying their account number. The auditors asked the customers to send copies of their most recent statements. A review of the statements confirmed the customers' assertions and raised new questions. The statements had not been printed on the standard preprinted form, nor had the usual high-speed laser printer been used. They had been created with a standard office laser printer.

The auditors extended their analysis, selected a sample of customer accounts, and generated confirmation letters, asking customers to verify their balance and the dates and amounts of the last three payments. Confirmation letters were also sent to a directed sample of all customers who had failed to make the minimum payment anytime in the last 12 months. Again, customers responded that their balances were not the same as the amount indicated in the letter. An unexpected benefit of the review: A number of customers who had failed to make the minimum payment included a check with their response to the confirmation letter.

One of the auditors looked at trends in the A/R department and found that the amount written off as bad debts had increased significantly in the last year. An aging, based on the number of days past due, was performed on all accounts that had been written off. The results showed that some accounts had been written off as a bad debt, even though the balance had only been outstanding for three months. The usual period was one year, and even then the accounts were to be written off only after three letters had been sent. A review of the accounts in question showed that not even one reminder letter had been sent. In each case Ivy had been responsible for writing off the bad debt and for creating the customer account.

The auditors presented their finding to the A/R manager. A search of Ivy's desk found blank statement forms, and her PC had a Word template that allowed her to type in customer statements and print them on the blank forms. Finally, a review of the canceled checks supplied by customers with statement balances different than on the accounting system revealed that Ivy had endorsed the checks. They also suspected, but were unable to prove, that Ivy had stolen the cash payments. The data analysis helped the auditor to highlight the perpetrator and obtain the evidence required. When presented with the evidence, Ivy confessed.

Scheme:	Clerk steals payment (or portion thereof); clerk sets up customer accounts and writes off bad debts.
Symptoms:	Customers with paid amount less than minimum were often processed by the same clerk; clerk who set up customer is same as clerk who wrote off bad debt.
Data Requirements:	A/R—customer number, payment, amount due, minimum payment, clerk. Bad debt write-off—customer number, customer name, clerk.

Sampling

Sampling has long been a great tool for auditors, allowing them to examine a subset of the data population, reducing the overall effort required to address audit objectives. The judicious use of sampling improves audit efficiency and effectiveness. However, improper sampling can lead to false conclusions.

One major attraction of software-driven sampling is that it makes existing sampling practices even more efficient and less time-consuming. For example, it may be corporate practice to verify signatures on all contracts or checks with values greater than $100,000 and on a random portion of the remainder. There is little that software can do to automate the final step of looking at the physical documents—even scanning checks or other papers into digital format will not completely eliminate this task. But the process of choosing documents for review can be much improved.

In the precomputer era, sampling would have involved a tedious and uncertain search through the files to find all high-value items, plus a crude sampling technique, such as selecting every tenth item regardless of the dollar amount. But filtering and monetary-unit sampling can ensure that all items above a threshold are reviewed and that all remaining items have a chance of being selected for review that is equal to their proportionate value. The auditor can then be sure that, at the end of the review, x percent of the company's total transactions were in fact reviewed.

There are two main types of sampling: judgmental (or directed) and statistical.

Judgmental or Directed Sampling

Judgmental or directed sampling is the selection of records based on auditor-determined criteria. The use of techniques such as summarization and stratification can help auditors develop a better understanding of the data and provide them with insights into the setting of criteria for judgmental samples. For example:

```
Quantity Received < 0 or Payments > $1M
```

Auditors use their knowledge of the business operations, data, and the risks and exposures to develop criteria to be applied. Assuming proper criteria are used, judgmental sampling can be very effective in uncovering fraud, but it will not necessarily determine the total materiality of the fraud. The errors found in the judgmental sample can only be extrapolated to the entire population as a minimum bound.

Statistical Sampling

Statistical sampling is the selection of items based on mathematical probability. Most audit software supports statistical sampling, including attribute and monetary (dollar unit) sampling, based on fixed or random intervals.

- Attribute sampling treats each record equally, so every record has the same chance of being selected for the sample. It allows the auditor to extrapolate the total number of records in error in the entire population.
- Monetary unit sampling treats each dollar equally, so larger dollar transactions have a higher likelihood of being selected. It allows the auditor to place an upper bound on the dollar amount of the error in the entire population.

Combining judgmental and statistical sampling often can be very effective because it allows the auditor to focus on areas of risk (judgmental sample) and still remain unbiased (statistical sample). Further, the total materiality of the detected fraud can be extrapolated, using the results of the statistical and judgmental samples.

The use of the statistical and judgmental samples will remove any judgmental errors or bias in the selection of items for review. However, care must be used in determining the sample size and selecting the sample transaction.

If only 100 transactions out of a total of 25,000 transactions are fraudulent, the likelihood of detecting the fraud with a sample size of 50 is not large.

One formula for determining the required sample size is:

$$n = N \times (1 - (1 - P)^{1/E})$$

where
n = sample size
N = population size
P = probability
E = number of errors

The probability of selecting an error in the sample is:

$$P = 1 - (1 - n/N)^E$$

Therefore, if there were 100 errors in a population of 25,000 and a sample of 50 was selected, the probability of finding a fraudulent transaction in the select sample is:

$$P = 1 - (1 - 50/25000)^{100} = 18\%$$

However, raising the sample size to 100 increases the probability of finding at least one fraudulent transaction in the sample to 33 percent and a sample size of 200 increases that probability to 55 percent.

Most audit software can calculate the sample size, given the population size, and the confidence level desired by the auditor. The auditor—taking into consideration the strength of the controls, the risk, and level of comfort with the likelihood of the sample containing a fraudulent transaction—should determine the size of the sample selected. At times, the auditor may be willing to accept that there is only an 18 percent chance that the sample will contain a fraudulent transaction. At other times, the auditor may want to increase the likelihood that fraudulent transactions will be sampled.

Sample sizes for fraud investigations will likely be larger, but the resulting workload may be reduced if the auditor is looking for specific evidence of fraud, making the review of the sample records faster.

A final point to keep in mind: The statistical assumptions used to generate the error-estimating equation do not fit very well with highly skewed, logarithmic distributions of actual data—that is, data sets in which there are large numbers of small items, and only a few large ones. Unfortunately, this is very common with financial data (and in fact, this is what causes such data sets to obey Benford's Law).

For example, consider a set of accounts payable transactions in which there are:

100,000 items of less than $100 each
10,000 items in the range $100–999
1,000 items in the range $1,000–9,999
100 items in the range $10,000–99,999
10 items of $100,000 or more in value

If there are 111 errors to be found (roughly 1 per 1,000 items), and we want a confidence level of 95 percent for the entire set of 111,110 items, we want the sample size S to be set according to:

$$0.95 = 1 - (1 - S/111,110)^{111}$$

which makes S = 2,959.

This is already a very substantial amount of work. We will have to review 2.7 percent of the transactions to achieve 95 percent confidence. However, when we examine the individual size strata, we see that this implied level of confidence really applies only to the smallest items, where the majority of errors are found. For example, if we considered only the items from $1,000 through $9,999 in value, we would see that we have 1,000 items, of which just one is expected to be in error. The sample size required to establish 95 percent confidence concerning this subset is given by:

$$0.95 = 1 - (1 - S/1,000)^{1}$$

which makes S = 950!

Sampling 2.7 percent of 1,000 items will give us only 2.7 percent confidence concerning whether there is one error present in this subset. Yet one error in the $1,000 to $9,999 range can be as materially damaging as 100 errors in the under-$100 range. Even more disturbing, the actual error rate is normally unknown, and is unlikely to be uniform across all values. It may be higher than 1 per 1,000, or lower. Thus, after examining 2,959 items in a large, skewed data set, we can have high confidence only about the number of small, individually unimportant errors; about large errors we can say very little.

The problem is that rare items in a data set (such as the handful of high-dollar items) wind up underrepresented by attribute sampling, so errors relating to those rare items stand little chance of being found. Thus, our real level of overall confidence winds up being much lower than indicated by the equation.

The reverse happens when we apply monetary unit sampling. The high-dollar items will tend to be strongly overrepresented, and errors pertaining to low-dollar transactions (which may be important for operating efficiency or other reasons) will have a much lower probability of being caught. Materiality in dollar terms is overemphasized at the expense of other concerns.

Sampling is a complex topic, and the "right" level of statistical confidence varies from one organization or auditor to another. However, there is one rule that should always be followed: When dealing with large, highly skewed data sets, auditors should not rely solely on either attribute sampling or monetary unit sampling. A common compromise is to apply monetary unit sampling above a certain dollar threshold and attribute sampling below it, calculating separate confidence levels for the two parts of the data set. Adjusting for size in this way requires little extra time when using the IDEA or ACL sampling tools and will greatly increase the real confidence level.

Case Study: A Confidence Boost for Management

Management at a medium-size manufacturing firm was very concerned about expenses, which were growing 2 to 3 percent per year faster than revenues. A large one-time audit of the entire accounts payable function was ordered, focusing on operating efficiency as well as fraud. The A/P data for the past 12 months amounted to three million transactions. Using the statistics tool, the team determined that just over 140,000 of these transactions were worth $500 or more, and in total these represented more than half of all expenditures (roughly $1.5 billion). A cutoff point of $500 was therefore established, and sample sizes required for a confidence level of 95 percent were computed separately for the two subsets.

For the 2,860,000 transactions under $500, using attribute sampling and an expected error rate of 1 per 1,000, a sample size of 3,000 was considered sufficient. For the 140,000 large items, a separate sample size of 2,600 was set using monetary unit sampling. The weeks of work involved in manually examining 5,600 individual transactions was considered well worth spending, if it would help identify problems in processing or ongoing frauds.

Eventually, some 24 bad transactions were found out of 5,600 tested. Of these, 19 were from the under-$500 range, and so in themselves they were barely worth the substantial labor cost of finding them. However, they pointed to several systemic problems that management could address:

- The majority of suspect items were paid late, paid twice, or contained processing errors. Changes were made to the training of A/P clerks to reduce the errors and delays, for an eventual savings of $35,000 in interest and $180,000 in other charges each year.
- Six of the small items involved repeated purchases of similar items that should have been consolidated and paid by a single monthly statement. These were just the tip of the iceberg: Searching outside the sample set, the team found more than 3,600 such transactions worth about $1.2 million. The resulting purchasing savings in the following year were at least $250,000.

(continued)

■ Two items were small tools or special materials for the shop floor that were not needed but were bought in duplicate due to poor communications between the purchasing department and engineering. Again this turned out to be representative of a much bigger problem in planning and scheduling.

Overall, management estimated that close to $600,000 per year would eventually be saved due to the "low-value" portion of the audit alone.

The remaining five high-value items represented a more serious problem. They were progress payments for $10,000 to $28,000 made on three different large service contracts where the vendor had not delivered the promised services on time or at all. Upon further investigation, the auditors found that two purchasing officers were receiving kickbacks in exchange for not terminating the nonperforming vendors. The total loss to the company was at least $750,000 per year.

Sadly, the audit could account for only a small portion of the firm's excessive cost growth. However, because of its thoroughness and carefully laid statistical foundation, the audit convinced management that the main causes of that problem did not lay in purchasing fraud or inefficiency in processing.

Scheme:	Inefficiency and fraud in a large database
Symptoms:	Numerous small transactions processed incorrectly and found by attribute sampling, plus a handful of large fraudulent ones found by monetary sampling
Data Requirements:	Accounts payable—amount paid (For purposes of sampling—follow-up investigation requires additional fields.)

Case Study: Sample Inventory

To conduct an analysis over the control of the receipt of goods, the auditors selected a monetary unit sample of inventory records. The sample size of 217 was based on the value of the population and their criteria for an acceptable error amount and confidence level. A sample of receipt records was extracted to a file, and the auditors started their review. The auditors studied the paper-based contracts, shipping bills, inventory records, and physical inventory related to the sampled items. The results established that one of the receiving clerks was using a variety of methods to intercept shipments, either when they arrived at the warehouse or when they were being shipped to project managers. The system controls were so weak that the inventory system could easily be compromised, and the data did not reflect the physical inventory.

Once the auditors identified the symptoms of the fraud schemes, they extracted all transactions meeting the defined criteria for further review. This determined that another clerk, who had left 10 months earlier, was also involved. In fact, interviews determined that the first clerk had taught the second everything he knew, just before he quit.

Scheme:	Clerk intercepts shipments and takes them out of inventory.
Symptoms:	Receipt records do not match actual totals.
Data Requirements:	Inventory receipt records—date, quantity, description, amount paid (Follow-up investigation requires physical count to confirm inventory totals.)

Quality Assurance

The theme that is repeated throughout this book is that CAATTs can significantly improve the investigation into possible frauds. However, care must be taken in applying the results. Initially, the analyses, approaches, and even data may be new to the organization, and the auditors and fraud investigators will still be on a learning curve. As the use of CAATTs increases, quality will remain an important issue, as the analyses will likely become even more complex. A good-quality assurance methodology, and adequate training and support, will help to provide an increased level of comfort and enhance the reliability of the analysis and interpretation of the results.

Simply providing auditors with the data, tools, and necessary training does not guarantee success. Errors in interpretation, logic, downloading, extracting, selecting samples, and so on, can and do occur. The potential for error is high unless the use of CAATTs is properly managed. It is important to perform ongoing quality assurance on the data, the analysis, and the interpretation of results. It would be a shame to go to all the effort of obtaining and analyzing data only to find out that "AND" instead of "OR" had been used when performing the initial extract.

Many factors can affect the validity of the results obtained from data analysis. Data collection, data analysis, and interpretation of results are all subject to their own errors. Although Exhibit 12.1 is not comprehensive, it highlights some of the important factors. (Note that there is overlap between areas.)

EXHIBIT 12.1   Factors Affecting the Reliability of Analysis/Results.

Data

Accuracy	Data contains errors (e.g., G/L Acct, Unit Price)
Completeness	Missing records; required fields not included or blank
Timing	Data from another period included; not all data from current period is included
Appropriateness	Data does not support audit objective (e.g., airline booking data used to determine travel costs—booked is not invoiced)
Definition	Data has not been properly defined, transferred, downloaded and read (e.g., date fields are improperly defined)

Auditor Analysis

Incorrect	Analysis not done properly (e.g., miscalculating dates; not removing duplicates)
Invalid	Analysis does not support audit objective (e.g., using wrong dates to calculate delivery times or interest payments)
Incomplete	Only a partial analysis was performed

Interpretation

Application	Wrong information source for given objective
Data	Data does not support audit objective
Auditor understanding	Insufficient understanding of application; poor understanding of the data; poor understanding of the results; incorrect interpretation of results

Adequacy

Data	Acceptance of data that lacks integrity (completeness, accuracy, and timeliness)
Analysis	Minimal analysis done—no verification of analysis or of data
Interpretation	Overvalues results supporting preconceived ideas; undervalues results not supporting them

Quality Assurance

Source	Failure to challenge/verify source data or extract
Existence	Failure to challenge data, results, and interpretation
Adequacy	Failure to seek advice and assistance

Quality Assurance Methodology

Assuring the reliability of the results requires a proper analysis plan and an assessment of the integrity of the data. Chapter 3 discussed how to develop a plan for the proposed analysis. Chapter 4 discussed how to ensure the integrity of the data.

Introductory-level knowledge of the data analysis software is not enough to ensure the reliability of results—nor is an advanced level of expertise that is not backed up by audit knowledge. Unless auditors know the objectives of the audit project, fully understand the data, are sure of its integrity, properly perform the required analysis, and verify the objectives and data, they cannot rely on the analysis or the interpretation of the results.

The first line of defense against improper results is the auditor performing the analyses. Every auditor has a responsibility to ensure the integrity of the proposed analysis and the validity of the logic employed. The auditor should develop an analysis plan that describes the objective to be addressed and the specific analyses to be performed. Team leaders are responsible for the overall fraud detection plan. They should review the proposed analysis plans and carefully review the results obtained against the planned objectives. The audit manager, as part of the planning process and during the file review toward the end of the audit or investigation, should be concerned with the nature of the analyses and the reasonableness of the results. Management is responsible for ensuring that proper controls to safeguard the data, the integrity of the analysis, and the interpretation of results are in place and are working.

There are three basic types of control: preventive, detective, and corrective. A quality assurance (QA) methodology should contain a mixture of all three types of control:

1. Preventive controls—to reduce the frequency of errors in the analyses performed by auditors and investigators
2. Detective controls—to highlight errors that occur as soon as possible
3. Corrective controls—to assist in identifying and determining the causes of errors in the analysis so they can be eliminated from future analyses

Preventive Controls

The most basic preventive control is knowledge—about the operational area, information system, data, analysis tool, objectives of the investigation, and techniques to be employed. Many audit organizations offer new staff training in audit, but few offer the new auditor any training aimed at understanding the key information systems used by the company. How many audit organizations have a good understanding of the company's financial information system? How many audit organizations are using standard reports developed by outside consultants, without understanding how they work or knowing what types of transactions are being selected, or worse, without maintaining the reports when changes are made to the financial system? Too many.

Chapter 4 discussed the utility of establishing computer-assisted audit tools and techniques (CAATTs) working groups to determine which applications will be supported by CAATTs and to develop an understanding of these systems and the ability to extract and use data from these systems. These working groups should also be responsible for communicating this knowledge to the audit staff.

Another preventive control is the ongoing involvement of individuals with expertise in audit and informatics. This can be accomplished through the establishment of an information technology support section (ITSS) with a mandate to provide ongoing support and advice. Many audit organizations colocate the ITSS with their information system auditors.

Detective Controls

The main feature of a detective control is the comparison of what happened with what was supposed to happen. In most cases, the results of the analysis are compared with the expected results or with another source of information. Fraud investigations are a highly sensitive issue. The potential impact on the reputation of those identified by the analysis demands that the results be carefully reviewed and, ideally, compared to source documentation and independent sources. A further detective control is the independent verification of the analysis and results. This would include peer and management review as well as the involvement of the ITSS staff.

Chapter 4 discussed the importance of ensuring the integrity of the data and the completeness and accuracy of any extraction. These form an integral part of the detective controls. In addition, most audit software packages log the analyses performed and the results. The log file should be retained and safeguarded as part of the working papers. A review of the log file can assist in determining the integrity of the analyses and the results.

Corrective Controls

It is important to make optimum use of the technology and to ensure the results are accurate and complete. When errors are made, the underlying causes should be determined and corrective action taken to prevent them from occurring again. Errors can be highlighted via regular communication with the auditors. Further, training courses can be tailored to address specific issues that have been identified as a source of errors.

Scripts can be seen as both preventive (ensuring new auditors perform the correct analysis) and corrective (addressing errors and ensuring consistency) controls.

Ensuring Reliability

In summary, data analysis reliability can be increased and a more valid interpretation of the results secured by:

- Developing clear analysis plans
- Challenging data received, the analysis done, and the results obtained
- Asking others, such as team members and experts, for input
- Keeping all team members informed of analysis, results, and interpretation
- Involving CAATTs experts at every step of the investigation—from the initial access to, and extraction of, the data, to the interpretation of the results
- Requesting that a CAATTs expert conduct a quality assurance review of any analysis performed by the team
- Verifying the results against another source (original documents, other system or report)
- Building scripts to ensure the consistency and accuracy of analyses performed

Audit managers, team leaders, and team members all have roles to play in ensuring the reliability of all investigation results. Good communication and professional skepticism are the main quality control methods.

A more detailed discussion on quality assurance and data analysis can be found in *Internal Audit: Efficiency through Automation.*

Data Analysis and Prosecuting Fraud

Auditors and fraud investigators using a proactive approach to fraud detection are uncovering more fraud than ever before. However, in most instances, the initial detection of the fraud still depends on police investigation, employee intervention, or internal controls. In these cases, auditors and fraud investigators will likely be involved only to ascertain the extent of the total monetary loss. This work is important, but auditors and fraud investigators usually prefer to prevent fraud rather than simply clean up after the fact.

The sizing of a fraud requires a detailed analysis of the transactions and an active search for evidence. The use of data analysis software to drill down into the details of the data will greatly assist in efforts to size a fraud. In addition, if the fraud has been going on for some time, there may be a requirement to extend the search into a prior year or years. Joining separate files and defining relationships can allow the auditor to combine information from several areas to find the source of the fraud and calculate the full cost.

Another critical advantage of using data analysis to analyze and identify the fraud is that the auditor or investigator can easily look for additional fraudulent acts committed by other perpetrators. Scripts can be used to search for the same symptoms in other areas or to look for similar schemes.

Once the fraud has been uncovered, the perpetrators identified, and the full scope established, the prosecution phase is entered in earnest. Preventing fraud is an admirable goal, but auditors and investigators must support the prosecution of criminals as well. Fraud detection will be an even more effective deterrent to others if the case is pursued and the criminals are prosecuted. It is vital, therefore, for auditors and investigators to be as diligent in the prosecution as they are in the detection of fraud. Auditors and fraud investigators will often be called on to assist the district attorney in preparing the evidence to support the case against the criminal and may even have to carefully explain the nature of the fraud and the losses incurred. It is not the intent of this book to delve into the issues of chain of evidence and other legal issues; these topics are best left to other books. However, data analysis tools and techniques can support the prosecution and ultimate incarceration of the perpetrators of fraud.

Given that the initial detection of fraud is an important first step, and not the final one, auditors and fraud investigators should also use technology to assist in the prosecution process. Auditors and fraud investigators must maintain vast amounts of information and data to support the successful prosecution of persons who commit fraud. To ensure maximum flexibility, many auditors and fraud investigators store related information in electronic databases. However, whether the fraud is large or small, the information must be protected, safeguarded, and readily accessible.

Data analysis software is ideally suited to the safeguarding and analysis of fraud-related information. Audit software has "read-only" functionality, protecting the integrity of the original information while allowing for complex analysis. Prosecution attorneys and auditors can use the analysis to explore various aspects of the cases and quantify the actual losses. This will assist in sentencing at the trial. Given that auditors and fraud investigators already have experience using audit software, it will not be necessary to train them or purchase additional software—another advantage in the use of data analysis software.

Case Study: Paper File Review

A possible incidence of fraud was brought to the attention of the audit manager. Allegations about kickbacks had surfaced and needed to be examined carefully. All paper files related to several high-value contracts were seized, and the audit team was attempting to reconstruct events that had occurred over a period of several years by examining paper files, letters, and other correspondence. The auditors had access to two file cabinets containing all the key hardcopy documentation but were experiencing problems coping with the sheer volume of paper information. Whenever they had a question, they were forced to search through mounds of paper files to find the answer. In the process of considering their problem, they realized that the computer could be used to simplify the file review process.

The auditors spent the next week creating a spreadsheet with key information about each piece of correspondence, such as file number, date, to, from, title, and keywords describing the context of the correspondence. When they were finished entering the data, they were in a position to review all correspondence from various perspectives. Using data analysis, they quickly and easily sorted the information into chronological order, identifying the logical flow of correspondence related to specific topics, by subject. They also identified all correspondence "to" or "from" specific individuals as well as all correspondence between any two individuals. Further, they identified all correspondence that referenced specific keywords, for example:

Correspondence Sent by "Jones"

Originator	Recipient	Date	Description
Jones	Smith	03/02/03	Reply to Stroby Incident
Jones	Smith	04/13/03	Reply to Stroby Incident
Jones	Black	03/12/03	Polaris Expenditures

Correspondence Related to "Polaris"

Originator	Recipient	Date	Description
Black	Williams	03/03/03	Polaris Expenditures
Black	Jones	03/03/03	Polaris Expenditures
Williams	Black	04/21/03	Polaris Expenditures
Jones	Black	03/12/03	Polaris Expenditures
Black	Coderre	04/16/03	Polaris Time Table
Coderre	Black	04/17/03	Exp/Time Table—Polaris

(continued)

The ability to search and sort volumes of data, on multiple criteria— date, subject, to, from—was greatly enhanced through the use of the computer. Questions could now be answered quickly, with assurance that all relevant files had been considered. Answers to a wide variety of questions could be determined easily without manually searching through all the files again and again. Detailed information related to a specific question was easily extracted from the manual file when required, using the file number as a reference. The days spent performing the data capture were more than recouped through the enhanced ability to analyze the information electronically.

Case Study: Debt Free?

A group of enterprising felons ran advertisements in the local newspaper informing readers that they would assume debts on car leases so that the owners could get out from under the high monthly payments. The crooks hoped that the persons unable to make their payments would be happy to have this financial burden removed, without any penalty. Usually, the people responding to the advertisement had signed a four-year car lease but found that they could not keep up their car payments. The crooks would stop by the house and tell the owner that they would assume the car payments and that the owners of the car simply had to sign over ownership to them. Sometimes the owners were even offered an incentive of a few hundred dollars. The owners were told that they did not have to obtain the approval of, or inform, the car dealership—so their credit rating would not be hurt. The crooks asked for the car keys. The original owners, unable or unwilling to make the monthly payments, handed over the keys and ownership papers.

Once the crooks had possession of the car, they would run a "car for lease" advertisement in the newspaper, lease out the car, and collect the monthly payments from the new driver. The fraud (known in some circles as equity skimming) occurred when they failed to make the monthly car payments. The crooks used this scheme on almost 150 cars, collecting approximately $40,000 per month from their victims, without making a single payment on the outstanding leases.

When the payments were several months in arrears, the car dealer-ships would contact the original owners to tell them that if the dealership did not receive all of the arrears, plus interest, immediately, they would repossess the car. The original owners told the car dealership that the crooks had taken the car and that they had assumed the crooks would be responsible for, and make, the payments. The owners even produced the signed, official-looking contracts. However, the crooks were not responsible for, and had never made, any payments to the dealerships. The car dealerships also argued that, since the transfer of ownership had not been approved, the original owners were responsible. They were on the hook for the payment arrears and were still responsible for the cars. The arrears amount was usually in the $2,000 to $4,000 range, and the owners did not have that kind of money on hand and did not know where the cars were now. The cars were reported as stolen and, when found, were repossessed from the new drivers—who then also became victims.

The original owners' credit ratings were destroyed when the car dealerships notified the credit bureaus of their failure to pay. Meanwhile, many of the new drivers had paid several months in advance and lost their money when the car was repossessed.

The crooks leased cars to unsuspecting drivers, who mailed their monthly car payments to post office boxes. Thus, when the crooks received the money through the U.S. Postal Service, they were guilty of mail fraud. (Mail fraud is committed when the U.S. Postal Service is used to further an illegal scheme.) In addition, the crooks sometimes used cell phones to call their new "leasees" when they were late in making their car payments and even threaten them with bodily harm if they would not pay up. This constituted wire fraud (using electronic means to commit a fraud).

The auditors developed several databases to maintain information related to the fraud. They also made extensive use of data analysis software to determine the size of the fraud and to prepare the court case for the federal authorities. The auditors subpoenaed the crooks' telephone records from the telephone company for a one-year period. They also built a database to track all the information for each defaulted car payment, including the name of the original owner, name of the crook, date the crook took possession of the car, payment due date, number of payments missed, amount of car payments collected, and so on. The database was used to support many lines of inquiry, including analysis to:

- Calculate the number of months the owner was in arrears (last payment date minus current date)
- Total the amount of arrears by owner (months in arrears times monthly payment)
- Total the amount of lease payments collected by each crook

(continued)

- Total the amount for car payments sent through the mail
- Count the number of phone calls by a given crook to a given leasee
- Assess the billed telephone number—to identify wire fraud
- Determine if calls were made to other states—to track crimes committed across state lines

The auditors were able to use the database to assist prosecutors in answering a wide variety of questions, leading to the successful prosecution of the crooks. The ability to analyze the data quickly was of tremendous value to the state prosecutors.

Scheme:	Crooks persuade individuals to sign over leased cars without permission of original leaseholder, then fail to make payments.
Symptoms:	Checks mailed to box number, threatening phone calls from crooks demanding payment
Data Requirements:	Telephone bills—date, time, number called. Check stubs and/or canceled checks—amount and payee.

Note

1. David Coderre, *Internal Audit Efficiency through Automation* (Hoboken, NJ: John Wiley & Sons, 2009).

Fraud Investigation Plans

Insurance Policies—Too Good to Be True

The auditors had identified sales commissions as a particularly risky area. First, there were known cases of fraud having been committed at ABC and in other insurance companies. Second, the inherent risk was high since commissions were closely tied to compensation, and even job security. Finally, the control framework was not as tight as it should be; there were weaknesses in the timing of commissions and in the determination of valid sales. So, while the project was treated as more of a preventive fraud measure, it was also given the same diligence and planning as an investigation of a suspected fraud.

Allegations—from Previous Audit Findings

Sales staff have defrauded the company by claiming for insurance policies that were fictitious or by delaying the reporting of policies to manipulate sales levels.

Objective

To ensure sales commissions are based on valid sales levels and accounted for in the period in which they were generated.

Audit Team

Lisa Marges will be the team leader and will be supported by Sam Bedford (financial auditor). Dave Crowley will provide CAATTs support and will interface with the systems people to obtain the necessary data.

(continued)

Schedule

All team members will cease other projects effectively immediately to concentrate on the investigation. An interim report will be presented to the audit committee on August 29 and a final report should be prepared for signature by the audit committee chairman on September 12.

Data/Information Source

The Administrative Manual (Chapter VI, Section 2.a) clearly states ABC's regulations regarding the reporting of policies in the period in which they are signed. As well, Section 6.d outlines the criteria for the payment of commissions on new policies.

The CAATTs cell within the audit department will create extracts of the data from the customer master, policy, and account receivable databases. The extracted data will be downloaded to the departmental server. The required fields are:

- Customer master—policy number, policyholder name and address
- Policy database—policy number, policy type, salesperson, policy amount, start date, end date, cancellation date, payment amount, terms
- A/R—policy number, payment amount, due date, payment date, payment type

Analysis

A review will be performed of company polices and regulations related to the basis for commissions and the reporting of policies to determine if any updates have occurred in the last year.

The data analysis will focus on the last completed fiscal year (2008) but will include data from three previous years (2005, 2006, and 2007) for trending purposes.

The customer master and policy data will be used to generate a sample of policies for which confirmation letters will be generated. The responses will be grouped for each salesperson to determine the validity of their policies sold.

The policy data will be used to examine trends in the number of policies sold—by salesperson, by month. The aim is to determine if the data suggests that sales staff have adjusted policy dates to inflate sales during contest periods. Additional analysis will be performed on policies raised in months where sales vary by more than 15 percent of expected values.

Policy payments and cancellation data will be used to review the length of time policies were held by policyholders. Additional analysis will be performed on policies where the salesman's average is below the industry standard.

A variety of digital analysis tests will be performed on payment date to look for anomalies.

Additional analysis will be performed as appropriate and detailed in annexes to this plan. In addition, a detailed audit program will be developed.

Audit Team Leader—Lisa Marges
Audit Director—Isabelle French
Date: July 16, 2008

Case Study: Insurance Policies—Too Good to Be True

At the beginning of every audit in the sales area, the auditors liked to review the personnel files of the top salespeople.

Bob was fairly new to the company, having started just over one year ago. He had excellent credentials and had brought a lot of his old policyholders with him. He was the only new salesperson to meet the targets for the first year and was continuing to sign up new policyholders. Since Bob had been performing so well, he was on the auditors' list for review. The first thing Jane noticed was that Bob had worked as an insurance salesman for three different companies in the last five years. This was not entirely unusual but was worth noting.

The auditors used the computer to select a random sample of policies and create confirmation letters. The confirmation letters were sent to each policyholder asking them to confirm the policy, payments, and terms. In previous years this technique had identified fake policies. Some confirmation letters came back "Addressee Unknown," others were returned by the addressee with a note to the effect that they did not have a policy with ABC Insurance Ltd. This year was no exception; six confirmation letters were returned, and the auditors followed up on them. Jane was pleased to see that none of the returned confirmation letters was from Bob's policyholders. He had been around earlier, talking with the auditors and stressing the importance of having good controls. He even shared some of his experience from working in a number of insurance companies over the last 20 years.

(continued)

ABC was in a very competitive business, and competition among sales staff was encouraged and rewarded by bonuses. Each year the top salesperson received a $10,000 bonus. Another audit test that had been successful in the past was to determine the total number and value of policies sold each month by each person. This provided the auditors with an easy way to determine if there was a sudden increase in policies sold just prior to the close of the sales contest. One year, a salesman claimed 48 policies in the last week before the end of the contest. This placed him first, and he received the bonus. Two weeks later he quit to join another company. One month after that, 44 of the 48 policies defaulted on their second payment. He had generated fake policies just to win the contest. Using a cross-tabulation of the sales staff, summarizing the number and dollar value of the policies by month, the auditors had a better chance at identifying this type of scheme. Also, since this had happened, the identification of the winning sales representative and the payment of the prize had been delayed until after the second month of payments on policies.

The auditors also performed other tests on policies sold, such as calculating (for each salesperson) the number of policyholders who failed to renew their policies after the first year. The rationale behind this test was tied to a risk the auditors identified in the way commissions were paid. The total of commission and expenses were about 105 percent of the total cost of the first year's premiums; the company would make money only if the policy was active for more than one year. This was not usually a concern, given that most policyholders maintained their policies for five or more years. However, the auditors surmised that, under the current commission plan, a salesperson could issue a policy, pay the premiums for a few months, and then simply default on the payments—and still make money. The use of confirmation letters helped to identify this type of scheme, but Jane had heard about one enterprising individual who actually gave away policies to people or sold them for ridiculously low premiums for one year. The salesman could justify the low premiums to the client by saying he would lose his job if he did not meet the quotas. The policyholders were happy with the price, and were told to direct any confirmation letters to the salesman, and he would take care of them. Thus, confirmation letters were not sufficient to identify the problem. When Jane reviewed the results of the test for "failure to renew policies," Bob was at the top of the list. More than 65 percent of the policyholders signed by Bob either defaulted on their payments or did not renew their policies.

Ted, one of the auditors on the team, wanted to run a few more tests on the data. For the first test, he talked to the sales manager and determined the amount of effort required (minimal, medium, and extensive) by the salesperson for each type of policy. The sales manager felt that the number of policies sold in each category should be approximately:

- Minimal—20 percent
- Medium—55 percent
- Extensive—25 percent

First Ted summarized the number of policies by the amount of work required: minimal, medium, and extensive. Then he performed a second analysis, breaking down the policies sold by each person into the same three categories. The first analysis supported the sales manager's opinion regarding the proportion of policies in the three categories. However, the analysis by salesperson revealed that 65 percent of Bob's policies fell into the minimal category. Two other salespeople also had higher-then-normal percentages of their policies fall in that category. One had also already been identified by a high rate of return of confirmation letters.

The next test Ted had devised was to examine the payment data for all policies. The premiums could be paid by cash, by check, by electronic withdrawal from the policyholder's bank, or by journal voucher. The analysis of the payments for all policies showed that the most popular method of payment was electronic withdrawal, followed closely by check. In less than 5 percent of the cases were policy premiums paid by cash, and company internal journal vouchers were used less than 3 percent of the time. A breakdown by individual and by type of premium payment was extremely revealing. Internal journal vouchers were used to pay more than 70 percent of the premiums on Bob's policies. Further, 100 percent of Bob's policies that had defaulted on premiums or had failed to renew had been paid by internal journal voucher. Ted totaled the premiums paid on these policies against the commissions and expenses received by Bob for them. The results showed that if Bob had paid all the premiums himself, he would still have netted $145,000 on the policies.

About a week after management and audit began questioning Bob about his policies and started the process of interviewing policyholders, Bob quit and started work with another insurance company. As a result of the audit findings, senior management revised the compensation policy. Commissions were paid out over a period of three years, and only if the policy was still in effect. For most of the staff, total income flow was not affected. However, this meant that it was no longer cost-effective for anyone to pay the premiums for the first year, collect the commission, and then default on the policy.

Paid by the Numbers

Allegations

On the last payroll run employees were overpaid.

Objective

To ensure payroll amounts for the last pay period (period 7, 2008) were accurate and complete.

Audit Team

Lyne Liberty will be the team leader and will be supported by Terry Roberts (financial auditor) and Sam Hurley (compensation specialist). Dave Brownley will provide CAATTs support and will interface with the systems people to obtain necessary data.

Schedule

All team members will cease other projects effectively immediately to concentrate on the investigation with the exception of Sam Hurley, who will provide support on an as needed basis. An interim report will be presented to the audit committee on March 1, and a final report should be prepared for signature by the audit committee chairman on March 12.

Data/Information Source

The Pay and Compensation Manual is the source for policy and regulations regarding pay and other forms of compensation.

The CAATTs cell within the audit department will use ODBC to access the payroll master file and will create an extract of the payroll transaction file for pay period 7, 2008. The extracted data will be downloaded to the audit team leader's PC. The required fields are:

- Payroll master—employee number, status, pay per period, department, payroll office, pay supervisor
- Payroll transaction file—employee number, gross pay, taxes, net pay, pay period

Analysis

The data analysis will focus on the last pay period (period 7, 2008). Data from the payroll master file will be joined to the pay transaction data for the pay period. The purpose is to identify cases where:

- Employees were on the master file but not paid
- Employees were paid but are not on the payroll master file
- The pay per period is different from the gross pay

A variety of digital analysis tests will be performed on payroll data to look for anomalies.

Additional analysis will be performed as appropriate and detailed in annexes to this plan. In addition, a detailed audit program will be developed.

Audit Team Leader—Lyne Liberty
Audit Director—Ron Milburn
Date: February 19, 2008

Case Study: Paid by the Numbers

The manager of the human resources (HR) department called the audit director into her office. She was concerned, as she had received complaints from two employees that they had not been paid last week. However, when she had her staff compare the payroll amount from last week with the master payroll file, the amount was thousands of dollars over. She was worried that, in addition to not paying some employees, others had been overpaid.

The master payroll file had been audited already. The audit manager was sure that it was accurate and that the problem lay in the period's payroll transaction file. First the auditors compared the amounts in the two files to verify that the totals were in fact different.

```
The total of Pay_Per_Period for Payroll_master is:
9,680,479.94

The total of Gross_Pay for Payroll_Mar08 is:
9,686,641.45

The difference is:
$6,161.51
```

(continued)

This proved that there was a problem with the last payroll calculation. Joining the files together would identify each record where there was a difference between the Pay_Per_Period on the master file and the Gross_Pay on the March 2008 payroll file.

Once the files had been joined, the auditors listed all records where the Gross_Pay was not equal to the Pay_Per_Period. The result was the table below.

The analysis identified three employees who had not been paid—employee numbers A9587, D4401, and D4715, and four people who were paid but did not match with a master record—employee numbers C3321, G4412, J3416, and L1413. Further, three individuals were paid amounts different from their established pay per period—employee numbers A1235, H2209, and M001.

The auditors did some additional checking and determined that employee D4401 was on leave without pay for a year; employees G4412 and L1413 were paid twice; and the other two employees, C3321 and J3416, were not even on the employee master file.

Pay Differences

EmpNo	Dept	Pay Per Period	EmpNum	Gross Pay
A1235	209	2,765.09	A1234	3,109.36
A9587	310	2,882.23		0
		0	C3321	2,100.32
D4401	102	2,691.03		0
D4715	100	2,110.81		0
		0	G4412	2,421.64
H2209	310	2,398.34	H2209	3,094.72
		0	J3416	3,472.62
		0	L1413	3,811.35
M0001	102	2,356.72	M0001	3,355.72
Total		15,204.22		21,365.73

10 out of 671 met the criterion: PAY_PER_PERIOD <> GROSS_PAY

Apart from D4401, who was on leave, the other two employees who had gone unpaid, as well as two of the three who had pay discrepancies, were all victims of innocent clerical errors in time reporting. The equally innocent error in M0001's pay revealed a separate weakness in how newly promoted employees were paid. The first pay in a new position was frequently input by hand rather than being determined by the payroll master table. The HR manager was glad to be able to tell all the affected employees that the problem had been identified and would not happen again.

Employees G4412 and L1413 were contacted and asked to return the overpayment. G4412 had not cashed the check, figuring that it was a mistake, and L1413 had already returned it to his pay officer. The canceled checks for C3321 and J3416 were obtained from the bank and the employee records were reviewed to find out who had cashed the checks. Two programmers from the payroll area were identified and fired.

APPENDIX B

Application of CAATTs by Functional Area

The tables in this appendix outline analyses that can be performed to identify areas of potential fraud, waste, or abuse. Some of the analyses are also applicable to audits of efficiency and effectiveness; others are more specific to fraud detection.

The CAATTs are presented by functional area for easier review, but should not be considered as a complete listing of all possible tests. A search of the Internet for additional tests is recommended. Also, auditors should always consider the unique exposures of their organization when determining which tests/symptoms are relevant.

The tests can be standardized, saved in scripts or queries, and run periodically as a proactive fraud detection measure. In addition, templates can be built to enhance the utility of scripts and make them easier for others to use.

Where such terms are applicable, the listing for a specific CAATT will include the relevant ACL, IDEA, and Excel terminology. Users of a specific software package should consult their user documentation for how the specific tests are applied, as details do vary from one package to another.

Accounts Receivable Tests

Test	CAATT
Calculate the age and value of receivables by range of days (30, 60, 90, 120)	Age
Calculate the average days from delivery of goods or services to billing date, to receipt of payment—by clerk and by customer	Age and Summarize
Calculate the days aged for receivables, by customer, to support contract negotiations	Age and Summarize
Identify bad debts and write-offs by customer or by department	Age and Summarize
Identify high-value credit notes, balances, and invoices—by customer and by clerk	Filter/Display Criteria
Generate confirmation letters to confirm customer balances	Export and Mail Merge
Report on gaps in the sequencing of invoices generated	Gaps
Identify duplicate invoices, credits, or receipts	Duplicates
Credits, receipts, and invoices not in proper sequence or range	Gaps or Sort
Variances between delivery documents and invoices	Join and Expression/Equations
Compare remittances to open receivables and report variances	Join and Expression/Equations
Generate invoice summaries by customer or invoice amount	Summarize
Identify high-value credit notes, balances, and invoices	Filter/Display Criteria
Calculate days to payment by client, by sales representative, or by region, and calculate carrying charges	Filter/Display Criteria and Summarize
Identify credits taken beyond discount terms of payment days	Filter/Display Criteria and Age
Identify accounts with oldest activity for sales follow-up	Age and Sort
Calculate average sales amounts by product, sales representative, or region	Summarize and Expression/Equation
Identify adjustments to discounts	Filter/Display Criteria
Examine bad debt account balances for increasing trends	Join and Expression/Equation

Test	CAATT
Examine amounts "in transit" to bank deposits for increasing trends	Join and Expression/Equation
Identify customer accounts with no address or telephone information	Expression/Equation
Identify credits/debits to dormant or unused accounts	Age and Expression/Equation
Identify customers with favorable credit terms (aged receivables)	Age and Expression/Equation
Compare purchase prices by vendor for same items	Join
Generate confirmation letters to verify customer payments	Export and Mail Merge
Perform ratio analysis (max/max2) by customer	Ratio Analysis
Identify accounts with even balances	Filter/Display Criteria

Accounts Payable Tests

Test	CAATT
Calculate age and value of payables by range of days (30, 60, 90, 120)	Age
Calculation of late payment charges	Filter/Display Criteria and Expression/Equation
Summarize large invoices without purchase orders (by vendor)	Filter/Display Criteria and Expression/Equation
Generate cash requirements by bank, by period, by product, and by vendor	Summarize
Create lists of vendors, with amounts, requiring 1099 forms	Filter/Display Criteria and Summarize
Compare recurring monthly expenses to posted/paid invoices	Join/Relate
Compare discounts available for prompt payment to discounts taken	Join/Relate
Compare voucher or invoice amounts to purchase order or contract amounts	Join/Relate
Calculate vendor rebates from total posted invoices for the year	Expression/Equation

Test	CAATT
Determine vendor unit price variances by product over time	Join/Relate and Expression/Equation
Isolate distributions to accounts not in suppliers' account ledgers	Join/Relate
Reconcile check register to disbursements by vendor invoice	Join/Relate
Identify duplicate purchase order numbers, credits, and invoices	Duplicates
Identify credits given outside of discount terms	Age and Filter/Display Criteria
Identify freight and tax overcharges	Expression/Equation and Filter/Display Criteria
Identify cash discounts not taken	Filter/Display Criteria
Generate confirmation letters to verify customer balances	Export and Mail Merge
Identify charges to dormant or unused accounts	Summarize and Filter/Display Criteria
Identify checks issued to vendors with names that sound like known vendors	Soundslike
Identify credits, receipts, and invoices not in proper sequence or range	Sort/Index
Report on gaps in the sequencing of invoices generated	Gaps
Identify high-value credit notes, balances, and invoices	Filter/Display Criteria
Summarize invoice amounts by account	Summarize and Sort
Report on variances between delivery documents and invoices	Expression/Equation and Filter/Display Criteria
Perform ratio analysis (max/max2) on payments to accounts	Ratio Analysis
Identify instances where one clerk has processed all the invoices for the account	Cross Tab/Pivot Table

General Ledger Tests

Test	CAATT
Calculate financial ratios, and changes, for sales/assets, and debt/equity	Expression/Equation
Track year-to-date activity for large operating accounts	Summarize
Calculate and compare variances in accounts between periods	Summarize and Join/Relate
Analyze and confirm shareholders' accounts and equity	Summarize
Compute weighted and average interest rates across periods	Join/Relate and Expression/Equation
Prepare trial balances and account reconciliation	Summarize
Identify large adjustment transactions	Filter/Display Criteria
Calculate free balances by account (Budget minus (Expenses plus Commitments)	Summarize and Expression/Equation
Prepare balance sheets, profit and loss statements, and cash flow analyses	Summarize

Materials Management and Inventory Control Tests

Test	CAATT
Reconcile unmatched pay and remittances to freight invoices	Join/Relate
Identify items below the standard margins	Filter/Display Criteria and Expression/Equation
Verify price compliance	Filter/Display Criteria
Select stock sample for reconciliation	Sample
Compare physical stock count with computed stock counts	Summarize and Extract
Identify negative receipt quantities	Statistics and Filter/Display Criteria
Report on items with high balances and age	Age and Filter/Display Criteria
Calculate stock turnover by item	Age
Identify duplicate items or serial numbers	Duplicates
Identify surplus or obsolete inventory	Join/Relate

Test	CAATT
Identify items with yearly volume over/under total quantity ordered	Expression/Equation
Report high value items purchased by buyer	Filter/Display Criteria and Summarize
Calculate current inventory based on last in, first out value or pool	Summarize
Determine percentage change in sales, price, or cost levels by product/vendor	Summarize and Filter/Display Criteria
Calculate the difference between actual and standard costs	Join and Expression/Equation
Isolate stock where cost is greater than retail price	Filter/Display Criteria
Compare historical standard to sales price to identify unrealized profits	Join/Relate
Identify items with negative quantities or zero/negative prices	Filter/Display Criteria
Match stock receipts with vendor ledger and report variances	Join/Relate and Expression/Equation
Calculate returns and shortages by vendor and by clerk	Summarize
Determine reorder levels for stock with slow turnover	Age and Expression/Equation
Compare reorder quantities by warehouse	Summarize
Compare book and tax depreciation values and report variances	Join/Relate and Expression/Equation
Show items depreciated to cost in order to highlight assets greater than cost	Expression/Equation and Sort
Analyze intercompany profit or loss on equipment sales	Summarize
Recalculate expense and reserve amounts using replacement costs	Expression/Equation
Calculate investment tax credits and compare to credit taken	Expression/Equation
Calculate inventory reordering volumes by item, by warehouse, or by vendor	Summarize
Select items from perpetual stock for reconciliation	Sample
Reconcile physical stock levels to computed amounts	Sample

Test	CAATT
Compare value of physical inventory to general ledger amounts	Join/Relate
Calculate turnover to determine usage and ordering efficiencies	Age
Highlight high-value balances	Filter/Display Criteria
Calculate turnover by stock class and/or item	Expression/Equation
Test for duplicate parts or descriptions	Duplicates
Calculate variances from standard pricing	Expression/Equation
Determine items with inventory levels under the minimum quantity	Filter/Display Criteria
Report on products in descending order of profitability	Sort
Identify variances between delivery documents and contracted amounts	Join/Relate and Filter/Display Criteria
Identify starting and ending balances by stock class or groups	Summarize
Compare speed and accuracy of delivery by product and by vendor	Age and Summarize
Profile supply usage by month or department	Join/Relate
Identify unusual delivery addresses	Summarize and Filter/Display Criteria
Match delivery addresses with employee addresses	Join/Relate
Calculate number and value of write-offs and strike-offs by location	Summarize
Calculate number and value of items with disposal followed by reorder transactions	Summarize
Identify items with quantities below reorder points	Filter/Display Criteria
Identify items with high return or allowance rates	Summarize
Calculate number and value of items sent to scrap (by clerk)	Filter/Display Criteria and Summarize
Calculate shortages and overages—by ordering and receiving clerk, and by vendor	Summarize

Salary and Payroll Tests

Test	CAATT
Match payroll master to employee master and report variances	Join/Relate and Filter/Display Criteria
Identify changes in exemptions, gross pay, hourly rates, and salary amounts	Join/Relate and Filter/Display Criteria
Extract all payroll checks where amount exceeds set amount (by category of employee)	Filter/Display Criteria
Report entries against authorization records for new or terminated employees	Join/Relate
Review special pay, overtime, premium pay, bonuses, and commissions	Filter/Display Criteria and Sample
Identify duplicate direct deposit numbers	Duplicates
Identify duplicate employee names, addresses, and phone numbers	Duplicates
Summarize payroll distributions and reconcile to general ledger file	Summarize and Join/Relate
Compare time card rates and pay rates to payroll and report variances	Join/Relate and Expression/Equation
Identify blank, false, invalid, and duplicate Social Security numbers	Duplicates and Filter/Display Criteria
Reconcile salaries by job or project	Join/Relate
Identify persons on payroll with no deductions for income tax, insurance, medical, pension, or benefits	Filter/Display Criteria
Identify persons on payroll with no time off for vacations or sick leave	Join/Relate and Filter/Display Criteria
Identify persons on payroll with no work address or telephone	Join/Relate and Filter/Display Criteria
Identify persons on payroll with no employment history and no performance evaluations	Join/Relate and Filter/Display Criteria
Compare payroll date with employee start and termination dates	Join/Relate and Expression/Equation
Compare pay rate with ranges for employee classification	Stratify
Perform ratio analysis of payroll (max/max2) by employee classification	Ratio Analysis
Compare trends in payroll amounts by G/L (by year)	Summarize and Join/Relate

Purchase Order Management Tests

Test	CAATT
Identify orders received without a purchase order or contract	Join/Relate
Compare purchase quantities and pricing to contract	Join/Relate
Analyze scheduled versus actual receipt dates	Age
Total purchases by order type (blanket, release, drop-ship) by vendor	Summarize
Identify duplicate purchase order numbers	Duplicates
Identify stale purchase orders, or purchase orders with only partial quantity received	Age and Filter/Display Criteria
Calculate late shipments, by vendor, and analyze impact	Age, Summarize, and Expression/Equation
Analyze open orders and open invoices (by clerk and by vendor)	Filter/Display Criteria and Summarize
Analyze product demand by summarizing orders by due date	Summarize
Determine percentage defective items shipped (by vendor)	Expression/Equation and Summarize
Reconcile booked items to inventory reserved (on hold) items	Join/Relate
Analyze overages and shortages (by vendor and by receiving clerk)	Expression/Equation and Summarize
Compare items ordered to items canceled (by employee)	Expression/Equation and Summarize
Reconcile receipts by comparing accrued payables to received items	Join/Relate

Conflict-of-Interest Tests

Test	CAATT
Compare rates for similar products from other vendors—ratio analysis on unit price by product (check high-ratio details)	Ratio Analysis and Expression/Equation
Total purchases by ordering clerk, by vendor	Summarize
Match contract price to invoice and report on variances	Join/Relate and Expression/Equation

Test	CAATT
Check for purchasing more than required: • Project requirements to contract • Inventory remaining at end of project • Order greater than quantity received	Join/Relate and Expression/Equation
Total number, and value, of contracts by contracting officer by vendor (bid rotation not followed)	Summarize
Calculate average value of contracts awarded by vendor (bids rotated, but highest contracts go to one vendor)	Summarize and Expression/Equation

Kickback Tests

Test	CAATT
Compare order quantity to optimal reorder quantity	Join/Relate and Expression/Equation
Total business volume (by agent and by vendor)	Summarize
Match quantities ordered to quantities received	Join/Relate and Expression/Equation
Total inferior goods (percentage returns by vendor)	Summarize
Check for purchases of more expensive items than required	Summarize
Ratio analysis on unit price—by product (check high ratio details)	Ratio Analysis
Ratio analysis on purchases—by vendor (check high ratio details)	Ratio Analysis

Bid-Rigging Tests

Test	CAATT
Compare inventory levels and turnover rates	Expression/Equation
Identify cases where inventory is written off and then new purchase is made (total write-off and purchase quantities by stock number)	Summarize
Calculate percentage contract awards by vendor (contracts won divided by number of bids)	Summarize and Expression/Equation

Test	CAATT
Percentage of sole-sourced contracts by vendor (contracts sole-sourced divided by number of contracts)	Summarize and Expression/Equation
Check for vague contract specifications: • Amendments, extensions, and increases in value • Total number of amendments • Delayed delivery (final minus original delivery date) • Percentage increase in value	Summarize, Count, and Expression/Equation
Check for contract splitting (same vendor and same day)	Duplicates
Fictitious bids (verify bidders and prices)	Confirmation Letters
Bids submitted after closing date	Age and Filter/Display Criteria
Last bid wins	Age and Summarize
Lowest bidder drops out and subcontracts to higher bidder (compare contractor with invoice payee)	Join/Relate

Policy and Administration Tests

Test	CAATT
Potential conflicts of interest, managers who have relatives working for them—check employee name, address, and phone number	Join/Relate
Analysis of pay adjustments and overtime by employee—frequency, rates, high payments compared to similar positions	Join/Relate
Comparison of vendor and employee addresses and phone numbers	Join/Relate
Analysis of travel expenses by employee—duplicates, high values, and frequency	Duplicates, Summarize, and Filter/Display Criteria
Analysis of education and training expenses by employee—duplicates, high values, and frequency	Duplicates, Summarize, and Filter/Display Criteria
Comparison of sales tax collected with calculation of sales tax	Expression/Equation

Vendor Management Tests

Test	CAATT
Identify duplicate vendor numbers on vendor master file	Duplicates
Identify vendors with more than one vendor number	Duplicates
Identify vendors with PO box addresses	Filter/Display Criteria
Identify vendor records where address changes are frequent	Summarize
Identify vendors with names spelled or sounding similar to well-known vendors (e.g., FedEx, UPS, USPS)	Soundslike(), and Filter/Display Criteria
Match vendor and employee names, addresses, and phone numbers	Join/Relate
Identify vendor with significant changes in activity (increase or decrease)	Summarize
Match vendor and company phone numbers	Join/Relate

Retail Loss Prevention Tests

Test	CAATT
Comparison of no sale transaction to cash voided transaction (by clerk)	Summarize
Test credit card balances against credit limits (by customer)	Join/Relate and Expression/Equation
Compare year-to-date allowances to net sales by customer	Summarize and Expression/Equation
Invoice tracking by dollar rank (by department)	Sort
Identify checks paid to more than one payee at same address	Duplicates
Compare amount of allowances by store	Summarize
Identify duplicate return transactions	Duplicates
Identify incomplete exchange transactions	Duplicates
Compare clearance sales of returned merchandise by markdowns, markups, and sales without receipts	Summarize
Identify price adjustments on returned merchandise (by department)	Summarize
Calculate inventory day sales by store	Summarize

Test	CAATT
Identify check purchases followed by cash refund (by customer)	Expression/Equation and Summarize
Identify credit card purchase and refund to different credit card	Expression/Equation and Summarize
Identify credit card purchase and cash refund	Expression/Equation and Summarize
Compare selling prices across stores by product	Join/Relate
Identify items selling for less than sales price	Filter/Display Criteria
Calculate (inventory items received minus items sold plus returns) and compare to inventory on hand	Expression/Equation
Calculate number and amount of refunds by clerk	Expression/Equation and Summarize
Calculate percentage of refunds by credit card	Expression/Equation and Summarize
Identify refunds that are greater than selling price	Filter/Display Criteria
Calculate number and amount of voids by clerk	Expression/Equation and Summarize
Compare no sale to cash voided transactions by clerk	Expression/Equation and Summarize
Compare amount of credit card payments by clerk	Summarize

Sales Analysis Tests

Test	CAATT
Generate sales and profitability reports by sales representative, product, and customer	Summarize
Calculate sales by region, customer, and category	Summarize
Compare current and previous periods to analyze sales trends	Join/Relate
Identify top dollar products, customers, and sales representatives	Index
Summarize sales performance over time by product and sales representative	Expression/Equation and Trend Analysis
Compare current product sales with booked sales for demand analysis/trends	Summarize

Test	CAATT
Calculate ratio of current sales to open receivables (high to low)	Expression/Equation and Trend Analysis
Analyze product distribution by calculating shipments by warehouse	Expression/Equation and Index
Compare ratio of current sales to open receivables (sort high to low and low to high)	Expression/Equation and Index
Select a range of products for current and period-to-date analysis	Filter/Display Criteria and Sample
Calculate profit variances by item	Expression/Equation

Work in Progress Tests

Test	CAATT
Monitor job progress by customer	Join/Relate and Expression/Equation
Calculate shortages based on allocations and deallocations against work orders	Expression/Equation
Identify stalled shop orders (aging on date) to improve productivity	Age
Total work pending by size, priority, for release to shop floor	Summarize
Total material usage by work order and compare to plans to identify misused materials	Summarize
Compare products on work orders and sales orders for net demand analysis	Join/Relate
Identify completed orders with shop floor orders still open	Join/Relate
Compare part requirements on contract with parts used on job	Join/Relate
Compare subassembly costs to outside costs for the same item	Join/Relate
Generate planned versus actual costs for labor, materials, and time	Expression/Equation
Compare master planning orders to capacity to improve schedules	Join/Relate
Reconcile job tickets or timecards to work order line items	Join/Relate and Expression/Equation
Reconcile time cards to payroll	Join/Relate and Expression/Equation

Test	CAATT
Compare actual job costs to standard costs, detail, or variances	Join/Relate and Expression/Equation
Identify items (labor, materials) charged to jobs not on master job list	Join/Relate
Compare budgets to expenditures plus commitments to identify projects that are over budget	Filter/Display Criteria and Expression/Equation
Identify duplicate time card or employee costs	Duplicates
Compare profitability by order	Sort/Index
Compute ratios such as cost of goods to revenue	Expression/Equation
Compare completed work order quantities to materials ordered for the project	Filter/Display Criteria and Expression/Equation

Cash Disbursement Tests

Test	CAATT
Total cash disbursements for consulting and professional services	Summarize
Total cash disbursements by account, by bank, and by vendor	Summarize
Identify high-dollar check requests	Filter/Display Criteria
Generate vendor cash activity summary to support rebate negotiations	Summarize

Customer Service Management Tests

Test	CAATT
Calculate length of service call (by employee)	Age
Calculate customer time on hold, waiting for service representative response	Age and Summarize
Compare arrival and service times for field service representative	Expression/Equation
Calculate average cost of service call by representative	Summarize and Expression/Equation
Calculate service call costs for labor, materials, and transportation by representative	Summarize and Expression/Equation
Compare reported service time to time card hours from payroll	Join/Relate

Loan Tests

Test	CAATT
Total number and value of outstanding loan balances (by branch, by employee)	Summarize
Trial loans balance (by location, by branch)	Summarize
Calculate unearned revenues from interest, discounts, and insurance	Expression/Equation
Total loans by type of security, purpose, class, and credit rating	Summarize
Identify write-offs and bankruptcies (by branch, by employee)	Filter/Display Criteria and Summarize
Highlight delinquent accounts by ranges of days aged	Filter/Display Criteria and Age
Identify loans where payments are less than regular amounts	Filter/Display Criteria
Identify loans where the terms were extended by more than the standard amounts	Expression/Equation and Filter/Display Criteria
Identify loans over a specific amount	Filter/Display Criteria
Identify loans with remaining payments that do not amortize to calculated balances	Expression/Equation and Filter/Display Criteria
Identify branches that are exceeding lending limits	Summarize and Filter/Display Criteria
Calculate defaulted loans (by branch, by employee)	Summarize
Identify accounts with balances exceeding credit limits by percentage overage	Filter/Display Criteria and Sort/Index
Compare original collateral, less depreciation, to outstanding loan amounts	Join/Relate

Deposit Tests

Test	CAATT
Arrange accounts by account number—check first and last accounts	Sort/Index
Calculate and compare interest and service charges by account	Expression/Equation
Identify accounts with continual overdrafts or dormant activity	Age and Filter/Display Criteria

Test	CAATT
Identify accounts with low balances, incorrectly exempted from service charges	Filter/Display Criteria
Generate frequency distributions by amount, interest, or maturity rates	Stratify

Real Estate Loans

Test	CAATT
Analyze mortgage loan file for principal and escrow balances	Filter/Display Criteria
Generate frequency distribution of loans by principal outstanding amounts	Stratify
Calculate days past due for loans and generate frequency distribution	Age and Stratify
Verify daily interest accrued, detail or summary, for specific criteria	Filter/Display Criteria
Arrange nonperforming loans by dollar amount	Sort/Index
Identify write-offs and bad debts	Filter/Display Criteria
Calculate market value of collateral for outstanding loans	Expression/Equation
Identify clients with more than one loan	Duplicates
Identify loans for same collateral (property, asset)	Duplicates

Credit Card Management

Test	CAATT
Identify accounts past due, largest amount first	Age and Sort/Index
Highlight accounts with balances over the credit limit	Filter/Display Criteria
Test for various conditions (excessive adjustments or credits)	Filter/Display Criteria
Calculate and verify monthly interest—report variances	Expression/Equation
Identify dormant accounts	Age and Filter/Display Criteria
Identify accounts that failed to make minimum payments	Filter/Display Criteria

Life Insurance Tests

Test	CAATT
Identify premium deposit funds, coupons left on deposit, suspense funds	Filter/Display Criteria
Calculate due, accrued, and unearned interest on policy loans	Expression/Equation
Total policy amount for loans with status other than active (by salesperson)	Filter/Display Criteria and Summarize
Calculate number and value of defaulted loans (by salesperson)	Summarize
Identify policies with a loan that also have a premium deposit fund	Filter/Display Criteria
Identify policies with a cash value less than the outstanding loan amount	Filter/Display Criteria
Calculate dividends due and unearned for current and subsequent years	Expression/Equation
Identify inactive policies with dividends paid	Filter/Display Criteria
Report unearned premium reserves for premiums due, deferred, or advanced	Filter/Display Criteria
Calculate number and value of policies (by salesperson)	Summarize
Calculate salesperson bonus amount compared to total premiums due for first year	Expression/Equation and Summarize

Travel Claims

Test	CAATT
Duplicate claims for same period	Duplicates
Claims for use of personal vehicle and rental car for same period	Join/Relate
Consecutively numbered hotel invoices or meal receipts	Gaps
Travel claims for time when employee was on vacation or sick leave	Join/Relate
Match expense claims amounts to amounts on corporate credit card	Join/Relate
Identify travel claims to exotic locations	Filter/Display Criteria
Identify business travel with departure on Friday or Saturday and return on Sunday	Filter/Display Criteria and Expression/Equation
Identify overlapping travel claims	Fitter/Display Criteria
Identify claims for even amounts	Filter/Display Criteria

APPENDIX C

ACL Installation Process

Step 1 Insert CD; at the main screen select **ACL 9 Education Edition** and click on install

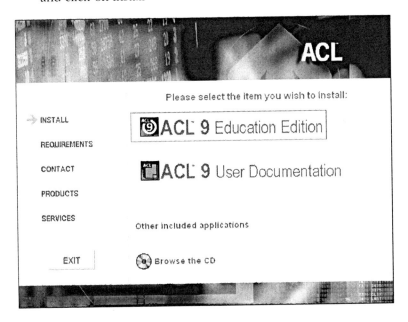

Step 2 Click on **Next**

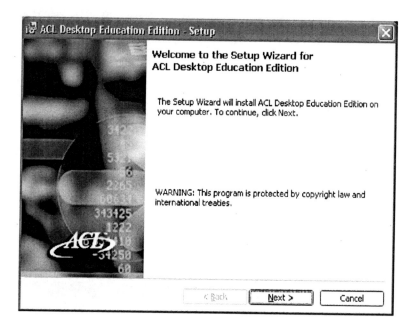

Step 3 Accept terms and click on **Next**

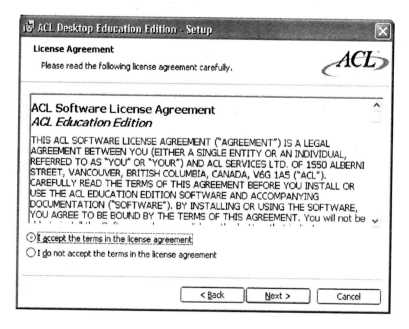

Step 4 Enter user name and company; click on **Next**

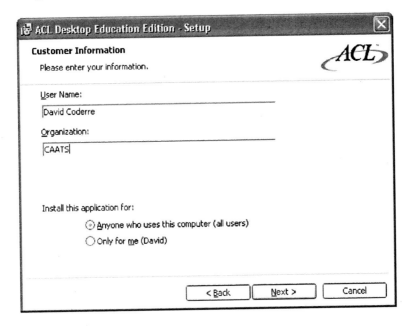

Step 5 Click on **Complete** install

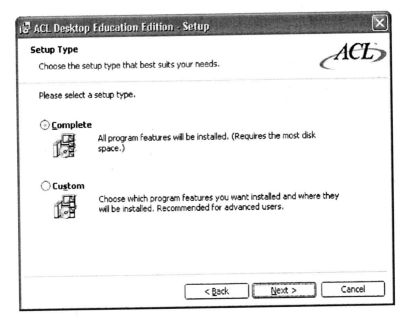

Step 6 Accept default directories; click on **Next**

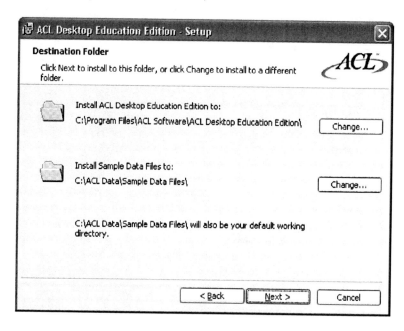

Step 7 Click on **Install**

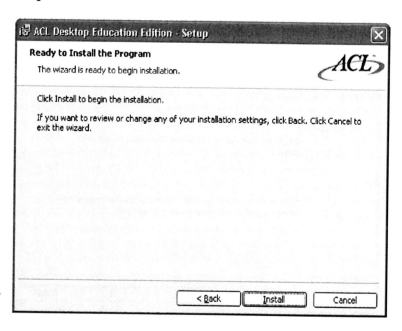

Step 8 Click on **Finish**

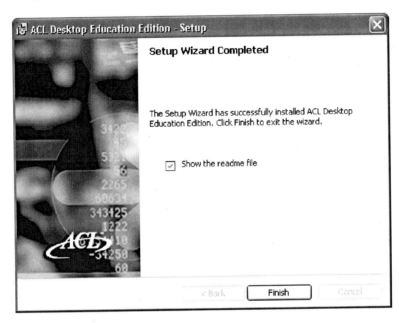

Double click on ACL icon on your desktop to run ACL

Refer to the documents ACL_in_Practice.PDF and ACLStart.PDF in the folder

"C:\ACL Data\Sample Data Files\"

for instructions on running ACL.

Note: ACL does not provide technical support for the Education Version of the software that comes with this book.

Epilogue

How can I end a book on detecting fraud using the computer except by saying good luck and good hunting? Always be wary of new types of fraud and new approaches to fraud detection. People committing fraud share their schemes and learn from other crooks, so they move along the learning curve at a fast rate. Auditors must strive to be ahead of the curve and the thieves if they want to prevent fraud or at least catch those who commit fraud. Therefore, share what you have learned, and try to learn from others.

The use of the computer and the power of audit software continues to grow. In addition, interface and data access issues are becoming easier for all auditors to overcome. You no longer need to be an Information Systems (IS) auditor to use audit software and access corporate systems.

The examples contained in this book are presented only to illustrate some of the types of frauds that may be occurring in your company and to serve as a background for the analysis techniques. They do not represent a comprehensive list of all possible frauds. Do not allow yourself to be constrained by the examples of analysis techniques discussed.

Audit software gives you the power to perform unlimited types of analysis. The techniques described may be relevant to your organization, or they may not. However, I hope that they have given you a vision of what you can be doing. You must take this vision and shape it to your own requirements, adding more techniques and approaches to your repertoire.

CAATTs can be used to perform routine functions or activities better suited to computers, allowing auditors time to think and to exercise audit judgment.

The use of automated tools and techniques in audit can result in many benefits:

- Increased audit quality
- Identification of materiality, risk, and significance
- Increased efficiency and effectiveness throughout the audit process
- Better audit planning and management of audit resources

The credibility of the audit function can be enhanced through improvements in the ability to access, analyze, and use data effectively. A well-designed and implemented fraud detection system, based on digital analysis, can reduce the occurrence of fraud going undetected.[1] The integrity of audit results can also be made more reliable by using computers to assess the full impact and significance of findings. In addition, the ability of auditors to conduct audits and fraud investigations in today's electronic environment will improve dramatically. As a result, the audit department will become a more appealing career choice, making it easier to attract and retain qualified audit staff. Finally, audit will detect and prevent more frauds, and do so earlier.

Note

1. ACL, *Fraud Detection and Prevention: Transactional Analysis for Effective Fraud Detection,* ACL Service Ltd., Vancouver, B.C. 2006.

References

ACFE. *Report to the Nation on Occupational Fraud and Abuse*. Austin, TX: ACFE, 1996.

Albrecht, W. S. *How to Detect and Prevent Business Fraud*. New York: Prentice Hall, 1982, 23.

Albrecht, W. S., E. A. McDermontt, and T. L. Williams. "Reducing the Cost of Fraud," *Internal Auditor, Institute of Internal Auditors* (February 1994): 28–34.

American Institute of Chartered Accountants, Statements on Auditing Standards (SAS)

SAS 47, *Audit Risk and Materiality in Conducting Audits*

SAS 53, *The Auditor's Responsibility to Detect and Report Errors and Irregularities*

SAS 56, *Analytical Procedures*

SAS 80, *Amendment to SAS 31, Evidential Matter*

SAS 94, *The Effect of Information Technology on the Auditor's Consideration of Internal Controls in a Financial Statement Audit*

SAS 99, *Considerations of Fraud in Financial Statements*

SAS 104, *Amendment to Statement on Auditing Standards No. 1, Codification of Auditing Standards and Procedures* ("Due Professional Care in the Performance of Work")

SAS 105, *Amendment to Statement on Auditing Standards No. 95, Generally Accepted Auditing Standards*

SAS 106, *Audit Evidence*

SAS 107, *Audit Risk and Materiality in Conducting an Audit*

SAS 108, *Planning and Supervision*

SAS 109, *Understanding the Entity and Its Environment and Assessing the Risks of Material Misstatement*

SAS 110, *Performing Audit Procedures in Response to Assessed Risks and Evaluating the Audit Evidence Obtained*

SAS 111, *Amendment to Statement on Auditing Standards No. 39, Audit Sampling*

Cerullo, M. V., M. J. Cerullo, and T. Hardin. "Auditing the Purchasing Function," *Internal Auditor* (December 1997): 58–64.

Coderre, David. *Internal Audit: Efficiency through Automation.* Hoboken, NJ: John Wiley & Sons, 2009.

Coderre, David. *Fraud Analysis Techniques Using ACL.* Hoboken, NJ: John Wiley & Sons, 2009.

Hill, Ted. "The First-Digit Phenomenon," *American Scientist* (July-August 1998): 358–363.

Hollinger, Richard C., and John P. Clark. *Theft by Employees.* Lexington, MA: Lexington Books, 1993.

Hylas, R. E., and R. H. Ashton. "Audit Detection of Financial Statement Errors," *The Accounting Review,* Vol. LVII, No 4, 751–765, 1982.

Institute of Internal Auditors, Statements on Internal Auditing Standards (SIAS)

SIAS 3, *Deterrence, Detection, Investigation and Reporting of Fraud*
SIAS 8, *Analytical Auditing Procedures*

Institute of Internal Auditors, American Institute of Certified Public Accountants, and Association of Certified Fraud Examiners. *Managing the Business Risk of Fraud: A Practical Guide.* Altamonte Springs, FL: IIA, 2008.

International Federation of Accountants, International Standard of Auditing (ISA) 240. *The Auditor's Responsibility to Consider Fraud in the Audit of Financial Statements.*

KPMG Peat Marwick Thorne. *Fraud Awareness Survey.* New York, NY (March 1992).

Lanza, Richard. *Payables Test Set for ACL.* Vancouver, BC: Ekaros Analytical Inc., 2003.

Lanza, Richard. *Payables Test Set for IDEA.* Vancouver, BC: Ekaros Analytical Inc., 2004.

Nigrini, Mark J. *Digital Analysis Using Benford's Law.* Vancouver, BC: Global Audit Publications, 2000.

Prawitt, Douglas, F., and Marshall B. Romney. "Emerging Business Technologies," *Internal Auditor* (February 1997): 25–32.

PricewaterhouseCoopers. *2003 Global Economic Crime Survey.* 2003.

Smith, Brian. *Best Practices: Managing Risk in a Managed Care Environment.* Chicago, IL: Arthur Andersen Consulting.

Wells, Joseph T. *Occupational Fraud and Abuse.* Austin, TX: Obsidian Publishing Co., 1997.

Wells, Joseph T. "An Unholy Trinity: Three Ways Employees Embezzle Cash," *Internal Auditor* (April 1998): 28–33.

Index

A

ACL, 59, 83, 97, 107–108, 124, 134, 148, 153, 195, 197, 208, 212–214, 227, 249
  installation 267–271
Aging, 78, 133–147
AICPA, 3, 8, 20–21, 37
Allegations flowchart, 10
American Institute of Chartered Public Accountants. See AICPA
Analysis techniques, 74–81
ASCII, 56, 61
Association of Certified Fraud Examiners (ACFE), 37
Audit objectives, 55–57, 133, 223, 230
Auditing standard #5, 20

B

Benford's Law, 80, 205–209, 225
Bonus, inappropriate, 179–180
Business risks, 7, 42

C

CAATTs:
  application by functional area, 249–266
  checklist, 56–57
  developing capabilities, 41–42, 44–48
  recognizing opportunities for, 49
Classify. See also Summarize, 32
Collusion, between vendor and employee, 29–30, 35, 88–89, 153, 186–187
Completeness, assessing, 82–100

Computer-assisted audit tools and techniques. See CAATTs
Confirmation letters, 81, 219–222, 241–243
Control:
  corrective, 232–233
  detective, 232
  internal, 5, 7, 14, 17–22, 38, 43, 130, 186, 233
  preventive, 231–232
  weaknesses, 27–30, 34, 37, 50, 130, 171
Corporate fraud policy, 2, 11–14, 18, 38, 65
Cross tabulation, 78, 11, 128–131, 242

D

Data:
  accessing, 58–59
  completeness, 82–100
Data file, attributes, 61–65
Data integrity, assessing 65–68
Data paths, 59–61
Data profiling, 194–199
Delimited file, 56, 61–64
Detecting fraud, 7–8, 12, 18–19
Digital analysis, 80–81, 193–209
Duplicate:
  check number, 72, 76, 103–104
  direct deposit number, 100, 174–175, 214–215
  home address, 175
  invoice, 88, 187–189, 191
  parameter, 212

Duplicate (*continued*)
  payment, 102–103, 187
  payroll check, 174
  serial number, 101–102, 105–106
  Social Security Number (SSN),
      174–175,
  transaction, 121, 125–126, 194, 216
  vendor number, 30, 103
  vendor, 188–189
  work location, 176
Duplicates, 32–33, 70–76, 100–106

E
EBCDIC, 56, 61
Error selection, probability of, 225
Even amounts, rounding, 197–198
Excess quantities, 191
Expected frequency, 205–207
Expressions / equations, 75, 85–92

F
File type:
  Delimited, 56, 61–64
  fixed-length, flat, 62
  multi-record type, 62
  relational, 62–63
  variable length, 61–62
Filter / display criteria, 75, 83–84
Fixed bidding, 190–191
Formula for sample size 224–225
Fraud:
  allegations flowchart, 10
  awareness training, 19
  cost of, 2
  definition, 3
  detection, 18–19
  detection, role of management
      7–11
  exposure, 18–23, 27–28
  impact on morale, 2
  investigating and reporting,
      37–38
  known symptoms of, 72–73, 193
  policy, 9, 12–14, 38
  policy, example, 14–15
  prevention, 17–18, 38–39

  prosecuting, 13, 233–234
  responsibility for detection, 7–11
  risk factors, 8, 23–27, 37
  risk factors, table, 22–23
  symptoms of, 18, 31–36, 73,
      171–173, 188
  symptoms, table, 35–36
  templates, 213–214
  triangle, 5–6, 27
  unknown symptoms of, 72–73,
      193–209
  who is responsible, 7–11
Fraud application, 213–216
  development, 217–218
Fraud awareness program, 1–12
Fraud investigation plan, 49–52,
      239–243
  example of, 52–54, 244–245
Fraud prevention, 38–39
Fraud risk assessment, 19, 25–26
Fraud risk considerations, 31–33
Fraudster's perspective, 18, 26–27,
      31
Frequently used values, 196–197

G
Gaps, 75, 93–96
Ghost employees, 174
Goods not received, 36, 86, 191

I
IDEA, 59, 93, 101, 112, 148, 195, 208,
      227, 249
IIA (Institute of Internal Auditors):
  Implementation Standard 1210.A2,
      43
  Implementation Standard 1210.A3,
      43
Index, 72, 76, 106–110
Inferior quality, 191
Inflated prices, 96, 161–163, 191
Information requirements, defining,
      57–58
International Federation of
      Accountants (IFAC), 8
Inventory shrinkage, 98, 159–160

J
Join. See also Relate, 79, 147–157

K
Key fields, 30–34
Kickbacks, 187–190

L
Least/most used categories, 198–199
Logarithmic distributions, 225

M
Monetary unit sampling, 223–224, 226–227
Multiple-record type file, 62

N
National Commission on Fraudulent Financial Reporting (Treadway Commission), 1

O
Open database connectivity (ODBC), 56, 62, 64–65
Overpayment (of employees), 178–185

P
PCAOB (Public Companies Accounting and Oversight Board), 20
Parallel simulation, 80, 168–170
Payroll fraud, 173–177
Pivot tables. See Cross tabulation.
Purchase card, tests, 194, 199, 215–217
Purchasing fraud, 185–191

Q
Quality assurance, 229–230
Quality methodology, 230–231

R
Ratio Analysis:
    current/previous, 201–202
    maximum/second highest, 201
    maximum/minimum, 200–201
    one business area/another, 202–203

Red flags, fraud, 25, 113, 124, 177, 190
Regression analysis, 73–74, 79–80, 165–168
Relate. See also Join, 79, 147–157
Relational file system, 48, 63–65
Reliability, ensuring 68, 233
Reliability of analysis, factors affecting
Reliability risk, 66–70, 230,
Report to the Nation on Occupational Fraud and Abuse, 3
Risk factors for fraud, table, 22–23

S
SAS #31, 91
SAS #47, 58
SAS #53, 8, 36
SAS #56, 43
SAS #80, 31
SAS #82, 8, 91
SAS #94, 34
SAS #99, 8, 21, 37, 217
SAS #104, 20
SAS #105, 20
SAS #106, 20
SAS #107, 20
SAS #108, 20
SAS #109, 20
SAS #110, 21
SAS #111, 21
SIAS #3, 8, 37, 217
Sampling 81, 223–229
    judgmental, 223–224
    directed, 223–224
    monetary unit, 223–224, 226–227
    statistical, 224–227
Sarbanes-Oxley, 20
Screening job applicants, 11–12
Scripts, 73, 86, 171, 177, 194, 211–218
Separation of duties, 22, 26, 29, 31, 87, 130, 186, 221
Sort, 72, 76, 106–110
Statistical analysis, 76, 96–100, 195
Statistics, 65, 96–100
Stratification, 77–78, 124–127, 195–196
Summarization, 35, 77, 111–123

Symptoms of fraud:
  Known, 72–73, 193
  Unknown, 72–73, 193–209

T
Terminated employees, 177–178
Trend analysis, 79, 159–164

V
Variable-length file, 61–62
Variance analysis. See Ratio
  analysis

W
Why Fraud Happens, 4–7

CPSIA information can be obtained at www.ICGtesting.com
Printed in the USA
LVOW10*0333140514

385666LV00001B/2/P